A Begi
Guide to

High-Risk, High-Reward Investing

From Cryptocurrencies and Short Selling to SPACs and NFTs , an Essential Guide to the Next Big Investment

ROBERT ROSS
Founder of TikStocks

ADAMS MEDIA
NEW YORK LONDON TORONTO SYDNEY NEW DELHI

Adams Media
An Imprint of Simon & Schuster, Inc.
100 Technology Center Drive
Stoughton, Massachusetts 02072

First Adams Media trade paperback edition May 2022

ADAMS MEDIA and colophon are trademarks of Simon & Schuster.

For information about special discounts for bulk purchases, please contact Simon & Schuster Special Sales at 1-866-506-1949 or business@simonandschuster.com.

The Simon & Schuster Speakers Bureau can bring authors to your live event. For more information or to book an event contact the Simon & Schuster Speakers Bureau at 1-866-248-3049 or visit our website at www.simonspeakers.com.

Interior design by Sylvia McArdle

Manufactured in the United States of America

2 2022

Library of Congress Cataloging-in-Publication Data
Names: Ross, Robert (Founder of TikStocks) author.
Title: A beginner's guide to high-risk, high-reward investing / Robert Ross, Founder of TikStocks.
Description: Stoughton Massachusetts: Adams Media, 2022. | Includes index.
Identifiers: LCCN 2021054814 | ISBN 9781507218235 (pb) | ISBN 9781507218242 (ebook)
Subjects: LCSH: Finance, Personal. | Speculation. | Investments. | BISAC: BUSINESS & ECONOMICS / Personal Finance / Investing | BUSINESS & ECONOMICS / Investments & Securities / Stocks
Classification: LCC HG179 .R697 2022 | DDC 332.024--dc23/eng/20211123
LC record available at https://lccn.loc.gov/2021054814

ISBN 978-1-5072-1823-5
ISBN 978-1-5072-1824-2 (ebook)

Dedication

To my parents, Pat and Terry Ross, who taught me the value
of money and negotiating from an early age on the streets of
New York City. While I still use these valuable lessons today,
even more important was that they showed me
how to work with the same tenacity I play.

CONTENTS

INTRODUCTION

When you hear the phrase "high-risk, high-reward investing," you likely think of hedge fund managers striking it rich on complex investment strategies. These cutthroat, super-rich members of the investing community use their superior intellects to see where the price of a stock is headed before anyone else. And as an individual investor, there's no way *you* could possibly replicate these strategies, right?

Wrong! This view couldn't be further from the truth. Technology has leveled the playing field, and now you can use many of the same strategies that top-notch hedge funds have at their disposal. And as renowned investor Peter Lynch wrote in his seminal work *One Up on Wall Street*, many individual investors can pick investments just as well as the average Wall Street expert.

There *is* one thing that separates Wall Street traders from individual investors: an ability to assess risk. As I'm going to teach you, the better you get at managing risk, the higher the investment returns you can reap. In this book, you'll learn how to use high-risk, high-reward investment strategies safely and effectively. I've culled all the key information, useful market indicators, and tips for avoiding losses that I've gleaned from my years of experience as a professional stock analyst and educator. You'll discover the inner workings of high-risk investments, determine when to buy and sell, and—if all goes to plan—watch your profits grow.

A few of the thirty topics that we'll cover are:

- Cryptocurrencies
- High-growth stocks
- Call and put options

- Special purpose acquisition companies (SPACs)
- Meme stocks
- Leveraged exchange-traded funds (ETFs)
- Double-digit dividend-paying stocks
- Futures trading
- Non-fungible tokens (NFTs)

Even if you're willing to start using high-risk investing strategies right away, I urge you to take your time to learn these strategies thoroughly before investing real money. I also recommend starting small. The entire purpose of using high-risk, high-reward strategies is to take a small amount of money and generate a large return. Betting too much money on a high-risk strategy is a mistake that many beginners make, and I don't want that to happen to you. That is why I mention the importance of controlling risk in every chapter.

To help you manage the associated risks, each chapter includes detailed examples showing you step-by-step how to employ these high-risk investment strategies. They will include stories about how investors have won (and lost!) on some of these high-risk trades.

The goal of *A Beginner's Guide to High-Risk, High-Reward Investing* is to teach you how to use these high-risk investment strategies responsibly so that you can achieve your short- and long-term investment goals. Let's get started!

CHAPTER 1

A Primer on High-Risk, High-Reward Investing

In most investing books, a grizzled Wall Street veteran extols the benefits of buying S&P 500 index funds, holding them for 40 years, and retiring with a few million bucks in the bank. The salt and pepper–haired old-timer then expounds on the virtues of holding gold stocks before bragging about how his "all-weather stock-picking system" will help you retire early.

And at some point—without fail—he'll mention that if you bought $5,000 of Amazon stock 20 years ago, you'd have enough cash now to buy a beach house.

Of course, buying and holding index funds over many years is a great way to build wealth in the stock market. As a millennial with many years left in my investing journey, I employ this approach with nearly half my portfolio. But you didn't buy this book to learn about the merits of index funds. As the title states, this is a book on *high-risk, high-reward* investment strategies.

I'm here to show you how to trade short squeezes like GameStop (GME) and discover cryptocurrencies that can surge 300% in a matter of days. Do you like dividend-paying stocks? I'll show you the best way to find double-digit dividend payers that will pay for themselves in a few short years. And if you're tired of financial talking heads telling you how much you could've made by buying Amazon 20 years ago, rest assured: My plan is to show you how to find the *next* Amazon.

But most importantly, I'm going to give you step-by-step instructions on how to use these high-risk strategies safely so you can try to avoid losing a lot of money.

UNDERSTANDING RISK

At its core, **risk is a study of uncertainty**. It's our attempt to figure out what the actual return on an investment will be compared to what's expected. The better you are at assessing risk, the better you'll be as an investor.

I've been a stock analyst for the better part of a decade. During this time, I've had the pleasure of learning from some of the world's best and brightest financial minds, including John Mauldin, Felix Zulauf, and Jared Dillian (many of these experts will make appearances later in this book).

I've also spent *a lot* of time talking to individual investors, mainly through direct messages on my popular social media channels. And if there's one thing I've learned, it's that new investors are *terrible* at assessing risk. That's why risk assessment is a major focus of this book.

Low-Risk versus High-Risk Decision-Making

Every person reading this book has likely made a risk assessment today. For instance, let's say that you're driving down a busy street during rush hour. You're running late for an important meeting, so you're trying to barrel through the upcoming intersection quickly. As you approach the bustling four-way intersection, you notice that the streetlight just turned from green to yellow. And in a few seconds, you know that light will flip to red.

What would you do in this situation? Your decision comes back to how comfortable you are with risk.

If you are a risk-averse driver, you would slow down and stop at the yellow-turning-red light. You would then wait for the light to turn green again and be on your way. While you've avoided a potential $75 red-light ticket, you will be late for your meeting.

Not everyone would respond that way. Let's say the driver in front of you decides to go through the yellow light. At that moment, you decide to increase your speed. You know that there's a chance you could get caught by the red-light camera, but your risk-reward calculation tells you that it's worth that risk to get to your meeting on time.

Investors make these same risk-reward calculations every day, although the options are less clear-cut than in the red-light example. For instance, let's say our driver is sitting at their desk later that day. They just received their paycheck for the month, and as usual they take $500 of that check and add it to their brokerage account.

Unlike the red-light example where there were only two options—stop or speed through the light—the person now has nearly unlimited options to consider. The most risk-averse investor would take that $500 and buy something ultra-safe, like US government bonds yielding around 1% or 2% per year. A slightly less risk-averse investor would buy something with tangible value, like gold, or—if they're feeling bold—a blue-chip dividend-paying stock such as International Business Machines (IBM) that may return 8% per year.

These risk-averse investors are the type of people who would stop at the yellow light. They don't want to assume the risk of potentially losing money on their investment, so they are compensated accordingly with lower returns. It is the same concept that motivated the driver who chose to be late to their meeting because they didn't want to risk getting a red-light ticket.

Not everyone is that risk averse, however. An investor more tolerant of risk sees that $500 in their brokerage account and immediately wants to maximize their returns. They know Boeing Co. (BA) has struggled to keep their planes airborne, which has tanked their stock price. While it's possible that the stock won't bounce back anytime soon, there's a possibility this *deep value* stock could return 50% if the company repairs its reputation.

Maybe this less risk-averse investor also saw a video on social media discussing a high-tech satellite company that recently went public via an initial public offering (IPO). Though these stocks are very risky, the return could be as high as 100% in a year, so they happily take on that risk. They may also remember that a coworker told them about a cryptocurrency called Ethereum, which could return 200% over the next year.

This investor is the type of person who speeds through the yellow light and risks getting a ticket. This person is willing to potentially *lose* money on their investment to potentially make *more* money in the future. They are interested in high-risk, high-reward investments.

Investment risk boils down to this: The higher the chance that you lose money, the more money you can potentially make.

Risk Impacts the Rate of Return

Understanding an investment's risk is a fundamental building block of investing. As a rule, the higher the risk in an investment, the higher the return, while the lower the risk in an investment, the lower the return. For example, if you buy shares of a blue-chip stock like McDonald's (MCD) or Johnson & Johnson (JNJ), you can't expect to double or triple your money in a short time period.

Although with a buy-and-hold strategy there's a good chance you could double or triple your money over the long term—say a decade or more—but blue chips are by definition low risk and thus yield lower returns. Everybody knows McDonald's and Johnson & Johnson will be around for years to come, so there's less risk in buying their shares.

On the other hand, you have high-risk assets like bitcoin. Bitcoin is the world's first cryptocurrency, a concept that has only been around for 10 years. There's no guarantee bitcoin (or cryptocurrency in general) will exist in another 10 years. That means investors in bitcoin are rewarded with higher returns for assuming this higher risk. But this rule cuts both ways, since there's a greater chance of severe losses when investing in high-risk assets.

BALANCING YOUR HIGH-RISK, HIGH-REWARD PORTFOLIO WITH LOWER-RISK OPTIONS

Many of you probably know me through my popular @tikstocks social media channels. My goal with that platform from the outset was twofold:

1. Demystify the stock market for individual investors and thus make investing more approachable.
2. Help others avoid making the same mistakes I've made in my investing career.

The first point is very important. Wall Street's goal is to intentionally make investing seem difficult. They want you to believe that only men in suits with big salaries can make money in the stock market. While these big firms may have more money and more resources at their disposal than you do, that doesn't mean you can't beat them at their own game.

I also want you to avoid making the same investing mistakes I've made. A common thread from my thousands of conversations with individual investors is that many people take on too much risk. While they have a general idea how to invest responsibly, they often don't diversify their portfolio well enough, or they bet too big on a risky strategy.

To avoid that, you should balance your high-risk investments with the long-term buy-and-hold investing approach espoused by silver-haired Wall Street veterans. Before starting my own company, I ran an investing service that showed people how to make money with low-risk dividend-paying stocks. If I hadn't made a name for myself with this strategy, I wouldn't be here writing a book for you today.

Even investors who want to dive deep into high-risk strategies should know that holding safe positions is a fundamental piece of high-risk investing. The math is simply too strong to completely ignore long-term buying and holding! For instance, over the last 90 years the S&P 500 grew in value in 74% of those years. That means that in nearly three-quarters of the years since 1940, investors who simply bought the S&P 500 saw their accounts grow in value!

THE STOCK MARKET IS STABLE

Though many in the doom-and-gloom crowd warn of imminent stock market crashes, the fact is these crashes are *extremely* rare. In fact, historically the S&P 500 rises for 9 years between every 30% market crash. And for all those looking to "time" the market, remember that more money has been lost anticipating market crashes than in the crashes themselves.

While this is a book on high-risk, high-reward investing, you want to make sure you have a solid foundation to employ these strategies. As a rule, **I keep 80% of my investment portfolio in reliable companies I plan to hold for many years**. These are stocks like Alphabet Inc. (GOOGL), Microsoft Corp. (MSFT), and even "trash" stocks like Waste Management (WM). These relatively low-risk positions provide a stable foundation on which I can employ higher-risk strategies.

It's important to maintain a core of lower-risk, lower-return assets in your portfolio because—frankly—if you *only* employ the strategies in this book, there's a good chance you could lose a significant amount of money. Having this solid foundation gives you the ability to take on extra risk without destroying your account.

HOW TO (SAFELY) BUILD ROCKETS

When Elon Musk and Jeff Bezos build their rockets, they know there's a good chance that the rockets might explode. In fact, NASA estimates there's a 1-in-60 chance that a rocket mission will fail, with a 1-in-276 chance that the mission will be fatal.

Musk and Bezos go to great lengths to make sure their rockets work properly. This is to ensure the viability of their business and to make sure they don't kill their employees in the process. They manage their risk by painstakingly reviewing launch protocols to ensure they don't literally blow themselves up.

To the Moon...When You're Ready

My goal with this book is to show you how to similarly manage risk with high-risk, high-reward investing. One of the most common investing phrases among the new crop of young investors is "to the moon." The phrase started in the cryptocurrency community to refer to when the price of a coin rises many hundreds of percent in a short time period. Now "to the moon" is a catchall for any investment that surges in value.

I want to show you how to build rockets to go "to the moon." But just like Musk and Bezos, you need to make sure your rockets are working properly before launch. That's why many sections in this book focus on investments that went south; you'll learn what works by analyzing what didn't.

WHAT IS DOLLAR-COST AVERAGING?

Dollar-cost averaging (DCA) is an investing approach where you invest equal amounts into an asset over regular intervals without regard to price. You'll see this term used frequently throughout the book; DCA is a good way to begin your involvement in a particular investment.

For instance, let's go back to the example of the investor with $500 in their brokerage account. The person feels like taking risks today, so instead of buying a blue-chip stock like Apple Inc. (AAPL), they opt to buy a special purpose acquisition company (SPAC; see Chapter 3) called Nikola Motors (NKLA). But 6 months later, this person loses 80% of their investment because, as it turned out, Nikola's upper management was charged with lying to investors.

Or instead of a SPAC, our hypothetical higher-risk-seeking investor decides to invest their $500 in a cryptocurrency (see Chapter 2) called XRP. They read an article showing how Ripple, the company that developed the XRP token, was going to revolutionize international transactions, so they plug their $500 into the speculative asset with hopes of tripling their investment. Unfortunately, US regulators come down hard on XRP not long after, sending its value down 90%.

To try and make the lost money back, our investor takes what little cash is left and bets it all on a microcap stock (see Chapter 6). A "microcap millionaire" on *YouTube* predicted that this stock could surge 1,000% in the next year. What the *YouTuber* didn't mention was how "share dilution" works for small companies. Although the share price of the microcap stock rose, our investor lost 50% on their initial investment because of dilution.

This book will spend a lot of time showing you how to manage the risks associated with high-risk, high-reward strategies. That starts with having a solid foundation of low-risk stocks to make sure you are diversified and protected from major market pullbacks.

After all, if you want to go to the moon, you must know how to build a rocket that will deliver you there safely.

CHAPTER 2

Cryptocurrencies

Cryptocurrencies are digital currencies in which transactions are monitored by a system that uses cryptography rather than a centralized authority. Cryptography is a discipline that explores how to securely transfer information while allowing only the sender and the recipient of the message to see the content. Think about the currency you're familiar with—dollars, cents, and so on. It's issued by and maintained by the federal government. That's not the case with cryptocurrencies such as Bitcoin and Ethereum.

Cryptocurrencies have their roots in a concept that may seem totally different: digital music. Back in the late 1990s and early 21st century, a new software program called Napster was blowing people away. Founded by Shawn Fanning and Sean Parker in 1999, the Napster file-sharing service allowed anyone in the world to easily send music to other people over the Internet. While Napster was eventually shut down due to copyright infringement, its legacy as the first widely used application of *peer-to-peer software* lives on. For the first time in history, the service made it possible for people outside the traditional brick-and-mortar music market to exchange music without the use of an intermediary.

Although peer-to-peer software was revolutionary at the time, Napster is hardly its most influential application. Just over a decade later, a mysterious figure named Satoshi Nakamoto applied the same concept to his project: Bitcoin. Satoshi's creation allowed people to send money outside the traditional banking system without the assistance of a financial intermediary. This digital currency, known as "cryptocurrency," now makes up a market that's worth more than $2 trillion.

And the world's first cryptocurrency is—you guessed it—bitcoin.

WHAT IS BITCOIN?

Let's start with some general points about cryptocurrency. A cryptocurrency is a digital asset that works as a medium of exchange. The idea combines two concepts: "crypto" (or computer code) and "currency," such as the US dollar. That makes "cryptocurrency" a digital medium of exchange backed by computer code.

Cryptocurrency is just like the dollar bill (a medium of exchange) you might have in your wallet right now. But unlike US dollars and other currencies like euros or yen, which are backed by governments and assets such as gold, cryptocurrencies are reinforced solely by computer code on something called a *blockchain*. A blockchain is a revolutionary way of recording information in a way that makes it nearly impossible for users to change, hack, or get around the security of the system. That makes bitcoin a "state-less" or "bank-less" money.

The Birth of the Bitcoin

It should thus be no surprise that bitcoin—the world's first cryptocurrency—was born out of the global financial crisis of 2008. The original Bitcoin white paper—or thesis statement for a cryptocurrency—was first published in October 2008. Titled "Bitcoin: A Peer-to-Peer Electronic Cash System," this landmark paper was published a mere month after the collapse of Lehman Brothers during the subprime mortgage crisis.

This tumultuous period shook many people's faith in the global banking system, as the US government blatantly cherry-picked winners (Goldman Sachs) and losers (Bear Stearns, Lehman Brothers). With the unprecedented money printing that followed via a new Federal Reserve policy known as "quantitative easing" (QE)—a central bank policy of buying government bonds to push down interest rates and inject more money into the financial system—a fresh approach to the concept of money was not only needed; it was a natural step forward. These initiatives made people uneasy because they involved untested monetary policies. In fact, the Fed was injecting so much money into the financial system that some economists were worried it could lead to hyperinflation.

Bitcoin developed in response to the extraordinary uncertainty in the traditional markets at the time. By design, only 21 million bitcoins will ever exist.

This is known as a "hard cap," and it distinguishes bitcoin from "fiat" currencies, which are government-issued currencies (like the US dollar) not backed or supported by a commodity like gold. This structure allows central banks to control how much money is printed at any given time. Bitcoin's creator rejected this idea, instead opting for a hard cap on its supply to make sure no government or central bank could dilute bitcoin's value by "printing" more bitcoin.

BITCOIN IN THE MIDST OF CRISES

Bitcoin has been a godsend for people in countries experiencing issues with their currency. For instance, when Venezuela's currency was experiencing hyperinflation, many of its citizens converted their assets to either US dollars or bitcoin to preserve their purchasing power.

People fleeing authoritarian governments did the same thing. Since a Bitcoin address is only a series of numbers, people were able to convert their cash assets to bitcoin and simply remember their Bitcoin address as they fled their native country.

Prior to bitcoin, people in such desperate situations had to convert their cash to other goods (e.g., gold) before fleeing, or else leave everything behind. Bitcoin provides a much more secure and easily executable option for transferring assets in times of crisis.

A Peer-to-Peer Cash System in Action

Bitcoin provides a simple way to move funds around quickly. For instance, let's say you live in Los Angeles and want to invest in a business run by a friend, Pierre, in France. But here's the catch: You need to send him $50,000 to secure an investment in the next 5 days, otherwise the deal is off.

You quickly run into a problem: Since Pierre didn't tell you about the deal until Friday afternoon, you didn't have time to contact your bank. Considering that it will take 3–5 days to wire the money, you will not be able to get Pierre his money in time.

That's where bitcoin comes into play. Since Pierre has a Bitcoin address, you're able to convert $50,000 into bitcoin and send him the money without the use of a bank. While it may take up to an hour to transfer the funds, it's still much faster and more efficient than waiting the 3–5 business days that the traditional bank route would require.

While this state-less and bank-less scenario works in a vacuum, the situation becomes more complex when you consider bitcoin's volatility.

Hold On for Dear Life (HODL)

One of the most common terms you'll hear in the cryptocurrency community is "hodl." While some might think of this as a variation on the word *hold*, it's actually an acronym that stands for "Hold On for Dear Life."

When it comes to bitcoin pricing, you often need to "hodl" because the cryptocurrency has famously high *volatility*. Volatility is an asset's price changes over a period of time. Basically, it tells you how often the price fluctuates and how steep those fluctuations are.

Few assets are more volatile than bitcoin. For instance, in 2017 bitcoin's price increased 1,400%. But that grind to the top included five separate 30% declines—and a 30% decline is a substantial drop. For instance, those who were invested in the stock market during the COVID-19 crash saw the S&P 500 fall 36% in March 2020. Imagine that happening five times in under a year!

Knowing this, let's revisit our earlier example. You tell Pierre that your bank is closed so you'll have to send the $50,000 via the Bitcoin network. Pierre agrees, but as you're completing the transaction, bitcoin has a steep sell-off. By the time your bitcoin arrives at Pierre's bitcoin wallet, that $50,000 is worth $40,000.

Clearly, if you can lose 20% of your principal in a matter of hours, bitcoin isn't a perfect medium of exchange. On the other hand, this volatility is one thing that has contributed to bitcoin becoming the best-performing asset in history. And it's also the reason why investors can make loads of money with bitcoin.

CASE STUDY:
A VALUABLE LESSON IN "HODLING"

I first heard of bitcoin back in 2014. A company I was working for as a junior research analyst had me dig deep into the technology and prepare a report for a client. During my research, it became clear bitcoin was some sort of "digital gold." But I concluded my report asserting that bitcoin was too expensive to invest in, as it was sitting at an all-time high price of $600.

Bitcoin was also difficult to buy back then. Anyone who wanted to buy bitcoin or other cryptocurrencies had to connect their bank account to shady exchanges. The largest exchange at the time was Mt. Gox, a Japanese exchange that would eventually lose 850,000 bitcoins—worth $42 billion as of this writing—in a cyber-hacking incident.

Because prices looked expensive, and without an easy place to buy, I decided to sit on the sidelines. That's what I did until 2017, when I found an exchange called Coinbase that made it relatively easy to buy bitcoin. So I hooked up a bank account to Coinbase and bought $500 worth of bitcoin. At the time, this represented 0.2 of one bitcoin. While I didn't know it at the time, this purchase would take me on a wild emotional and financial ride over the next 4 years.

Prelude to a Crypto Winter

Bitcoin continued to surge through the remainder of 2017. Since my $500 buy that summer, bitcoin had surged over 500%. Now my initial $500 investment was worth over $3,000!

I continued to add to my position. In fact, by the end of the year I'd become a "whole coiner," which is crypto slang for owning an entire bitcoin rather than a fraction of one. Despite the big run-up, I still believed I'd gotten in early on this novel technology and prices would keep rising. And if I kept "hodling" bitcoin—and buying more—it could make me rich.

Similar to many assets that quickly rise in value, bitcoin experienced a sharp "mean reversion." After peaking at $19,650 in December 2017, bitcoin rapidly lost value. In fact, by the end of 2018, bitcoin had crashed 81%. Since I'd been buying at as high as $15,000 per bitcoin, my initial 500% gain had turned into a massive loss.

Losing money is demoralizing for any investor. Nevertheless, since I had experience with investing and kept a long-term view, I decided to "hodl" my bit-coin positions. Plus, I knew that bitcoin's net unrealized profit and loss (NUPL) and bitcoin dominance indicators were now near cycle lows (more on that later in this chapter). Since these indicator readings meant it was a great time to buy, I decided to "hodl" my position.

Don't Flinch When Your Face Gets Ripped Off

I held my "whole coin" throughout all of 2018. While the news media coverage and general interest in bitcoin had faded, I kept my bitcoin in my Coinbase wallet.

In 2019, I decided to buy *more* bitcoin. I believed in the project's long-term goals of allowing people to keep money outside the financial system. By January 2020, I'd acquired another bitcoin. Now I held two bitcoins with an average cost of $8,000. At $16,000, bitcoin was now the largest position in my portfolio.

I also knew that bitcoin was a "risk-on" asset. This meant that people would buy bitcoin when they wanted to take on more risk with their portfolio. With the US economy in its longest growth streak since the 1950s and stocks at all-time highs, it seemed like the perfect time to increase my bitcoin position.

Then the COVID-19 pandemic struck. In March 2020, the S&P 500 fell 36% as the global economy braced for lockdown. Investors lost their appetite for risk in a big way, and the bitcoin price fell more than 50% in a matter of days.

While I saw my largest holding get cut in half, I reminded myself that nothing with my thesis had changed, so I should continue to hold my position. This strategy would pay off: By the end of the year, bitcoin had hit a new all-time high of $42,000. And by early 2021, my two bitcoins were worth $120,000.

INVESTMENT STRATEGY:
BITCOIN

When it comes to high-risk, high-reward investments, few offer better prospects than buying and holding bitcoin. While there are certainly faster blockchains with better technology, bitcoin is the best-known cryptocurrency and has "first mover advantage" in the cryptocurrency market.

This name recognition and "network effect" makes bitcoin a great long-term investment. That's especially true because of the "hard cap" of 21 million coins that cannot be exceeded.

CRYPTOCURRENCIES AS LEGAL TENDER

I'm not the only one who believes in the long-term prospects of bitcoin. In 2021, El Salvador was the first country to adopt bitcoin as legal tender. This means that all businesses in that country must accept bitcoin for goods and services. It's possible that other countries will follow El Salvador's lead in the future.

How to Identify a Good Time to Buy Bitcoin

Similar to all cryptocurrencies, bitcoin is a highly volatile asset. But if you can stomach the steep declines, the payoff can be very rewarding. It may often seem like bitcoin's price moves at random. Rest assured, there are large players, known as "whales," who will influence the market. Although it's a difficult market in which to invest, there are a few key technical indicators to keep an eye on that help determine where bitcoin's price is headed. If you learn how to read and interpret these metrics, you can make tons of money. Here are the key indicators:

1. Net Unrealized Profit and Loss (NUPL)

The net unrealized profit and loss (NUPL) is the difference between the relative unrealized profit and the relative unrealized loss for all bitcoins in existence. When bitcoin's unrealized profits are high, this implies that bitcoin investors are greedy. This makes sense, as the more unrealized profit in bitcoin, the more likely it is that investors will take profit on their positions.

This indicator has a great track record. A NUPL reading of 75% or higher—also known as the "euphoria zone"—has coincided with the last five "tops" in bitcoin's price.

Fortunately, the opposite is also true. When NUPL is low, it means that few investors are sitting on gains with their bitcoin positions. This is known as the "capitulation zone" and has coincided with a bottom in bitcoin's price for the last five cycles.

Investors looking to open a position in bitcoin would be wise to wait until bitcoin is in the capitulation zone, or when NUPL is below 0%. On the flip side, it's a good idea for investors to take profits on bitcoin when the NUPL index is 75% or higher. Investors can find NUPL data on LookIntoBitcoin.com and Glassnode.com.

2. Bitcoin Dominance

Bitcoin dominance tells you how much of the total cryptocurrency market is composed of bitcoin. A downtrend in bitcoin's dominance happens during cryptocurrency bull markets, as prices for "altcoins" (which we'll discuss in the next section) rise faster than the bitcoin price.

On the other hand, an uptrend in bitcoin's dominance happens during a cryptocurrency bear market. This is a good time to either sell your cryptocurrency positions for bitcoin or convert your cryptocurrency to cash.

As a rule, you want to buy bitcoin when bitcoin dominance is low and sell when bitcoin dominance is high (and vice versa for altcoins). Historically, when bitcoin dominance falls *below* 40% of the cryptocurrency market, it's a good time to buy bitcoin. And when it rises *above* 65%, it's a good time to take profits. You can find bitcoin dominance information on TradingView.com.

3. Unique Wallet Addresses

When you decide to open a Bitcoin wallet, the first action you must take is to establish a crypto wallet address. This is the address with which a person can send and receive cryptocurrencies.

It follows that one of the best indicators for how many people are using cryptocurrency and adopting blockchain technology is tracking how many addresses are being created.

Keeping track of the number of new addresses created (and how many are active) is a great way to measure cryptocurrency sentiment. These metrics tell you how many new investors are entering the crypto market in addition to how many accounts are active. You can find this information on Blockchain.com.

How to Invest In Bitcoin

Once you've decided to buy bitcoin, you want to dollar-cost average into your position. As discussed in Chapter 1, dollar-cost averaging is an investing approach where you invest equal amounts into an asset over regular intervals without regard to price. Therefore, if you have $1,000 to invest in bitcoin and want to spread your buys over a few months, you can select to buy $100 worth of bitcoin every Monday at 5 p.m., for example. For new investors, it's a good idea to have a set amount you want to invest every month and have your broker buy it for you. This reduces volatility in your entry price.

You are not required to have the broker make the purchase for you, but at first, it's not a bad idea to get a little help. It's a personal choice.

Depending on your risk tolerance, allocating 5%–8% of your portfolio to bitcoin is advisable, and for beginners, perhaps even less.

When opening your position, you want to make sure that the NUPL index is not near the "euphoria" stage. If that's the case, it's best to sit on the sidelines until bitcoin pulls back. If there is anything we know about bitcoin, it's that another major pullback is inevitable.

In the same vein, you want to invest in bitcoin when bitcoin dominance is high. This will ensure you're not buying during the throes of a bull market. Investors can find bitcoin dominance information on TradingView.com.

When both bitcoin dominance and NUPL are at their cycle peaks, that's a good time to take some profits off the table.

ALTCOINS

WHAT ARE ALTCOINS?

While bitcoin makes up most of the cryptocurrency market, the rest of the market is made up of something called altcoins.

The term *altcoin* is short for "alternative versions of bitcoins." An altcoin is simply any cryptocurrency other than bitcoin. And there are *loads* of altcoins on the market. As of February 2021, there were nearly 9,000 altcoins available for trading.

Altcoins fall into four broad categories:

- **Mining:** These altcoins use a proof-of-work (PoW) structure in which complex systems generate new coins and keep track of transactions.
- **Stablecoins:** These altcoins are pegged to a value of goods, such as a currency or precious metal. These have low price volatility, as their value is designed to be tied to fiat currencies like the US dollar, commodities, or even other cryptocurrencies. For instance, the largest stablecoin, known as "tether," stays at a level of $1.
- **Utility tokens:** These altcoins provide a function within a cryptographic network. They are typically not for investment purposes; rather they are designed to be used to buy products within a certain platform.
- **Security tokens:** These altcoins represent a form of ownership in a crypto project or company, much like a share of stock represents an ownership stake in a company. Security tokens give holders voting rights, dividends, and partial ownership in the company.

Like the mining category of altcoins, bitcoin is a proof-of-work (PoW) token. This means that in order for new bitcoins to be created, they need to be mined by a decentralized system of computers solving increasingly difficult math problems. Since it takes increasingly more powerful computers to solve each problem, these computers use lots of energy.

Many altcoins improve on this proof-of-work process by using what's known as "proof of stake" (PoS). Just like PoW, this other "consensus mechanism" is used to verify new transactions, add them to each altcoin's blockchain, and create new tokens. Basically, a consensus mechanism is a way to make sure that people aren't spending their cryptocurrencies twice, what's known as the "double-spend" problem.

Both PoS and PoW solve cryptocurrency's double-spend problem. That concept is best explained with an example. Say you want to buy a $200 pair of Air Jordan 7s. In the brick-and-mortar world, you would simply swipe your Visa to purchase them. In this case, Visa acts as the central authority and serves as intermediary between you, your bank, and the merchant. This ensures that you don't take that same $200 and spend it on a steak dinner down the street.

In the altcoin and crypto universe, there are competing theories on how to solve this double-spend problem. And as I'll show you in the case study later in the chapter, a failure to pay attention to these nuances can land you in court.

Double, Double, Toil and Trouble

Cryptocurrencies aim to replace the middleman for financial transactions. But proof-of-work (PoW) and proof-of-stake (PoS) systems go about solving this issue two different ways.

Proof of Work (PoW)

Let's circle back to the sneaker example. Instead of using your Visa card to buy the pair of Air Jordan 7s, you decide to pay with bitcoin. Bitcoin is underpinned by a type of "distributed ledger" known as a "blockchain." Every time someone makes a transaction on this network, the transaction is recorded on this blockchain, sort of like a ledger.

To ensure nobody is spending their holdings twice, the ledger is distributed (or shared) between millions of computers. These computers solve increasingly difficult mathematical problems roughly every 10 minutes to verify that nobody on the network has double spent their bitcoins. And if a miner solves the problem, that miner is rewarded with bitcoins.

The issue with PoW is that it uses lots of energy. In fact, some estimates claim the Bitcoin network uses 54 terawatt hours per year, or the equivalent of powering 5 million US households or the entire country of New Zealand.

Therefore, when you buy your Air Jordan 7s with bitcoin, the transaction is verified by this series of decentralized computers using *loads* of energy. There is no Visa or Mastercard verifying the transaction, only the Bitcoin network and these mining operations.

Proof of Stake (PoS)

Proof of stake works under different parameters. While PoW systems are powered by decentralized mining operations, PoS uses a series of "validators" to ensure that no person is double spending. The system selects a node—a computer linked to a computer currency network—to validate each transaction. This bypasses the wasteful energy usage employed by PoW.

CASE STUDY:

RIPPLE LABS AND XRP

In September 2017, a friend of mine who was a successful software engineer came to me excited about a new cryptocurrency project. He started telling me about a company called Ripple Labs. Their goal was to make it easy for banks and other large institutions to send money quickly and seamlessly across borders. Since the 1970s, banks have had to use something called the Society for Worldwide Interbank Financial Telecommunication (SWIFT) system to send money across borders. The system allows 11,000 financial institutions from 200 countries to send money via a messaging network.

Unfortunately, the SWIFT system is *very* slow. It takes 3–5 business days to transfer money, and you must pay foreign transaction fees. By the time a $100,000 transaction is transferred from a bank in the US to Canada, it might be worth only $98,000 as a result of fees and exchange rate issues.

Ripple Labs wanted to change this procedure with their XRP cryptocurrency. This token would allow individuals and banks to conduct large financial transactions instantly. There would be no wait times (like with the SWIFT system), and the platform fees would be minimal, making XRP—in the eyes of Ripple Labs—a utility token.

I bought my friend's sales pitch. After he showed me how to buy the tokens on a Chinese crypto exchange called Binance, I bought a $500 position at $0.18 per token.

Ripple Goes to the Moon

XRP was largely unknown at the time. While Ripple Labs was founded in 2012, the XRP token had only started trading in 2014. Since cryptocurrency was still a relatively unknown topic for people outside of finance and tech, it was under most people's radar.

That changed in the weeks after I bought my position in XRP. Interest in cryptocurrency started to swell as bitcoin's price kept surging. Once people realized there was an entirely different set of digital assets known as "altcoins," a flood of money poured into these newfound digital assets.

Between December 2017 and January 2018, XRP surged 1,135% to as high as $3.84. Ripple had pre-mined 38.7 billion XRP tokens, bringing the company's total market value to nearly $150 billion. For a brief time, this made Ripple cofounder Chris Larsen (who owned 37% of the company) one of the richest people in the world.

The key word here is *briefly*. While Ripple and XRP had their day in the sun at the start of 2018, the next 3 years would be tumultuous for the company.

What Goes Up Must Come...

The $500 XRP position I opened in September 2017 had grown to over $10,000 by early January 2018.

But just like Chris Larsen's stint as the world's richest man, my gain was short-lived. By September 2018, the value of my XRP holdings had dwindled to a mere $1,000. If you included all the times I added to my position while XRP's price was falling, this trade was officially in the red.

Things were about to get worse for Ripple and its founders. Unlike bitcoin and most altcoins, which are either proof of work (PoW) or proof of stake (PoS), Ripple uses a "consensus mechanism." This means that Ripple selects its "validators" to prevent double spending on its system.

Ripple had produced and sold XRP tokens to the tune of $1.3 billion. The problem was that, in addition to operating as a centralized exchange, the company was selling tokens to fund its operations. This drew the attention of the Securities and Exchange Commission (SEC), which claimed XRP was a "security."

In December 2020, XRP was delisted from Coinbase, the world's second-largest crypto exchange. While bitcoin and other cryptocurrencies surged during this period, XRP has yet to reclaim the all-time high it hit in January 2018.

You may wonder how XRP got into so much trouble. Basically, Ripple was issuing unregistered securities, which fell under the jurisdiction of the SEC. Unlike Ethereum (another altcoin, which we'll discuss in the next section), which is not considered a security because it is decentralized, XRP is currently seen as a security token by the SEC. The good news for XRP is that they are still negotiating with the SEC to decide if they are a utility token or a security token.

INVESTMENT STRATEGY:

ALTCOIN

The altcoin market is very diverse and rapidly evolving. In fact, by the time this book is published, there will likely be new types of altcoins hitting the market.

How to Identify a Good Altcoin Investment

In such a changing marketplace, it's important to know what you're investing in. Do your due diligence research before buying; the altcoin market is rife with scams. Investors venturing into this high-risk, high-reward market should keep this in mind before investing in any altcoin.

Finding and capitalizing on movements in altcoins is the epitome of a high-risk, high-reward trade. As seen in the XRP example, you can gain, and lose, thousands quickly. With altcoins, the data is not in your favor: A study from Messari, a crypto research firm, showed that 83% of altcoins that hit all-time highs in January 2018 were trading more than 90% below their all-time highs during the next bull market, which started in 2020.

This makes sense because during speculative manias, people typically pile into assets they don't understand out of a fear of missing out, or FOMO. This leads to a feeding frenzy in many tokens, pushing prices up to unsustainable heights (as we saw with XRP).

But if you use the following three guidelines, you'll increase your odds of making money.

1. Assess Token Utility

Before diving headfirst into buying an altcoin, you want to understand why it has value. For example, the value of bitcoin is that it allows its users to hold and transfer money peer-to-peer without the use of a traditional financial institution. Another example is XRP; this token can be used to send money around the world more quickly than through the traditional SWIFT system.

Note: "Token utility" should not be confused with "utility token," which is a type of cryptocurrency. Token utility refers to the intrinsic value of the cryptocurrency.

UNDERSTANDING VALUE

It's important to remember that *most cryptocurrencies do not have any intrinsic value*. While there are thousands of cryptocurrencies, only a handful perform a function that requires the token to be used and have value.

If your cryptocurrency of choice is simply a "meme coin" like ShibaCoin or Dogecoin, there's a good chance it will end up having little to no value. I'd recommend staying away from these coins; it's better to focus on projects with intrinsic value and real applications.

2. Study the Technical Specifications

Once you know that your altcoin has utility (i.e., it is worth something), you will want to start digging into the project's technical specifications.

First, it's important to determine whether the project is a proof-of-work (PoW) or proof-of-stake (PoS) system. This will tell you whether the project is centralized, thus confirming the stability of the project (the decentralized PoW is always preferred).

Second, you want to dig into the cryptocurrency's *tokenomics*, which is an explanation of how a cryptocurrency project works within the cryptocurrency ecosystem. This is incredibly important, as it tells you whether the supply of the token is inflationary or deflationary (among other factors). For instance, bitcoin is a *deflationary* (i.e., finite) cryptocurrency, which means that only 21 million bitcoins will ever exist. On the other hand, you have *inflationary* (i.e., infinite) cryptocurrencies like Dogecoin, which creates 10,000 new tokens every minute. For supply and demand to work in your favor, it's always better to hold deflationary assets.

3. Research the Project Team

Whether you're investing in start-ups, stocks, or cryptocurrencies, you *always* want to make sure your asset has a top-notch team behind it.

Even if you have a cryptocurrency with a solid use case and great tokenomics, it means nothing if there isn't a team to capitalize on the opportunity. For instance, many "shitcoins" like SafeMoon or CumRocket are created solely to rip off or "rug pull" investors. But if you buy the cryptocurrency only because the price is rising, you might think it's a legitimate project.

When looking at a cryptocurrency project, you want to see where the leaders of the team have previously worked. Those who have developed other successful cryptocurrency projects often held senior positions at major technology companies (Google, Microsoft, etc.) or come from top-tier universities (MIT, Harvard, etc.). Choosing projects where the management team has excellent credentials will increase your odds of hitting it big with an altcoin.

How to Invest In Altcoins

Once you've found a cryptocurrency project that checks all these boxes, it's a good idea to dollar-cost average into your position. Altcoins are famously volatile; by dollar-cost averaging, you spread your risk over the long term and minimize the damage to your position that can be caused by any major pullbacks.

After you've acquired your tokens, watch your position closely. Except for a few high-conviction long-term holds, I always include a 35% *stop loss* on my altcoins, meaning that I prearrange a sell order once the altcoin reaches a 35% loss. This is to make sure I don't let a bad loss turn into an insurmountable loss. And considering that most altcoins fall by 90% after a bull run, it's extremely important to take steps to protect your capital.

Let's say that one of your altcoins "pumps." This is cryptocurrency slang for a swift upward movement in price. When this happens, you want to avert excessive greed and "respect the pump." You should keep a close eye on the cryptocurrency's volume because once volume starts to decline, it could be time to scale out—or start selling—some of your position.

ETHEREUM

WHAT IS ETHEREUM?

Ethereum is the world's second-largest cryptocurrency and largest altcoin. While Ethereum's market capitalization is roughly half the size of Bitcoin's, it's 6 times larger than the third-largest cryptocurrency. At the time of this writing, it has a larger market capitalization than stalwart companies like Coca-Cola (KO), International Business Machines Corp. (IBM), and McDonald's (MCD).

Ethereum cofounder Gavin Wood described the proof-of-stake (PoS) platform as "one computer for the entire planet." This makes sense when you realize Ethereum users can:

- Access a broad range of financial services (brokers, exchanges, banks, etc.)
- Create and exchange non-fungible tokens (NFTs)
- Build real-world cryptocurrency tokens via ERC-20, which is Ethereum's "smart contract" system (discussed later in this chapter)

One way to describe Ethereum is that it's a *decentralized operating system for the cryptocurrency market.* An operating system is software that supervises a computer's hardware and provides critical services for computer programs. Anyone who uses a computer uses an operating system. For example, a Microsoft laptop uses Microsoft Windows as its operating system. To get this operating system, you went to a store and bought a computer that was preloaded with Microsoft Windows. You can do everything from writing software, browsing the Internet, to opening an Excel spreadsheet—all on this operating system.

The operating protocol for your phone is the same. For example, if you're using an iPhone, your phone comes preloaded with the iOS operating system. The operating system on the phone allows you to send text messages, watch videos, and download applications.

The key difference between Ethereum and Windows/iOS is that, with Ethereum, the applications (like browsing the Internet and texting) are not stored on one computer. In fact, Ethereum is spread over thousands of computers working together to run the Ethereum operating system. That means that Ethereum's infrastructure is "trustless" and not dependent on a third party to run the app. Instead, all transactions are stored and executed via something called "smart contracts," all of which are stored on the highly secure Ethereum blockchain.

This is a revolutionary idea in computing. No longer do those running applications need to worry about downtime, fraud, or interference from a third party. Because they are spread out, they are less vulnerable to interference.

Your Contracts Just Got "Smart"

Ethereum's smart contracts are arranged between the buyer and seller (i.e., self-executing contracts) with defined terms embedded in their code. They are just like contracts in the real world; the only difference is they're completely digital and stored on the Ethereum blockchain.

One way to think about a smart contract is that it's a tiny piece of software that executes when a task is complete. Let's use an example: Say you want to take a cab from your hotel in Manhattan to LaGuardia Airport. You open your Uber app, order your car, and get picked up by your driver. Once you arrive at the airport, you pay the driver via the Uber app.

Uber acts as the middleman between you and the driver and collects a fee for facilitating the transaction. That means both you and the Uber driver need to "trust" that Uber will make sure both parties receive what was agreed upon.

Now let's say there's a new ride-hailing app or "dapp" (i.e., decentralized application) built on the Ethereum network called Super. Just like before, you need a ride to the airport. So you open your Super "dapp" and order a car. When a Super driver sees your order come through, he accepts—which immediately creates a smart contract.

Notice that Super is not a company. It is simply a decentralized app that is connecting you to your driver. They are not taking a fee for this transaction and there is no one on the other end facilitating the contract. Instead, you and the driver created a contract that is locked until it's complete. It cannot be changed by either party and is stored on the Ethereum network. When you arrive at LaGuardia Airport, the smart contract recognizes the terms have been met and releases your funds to the driver.

While this is a revolutionary idea for making transactions, there are a variety of moving pieces that make this network run smoothly.

You'll Need Some "Gas" to Run That Dapp

This Ethereum network doesn't run on its own. Instead, it's run by a series of computers called "nodes." There's even a special group of these nodes, known as "miners," that make sure the Ethereum network is secure and working properly.

But these miners don't do this out of the goodness of their heart; they're paid in something called "gas," which is a percentage of "ether," or the cryptocurrency that underpins the Ethereum network.

These miners are the gatekeepers of the Ethereum network. They're tasked with prioritizing which processes on the network are executed first. To get to the front of this line, those running dapps on the Ethereum network pay "gas."

This gas is what makes Ethereum run efficiently. Since Ethereum is both the operating system for the cryptocurrency community and a haven for smart contracts, it's important to make sure this system can function as effectively as possible. It's also a key reason why Ethereum has so much value.

CASE STUDY:

BUY ETHER WHEN THERE'S BLOOD IN THE STREETS

I'm the "investing guy" in my family. So when I was at our annual Christmas party in December 2017, everyone was asking me about cryptocurrency.

Bitcoin had hit a new all-time high of $19,650 a few weeks earlier. Since prices had pulled back 30% after an incredible 900% gain over the previous 6 months, many in my family were asking if they should "buy the dip." Despite my warnings about the dangers and volatility in cryptocurrency, many decided to take the plunge.

A few weeks of glee followed, especially for those who bought Ethereum. Between December 22, 2017, and January 12, 2018, the price of ether—the cryptocurrency token used on the Ethereum network—nearly doubled. I was getting text messages from my family showing their Coinbase accounts and how much money they'd made.

Not long after, the messages stopped completely. Ether prices—and the rest of the crypto market—started to collapse. This got so bad that ether prices fell 91% over the next year.

Suffice to say, none of my kin wanted to talk about cryptocurrency at the family Christmas party the following year. But if you understand market sentiment, this was precisely the right time to buy.

There Will Be...Gas

One of my investing mentors, Jared Dillian, is a master of gauging market sentiment. While working as his analyst for many years, I saw how he would often do the opposite of what the market consensus was at the time.

For example, Mexican restaurant Chipotle (CMG) had a major *E. coli* scare in 2016. This caused the stock to crash 64% over the following year. Not long after this epic collapse in Chipotle's share price, Jared had me prepare a research report on the company.

In my report, I detailed how the Mexican burrito chain had a strong brand, solid sales growth, and high sales per square foot. Also, there was little chatter online about Chipotle and *E. coli*, implying the downward catalyst for the stock had faded. After reading my report, Jared was convinced that the reports of Chipotle's demise were wildly exaggerated. He soon recommended the stock to his subscribers, which was great timing, as the stock surged 500% over the next 4 years.

I applied this same "buy when there's blood in the streets" approach to the cryptocurrency market in early 2019. At that time, most pundits had chalked up the cryptocurrency boom in 2018 to a speculative bubble akin to the Dutch tulip mania in the 17th century. If you looked at Google Trends—which shows you how many people are searching for a particular subject—searches for "crypto" or "bitcoin" were back to pre–2018 run levels.

Thinking this could be an indicator that sentiment for the cryptocurrency market was reviving, I began investing heavily in the cryptocurrency market.

Return of the Cryptocurrency Bull Market

Between February 2019 and January 2020, I began dollar-cost averaging into my highest-conviction cryptocurrency projects: Bitcoin and Ethereum. Ether had lost more than 90% of its value during this bear market. Since I knew ether was an "operating system" for cryptocurrencies, it followed that a bet on ether was a bet on long-term growth in the cryptocurrency market. After a year of dollar-cost averaging into ether, it was now 8% of my investment portfolio.

However, I wasn't done being tested by the cryptocurrency market, as Bitcoin and Ethereum crashed near 4-year lows during the COVID-19 crisis. Even though there was so much uncertainty, I kept dollar-cost averaging into my position without selling any of my holdings.

This turned out to be one of the best investment decisions I ever made, as by the end of 2020 we'd entered another cryptocurrency bull market. And by early 2021, my Ethereum position was up more than 800%.

ETHEREUM

As you'll notice throughout this chapter, the best time to buy cryptocurrency—and really any high-risk, high-reward investment—is when nobody else wants it and when negative sentiment is at a fever pitch. In retrospect, I should have taken it as a sign that we were near the top of the bull run when my family was talking nonstop about cryptocurrency.

How to Identify a Good Ethereum Investment

"Sentiment indicators" can be very useful when you are able to identify them. After all, if everyone is thinking negatively about an investment, who will be left to buy and drive the price higher? To help you keep track of sentiment (and other factors), I outlined a few tools you can use to stack the deck in your favor.

Fortunately, trading ether is much more straightforward than trading bitcoin or altcoins. In the earlier section on altcoins, we discussed three factors you should focus on when analyzing altcoins:

- Value
- Technical specifications
- The project team

These considerations are also relevant when it comes to assessing an Ethereum investment. For ether, the token has intrinsic value (i.e., it is worth something) since it's the operating system on which many cryptocurrency projects are built. It also has favorable "tokenomics," as EIP-1559 introduced a deflationary feature to the network. This created a base fee for using space on the Ethereum network, which "burns" ether after its use (thus lowering the total supply). And since Ethereum is led by early crypto adopter and founder Vitalik Buterin, the network has a solid management team.

The following additional factors will help you enter and exit your Ethereum position at opportune times.

1. Monitor Google Trends

Google Trends allows you to track how many people are searching for a particular topic. For instance, at the end of every January you will see searches for "Super Bowl" surge and then fall back down after the game.

You can use this same idea when investing in Ethereum. For example, I started dollar-cost averaging into Ethereum when Google Trends activity had fallen to pre–bull run levels. This is typically a good time to buy into cryptocurrency—when interest is low and so are prices.

2. Use Technical Analysis

Technical analysis is a trading technique that evaluates investments based on price trends and patterns seen on charts. While you could write an entire book on technical analysis, the discipline is important for Ethereum and all other cryptocurrencies as well.

One way to determine a healthy technical picture is to look at a security's moving averages. These are the average prices for a security during a specific period. I prefer to buy ether when it is in an uptrend, which is when its 15-day moving average is above its 50-day moving average, for example (and both are above the 200-day moving average). You can find this information on TradingView.com.

3. Research Corporate Adoption

Since the Ethereum network is the gold standard of decentralized blockchains, the platform has courted many big companies. Recently, companies using Ethereum to build products include JPMorgan Chase, Amazon, and Microsoft.

When a company announces that it is going to use the Ethereum network, that is almost always bullish for prices. That's why it's a good idea to keep track of press releases for any company announcing partnerships with Ethereum.

ETHER IS BEST FOR LONG-TERM GROWTH

Remember that investing in Ethereum and its ether cryptocurrency is a bet on the long-term growth in the cryptocurrency market. Since it's very likely the market will grow and mature over many years, it makes sense to ignore most short-term fluctuations with ether's price and—as crypto traders say—"HODL."

How to Trade Ethereum

As with other altcoins, you want to dollar-cost average into your Ethereum position. I would recommend defining how much you plan to invest in ether and spread your entry out over 2–3 months. This will smooth out any volatility in ether prices over that period.

Assuming you're buying when interest in cryptocurrency is low, you should have an ideal entry point for prices. This means that you don't need to "trade" ether. Rather, you simply buy and hold your investment for many years and let your gains compound.

Investing Quick-Start Guide:
BITCOIN, ALTCOINS, AND ETHEREUM

These step-by-step instructions can be used to trade any cryptocurrency, including altcoins and Ethereum.

1. Open an account with an exchange (e.g., Coinbase, Binance, etc.).

2. After your account is approved (which can take at least a week), fund the account.

3. Take your time to learn the mechanics of buying and selling cryptocurrencies. At first, start small. It's possible to buy just a few dollars' worth of a cryptocurrency.

4. Gain access to your Bitcoin address and password.

5. Do your homework and avoid buying unknown cryptocurrencies. At first, stick with the ones mentioned in this book, such as Bitcoin and Ethereum.

6. After buying a cryptocurrency, keep your coins on the exchange. And if you are worried about getting hacked, you can always transfer your digital assets from the exchange to a personal cold wallet (i.e., an offsite location not connected to the Internet). Fortunately, cryptocurrency exchanges have taken steps to improve security, and the likelihood of getting hacked is minimal.

CHAPTER 3

Volatile Stocks

Stocks are securities that represent a fraction of ownership in a company. Think of a share of stock as a small piece of a company that fluctuates in value. This chapter will cover highly volatile stocks like growth stocks, initial public offerings (IPOs), special purpose acquisition companies (SPACs), and deep value stocks. If you don't know what any of those are, don't worry, as I'm going to review each in great detail.

One of the best parts of my job is that I get to travel all over the world. I've been lucky enough to sit with central bankers in Brussels, wealth management professionals in Buenos Aires, and astrophysicists in Vienna. But my favorite work trip of all time was spending 3 hours with the Swiss billionaire Felix Zulauf.

Felix started his investing career as a trader for Swiss Bank Corporation (now part of UBS). After proving that he could manage a multi-asset portfolio, he became head of institutional portfolio management for Switzerland's largest bank. When I met Felix, he was near retirement and running his family office in Zug, Switzerland. Even though he was a man managing $1.3 billion of his own money, he was happy to take a few hours to talk with me when I was in Switzerland on business.

While he is a traditional value investor, Felix told me that people who can find high-growth stocks with long-term growth prospects could make life-changing money. Buying and holding these unique companies would "cover up losses" as their gains compounded over many years.

Knowing how to spot the fakers from the real deal was the difficult part. That's when I dedicated myself to researching and investing in high-growth and other volatile stocks.

HIGH-GROWTH STOCKS

WHAT ARE HIGH-GROWTH STOCKS?

There are two ends of the spectrum when it comes to stock investing: value and growth.

Value Investing

Value investors try to find companies that are trading below their "intrinsic value." Popularized by Warren Buffett and his mentor Benjamin Graham, this technique uses fundamental research to determine if a company's stock is cheap relative to its market value. This approach commonly employs valuation techniques such as discounted cash flow, dividend discount model, and comparative analysis. Value stocks also tend to trade at low or "cheap" valuation metrics like price-to-earnings, price-to-sales, and price-to-book.

There's a catch, however. Stocks trading at a good value are typically slow-growth companies operating in mature industries. They are also relatively low risk compared to growth stocks and will theoretically hold their value better during market downturns.

For example, Procter & Gamble (PG) is a classic value stock. The company sells goods like Charmin toilet paper, Pampers diapers, and other items consumers will buy no matter what is happening in the broader economy. After all, people always need toilet paper and diapers, so investors are happy to invest in Procter & Gamble and hold their shares even during market downturns.

That also means Procter & Gamble's upside is lower than what you'd find in a growth stock counterpart. While the company grows its earnings at a steady 4%–5% per year with little volatility, its share price will likely either track or underperform the S&P 500 in most years.

Growth Investing

On the other end of the spectrum is growth investing. This approach looks for companies that have the potential to grow earnings and share prices quickly and—ideally—beat the S&P 500 over the long term.

Growth stocks are typically in fast-growing industries with exposure to what I call *secular trends*. A secular trend is a market dynamic that unfolds over many years. This could involve companies benefiting from things as simple as aging populations, global Internet adoption, or conversion to electric vehicles.

These are undeniable trends, and the best growth stocks tend to have the prospect of profiting from these trends over the long haul.

A growth stock that I've held for many years is Alphabet Inc. (GOOGL), the parent company of the popular search engine. The company is the largest digital advertiser in the world and grew earnings at an average of 17% per year between 2012 and 2021. And since digital ad sales will continue to grow as more people use the Internet, Alphabet's business has exposure to a long-term secular trend, which should translate to lots of profits. Because of this robust earnings growth, Alphabet shares have outperformed the S&P 500 but also trade at a "premium" relative to other stocks in the S&P 500. That means shares tend to be relatively expensive based on valuation metrics like forward price-to-earnings, price-to-sales, and price-to-free cash flow.

Unlike Procter & Gamble, which will perform well during bear markets, Alphabet would struggle, as digital advertising sales tend to crater in recessions (unlike demand for toilet paper). So, while shares of Alphabet may beat the S&P 500 during bull markets, they would be expected to underperform during bear markets.

If You Want a Higher Reward, You Need More Risk

Value and growth investing are the two pillars of stock investing. For both, the further out on the "risk pyramid" you go, the more high-risk, high-reward opportunities you find. In general, when I talk about the risk pyramid, I'm referring to how risky certain assets are compared to others. The hierarchy I use for the risk pyramid is as follows (listed from least risky to most risky):

- Cash
- Savings accounts
- US government bonds
- US investment-grade bonds
- Gold and silver
- Junk bonds
- Value stocks
- Alternative assets (REITs and business development companies)
- Growth stocks
- Deep value stocks
- High-growth stocks

- Small-cap stocks
- Microcap stocks
- Special situations (meme stocks, bankrupt stocks)
- Cryptocurrencies
- Non-fungible tokens (NFTs)

High-growth stocks fall on the higher-risk end of the risk pyramid, or what I like to call "the meaty part of the curve." Unlike growth stocks such as Alphabet, which are steadily growing earnings, many *high*-growth stocks are unprofitable. In fact, many companies readily admit they will lose money for many years before reaching profitability!

Arguably the most famous high-growth stock of the last decade is Tesla, Inc. (TSLA). The performance of the electric vehicle company headed by Elon Musk left investors—especially value investors—scratching their heads for years.

Value investors put a strong emphasis on earnings growth. This makes sense, as buying a share of a company's stock is akin to buying a piece of that company's earnings. The logic followed that if a company generated no earnings, how could it be highly valued?

Tesla upended this logic; between 2011 and 2015, the company sold $10 billion worth of electric vehicles, with sales growing more than 100% per year. But despite the impressive "top line" growth (i.e., sales), its "bottom line" (i.e., earnings) was lacking. Over the same time frame, Tesla *lost* nearly $2 billion! Even though Tesla was chronically losing money, the company's stock price kept rising. In fact, Tesla shares rose 900% between 2011 and 2015, more than 7 times the return on the S&P 500 during that period.

The market rewarded high-growth investors in this instance. They overlooked that Tesla was losing money in the short term because they calculated that over the long term the company would likely be the global leader in electric vehicles.

That's not to say all companies with a promising future will be rewarded by the market. For every Tesla, there are a hundred other high-growth companies that struggle or fail. But if you study the world's best high-growth investors, you, too, can find the next Tesla.

CATHIE WOOD AND THE ARK INNOVATION FUND

Back in 2018, I was preparing to make a presentation at an investment conference. At the time, I was a twenty-nine-year-old stock analyst who was predictably nervous to present my ideas to an audience full of seasoned hedge fund managers and high-net-worth individuals.

My presentation was scheduled for the afternoon. To help get an idea of the audience, I sat in the conference room. That was when I heard a woman named Cathie Wood calmly discussing her outlook for what she dubbed "disruptive companies."

I was drawn to the presentation because it was getting rather heated. One of the panelists—a well-known value investor—kept calling her holdings "bubble stocks." That's because they were high-growth companies that had yet to turn a profit but were trading at *extremely* high valuations.

The value investor had recently done an entire presentation on how Tesla was a Ponzi scheme that would be the next major short opportunity. Tesla also happened to be Wood's largest position in her flagship fund, the ARK Innovation Fund.

Little did I know that I was watching one of the world's top investors defend her portfolio. And a few years later, she would be vindicated.

Cathie Wood Lays Out Her Bold Thesis for the World

Wood's investment management company, Ark Invest, was focused on finding high-growth, disruptive companies that delivered the greatest returns relative to the risk. For instance, she'd often talk about how she was an early proponent of streaming company Netflix Inc. (NFLX).

In 2014, Wood surmised that the company would become one of the world's dominant media companies. That's because Netflix was providing a revolutionary—or *disruptive*—service to consumers. While a bizarre prediction at the time, Wood was vindicated as Netflix's stock returned over 700%—more than 4 times the S&P 500 return—between 2014 and 2021.

But Netflix was far from her boldest call; Wood made headlines in February 2018 when she stated on CNBC that Tesla stock would hit $4,000 within 5 years. Not only did that represent a gain of 1,100%, but Tesla also had yet to turn a profit. In fact, it was one of the most shorted—meaning investors were betting the stock would fall—stocks in the market!

Wood's Conviction on Tesla Pays Off

Wood was maligned in the financial media for her bullish call on Tesla, just like when she stated her case on stage at the investment conference.

By May 2019—18 months after Wood's appearance on CNBC—Tesla's stock had fallen 29%. Yet Wood and her team weren't deterred. In fact, she went back on CNBC to reaffirm her bullish outlook on Tesla. According to her detractors, Tesla was a car company and should trade closer in value to peers like General Motors (GM) or Ford Motor Company (F).

But in Wood's view, this comparison was misplaced. She kept reiterating her claim that GM and Ford were relics of the internal combustion engine age. On the other hand, Tesla was the market leader in electric vehicles and had a large "total addressable market" (TAM), meaning the market size that can theoretically be captured by the company. She also noted that Tesla could generate massive sales from high-margin "software as a service" (SaaS), such as their full self-driving technology—products GM or Ford could not offer.

And while her CNBC interviewers didn't grasp the thesis, it didn't matter. Three years later (and 2 years ahead of Wood's prediction) Tesla share price would surpass the lofty $4,000 price target she had forecast.

Not only that, but in 2020 Cathie Wood's ARK Innovation Fund (ARKK) was the best-performing actively managed exchange-traded fund in the world.

INVESTMENT STRATEGY:

HIGH-GROWTH STOCKS

Many high-growth stocks can go years without delivering returns. For instance, Cathie Wood is one of the greatest high-growth investors on record. In 2020, her fund returned an incredible 152%, which is equal to the returns on the S&P 500 from 2013 to 2020. Only investors with conviction were rewarded, though. From 2015 to 2019, Wood's fund did not have such stellar returns, either matching or underperforming the S&P 500. But if they stuck around, patient investors were rewarded in 2020.

How to Identify a Good High-Growth Stock

If you have patience and use the following three guidelines as factors to help you decide what to buy and when, you, too, can earn huge gains with high-growth stocks.

1. Look for High Sales Growth

High-growth companies will likely not have any earnings or positive cash flows at the time of your investment. This corporate strategy makes sense, as these companies are currently unprofitable by design and are choosing to reinvest their cash flows to grab as much market share as possible. This is so the business can "scale" (i.e., grow as fast as possible). Eventually, when the business is large enough and "hits scale," the profits will materialize, and the company will grow into its valuation.

That's only possible if you're growing sales quickly at the top line. When looking for a high-growth stock, I typically look for a company growing sales at a minimum of 15% per year. You will also want to look at what sales growth is relative to the "price-to-sales" valuation metric. This will tell you how much you're paying for each percentage of sales, or "sales per share." As a general rule, you want the company's 3-year average sales growth to be less than its forward price to sales multiple.

2. Evaluate the Total Addressable Market (TAM)

High-growth companies are typically trying to capitalize on a lucrative market opportunity. Whether it's Tesla with electric vehicles or Netflix with streaming video, these companies are going for a big piece of a big pie.

That "pie" is the TAM. You always want to invest in high-growth stocks with large (and growing!) total addressable markets.

A large TAM goes hand in hand with high sales growth. If the market opportunity (i.e., TAM) is being captured quickly (i.e., high sales growth), that means the business will likely scale and grow into its valuation.

In addition, look for companies with "optionality." This means that the business has more than one application. For instance, Unity Software (U) is a video game development company. While currently focused on video games, it has "optionality" outside the gaming industry since its platform can be adapted for aerospace, architecture, and other industries, thus enhancing its long-term TAM.

3. Choose a Company with Founder-Led Management

Once you've found a company that is growing sales and has a large total addressable market, you want to make sure the business has the right team in place to capitalize on the opportunity.

That's when vetting the management team comes into play. According to a 2016 study from *Harvard Business Review*, S&P 500 companies led by founders outperformed their non-founder-led peers 3-to-1 over the previous 15 years.

The reasons listed in the study are more qualitative than quantitative. For instance, the report claims that the founders of the company have a concrete vision for where they want the business to go. This single-mindedness directed toward conquering an industry is only fully articulated by the person who had the initial vision. This tirelessness is a classic founder trait; two good examples are Jeff Bezos (Amazon) and Reed Hastings (Netflix). When a business like a high-growth company is in its early stages, having a founder with a concrete vision for the company pays off tremendously.

How to Trade a High-Growth Stock

You need to be very picky about the high-growth stock you decide to buy. A large majority of high-growth companies—even if they're founder-led—will *not* capitalize on their market opportunity.

But once you've found one that meets the criteria I just laid out, begin dollar-cost averaging into your position. Since high-growth stocks are often very volatile, you want to make sure you are getting in at the best possible price.

Once you've acquired your shares, hold your position. This is especially true if the market is in a low inflation (i.e., 2% or lower) and low-interest-rate environment. Since most high-growth stocks will not generate earnings for many years, those earnings are worth less if inflation rises. For that reason, keep a close eye on the trajectory of the 10-year US Treasury yield. Why? If investors see a major uptick in inflation expectations—and thus bond yields— growth stocks will underperform. In that event, it's a good time to scale back on your growth stocks.

Investing Quick-Start Guide:
HIGH-GROWTH STOCKS

1. Identify a secular growth trend that the high-growth stock will capitalize on over the long term.

2. Once you've found a suitable company, allocate up to 3%–5% of your investable assets to the position.

3. To smooth out your entry price, I recommend scaling into your position over a few weeks via dollar-cost averaging.

4. Before buying, look at technical indicators to determine what stocks to buy and when.

5. My preference: A stock must fall below its 50-day or 200-day moving average before I open the position. As the stock falls below these key technical levels, I scale into the position with one-third of my position until I own 100% of the position.

6. Hold on to the stock even during volatile market conditions.

7. My stop loss for these stocks is 30%, which means I sell when I incur losses of 30% or more. I refuse to let a relatively small loss turn into a large loss (50% or more).

INITIAL PUBLIC OFFERINGS (IPOS)

WHAT ARE INITIAL PUBLIC OFFERINGS (IPOS)?

An initial public offering (IPO) is when a private company "offers" shares to the public. This means that anyone with a brokerage account can buy shares. Prior to an IPO, only private investors were able to invest in the company.

Most companies "go public" to raise money that can be used to invest in their business. Here's an example: Let's say you're the founder and CEO of a software business called Big Data Inc. Your business helps small businesses all over the world collect and interpret data on their customers. And since your software is based on a proprietary algorithm you developed while living in your parents' basement, it's been difficult for competitors to emulate your products.

Since you're the only game in town for this niche type of data analytics, your business is growing very fast. That means you need cash to take Big Data Inc. to the next level. Before soliciting outside investment, you ask your friends and family if they'd like to invest in your business. They agree, and you raise $200,000 in exchange for 5% of the company. With this new infusion of cash, your business is now valued at $4 million.

Things Start to Get Real for Big Data Inc.

Now let's say a year later, your business is booming and Big Data Inc. is expected to hit $10 million in sales. That's great news! On the flip side, you have a problem: If you want to hit that $10 million in sales, you need to hire twenty more employees to analyze data and buy more computer servers.

That's when investors from Redwood Capital—one of the most prestigious venture capital firms—come knocking at your door. This is a major vote of confidence, as Redwood Capital invested in other technology companies like Apple, Google, and PayPal in the early days. Redwood Capital offers you $10 million in exchange for 10% of your business. You're blown away, as that values your business at a whopping $100 million!

You take the $10 million from Redwood Capital and make the necessary hires and capital expenditures. A year later, Big Data Capital needs another cash injection. Since your sales projections have tripled to $30 million, Redwood Capital is happy to increase their investment to $50 million for an additional 5% of your business. This values your business at $1 billion—officially making Big Data Inc. a "unicorn," a start-up worth $1 billion or more.

At this point, you've sold 20% of your business's equity to family, friends, and venture capitalists. For your next round of funding, however, you decide to sell shares to the public via an IPO.

Big Data Inc. Goes Public

As the founder and CEO, you are now working with investment bank Goldman Sachs to underwrite the Big Data Inc. IPO. They help you file your S-1 registration statement, set up a board of directors, and lead a "road show" where they go around soliciting investment from institutional investors.

After this long drawn-out process, you've completed the steps necessary to start an IPO. Since your business is growing so fast, there is a lot of hype around the IPO. Guest analysts on CNBC keep saying that Big Data Inc. is the next hot stock, so retail investors can't wait to buy your shares. You head over to the New York Stock Exchange to ring the bell as many founders do on IPO day. Your shares then begin trading on public markets at a valuation of $10 billion.

Since you still own 60% of the company, you're now a billionaire with net assets of $6 billion.

Your friends and family have also realized a spectacular 250,000% return on their initial investment at a $4 million valuation. While not as eye-popping, Redwood Capital also scores with a 10,000% return on their initial $10 million investment. To lock in these gains, your friends, family, and Redwood Capital sell a good chunk of their initial investment on IPO day.

While this is great for these early investors, it's not so great for those buying on the day the IPO is launched. Once these new investors realize Redwood Capital and other "insiders" are selling their shares, they begin to sell as well. And within a few months of your IPO, Big Data Inc.'s market value has plummeted back down to $1 billion.

This is a very common occurrence with IPOs. While insiders tend to get very wealthy on IPO day, those retail investors who buy IPOs often get burned. The hype soon wears off, and when individual investors see insiders selling, it can often spook the markets and tank your stock price.

That's why it's important to be stoic with newly listed companies. Often, patient investors are rewarded with *huge* returns—even if the IPO is seen as a "failure" at first.

FERRARI AND THE LESSONS OF A "FAILED" IPO

Enzo Ferrari started the car company that displays his name in 1939. A veteran of the Italian military in World War I, Enzo dreamed of building the perfect race car. In the late 1940s, Luigi Chinetti approached Ferrari about building cars for the public. A few years later, Chinetti would open the first Ferrari showroom in the US.

Winning is a part of the culture at Ferrari. The racing team won a record 238 Grand Prix races. In addition to its winning reputation, Ferrari is synonymous with style. You can't help but do a double take when seeing a Ferrari drive down the street. This mix of artistry and performance is one reason Ferrari is a unique luxury brand. And this all played into the company's sky-high valuation when it went public on October 20, 2015, as individual investors could now own a piece of the iconic brand.

Unfortunately for Ferrari, it would soon be a "loser" on public markets.

Ferrari Stalls at the Starting Line

Ferrari shares were hyped before going public. CNBC was all over the IPO, broadcasting that both institutional and individual investors couldn't wait to buy shares. And while shares rose on IPO day, the party didn't last for long. After its first week, Ferrari saw its shares slip 6%. And by the end of the year, shares had lost 40% of their value!

This debacle was predictable if you knew what to look for. Ferrari went public at a nearly $10 billion valuation with a price-to-earnings (PE) ratio over 30. That implied Ferrari was growing very fast. The problem was that Ferrari—and most luxury brands—are all about exclusivity. Ferraris command a high price because they're rare. (The company had been limiting production to 7,000 cars per year, but in 2020, sales topped 10,000 for the first time.) Expecting the company to ramp up production to meet lofty expectations suggested by the high valuation didn't make much sense.

Ferrari shares had lost nearly half their value by early 2016. The hype had faded, and—at least in the investing community—Ferrari had become a joke.

But this was actually the perfect time to buy.

Ferrari Shares Get in Gear

Ferrari management was doing their best to ignore the noise around the stock. They needed to make sure to keep up the exclusivity that Enzo Ferrari and his team had created. Without that, the brand would lose value.

Management did its best to meet its growth projections. In 2016, the company produced 9,200 cars—an increase of 31%. While this was chump change compared to General Motors and their millions in sales, Ferrari made it clear that they could also grow revenue.

And with the share price decimated after such a hyped IPO, the stock was cheap relative to the company's earnings growth. Wall Street soon caught on; by the end of 2016, Ferrari share price had returned 50% and was back at its IPO point.

Just like the Ferrari car, the stock kicked into high gear, and by 2021 the luxury carmaker's stock was up 350% since its "failed" IPO.

INVESTMENT STRATEGY:

INITIAL PUBLIC OFFERINGS (IPOS)

This section will help you find an IPO that fits key criteria for a sound investment.

How to Identify a Good IPO

Bringing a company from humble beginnings to an IPO is a major milestone. Naturally, these firms waste no time promoting the fact that their shares will soon be traded on major exchanges.

You can find IPO calendars for free on websites like *Forbes*, *Nasdaq*, and *MarketWatch*. The investment banks leading the road shows *want* people to know these companies are going public, so you shouldn't have much trouble finding this information.

That said, you don't want to select any old IPO to buy. Therefore, if you evaluate the following three criteria, you'll increase your odds of making big gains in the IPO market.

1. Seek Out Strong Underwriters

An underwriter is the bank that evaluates and assumes the risk associated with the company going public. They are the ones evaluating how risky the company is, how the stock should be priced, and other criteria for bringing the company to market.

In the Big Data Inc. example earlier in this section, the underwriter for the IPO was Goldman Sachs, considered by many to be one of the most reputable IPO underwriters. Having a company like Goldman Sachs underwrite your IPO is a vote of confidence since they can be very picky about which companies they choose to bring public. Most companies would love for Goldman to bring them public, and since Goldman can choose what they believe are the best IPOs, it follows that any company they bring public is of good quality.

In addition to Goldman Sachs, Bank of America, Morgan Stanley, and JPMorgan Chase are also top-tier underwriters. If one of these companies is bringing your prospective IPO public, you're in good hands.

2. Know the Lock-Up Period

One thing that every IPO investor needs to know is an IPO's lock-up period. When a company goes public, insiders—like Redwood Capital in our example—must wait a mandated period of time before selling any of their shares (dubbed the "lock-up period"). This can be 90–180 days after the IPO date, or even as long as 12–18 months.

Lock-up periods are meant to prevent insiders from dumping large amounts of shares on the public at once. Most companies sell roughly 20% of their equity when going public. Therefore, if a single large shareholder—like Redwood Capital—dumped their 15% stake on IPO day, that would potentially send the stock price spiraling. A study from New York University showed that after the end of a lock-up period, stocks tend to fall 1%–3% on that given day.

Plus, if there's lots of "insider selling" on an IPO, that would send a negative sign to investors looking to buy the IPO. So if you're an individual investor seeking an IPO, you want to keep a close eye on the end of this lock-up period and wait until *after* the lockup expires before opening a position.

3. Evaluate the Fund Ownership

Managers of institutional investment funds (such as hedge funds and pension funds with assets over $100 million) file something called a Form 13F with the SEC every quarter. These filings disclose all stocks owned by these institutions.

Most importantly, this form shows *changes* to their stock holdings. Since these filings are published every 3 months, you can see if any of the top hedge funds bought the IPO you're monitoring. If the top hedge funds are investing in your IPO candidates, you should take note. After all, I'm a big believer in following the world's top investors. Some of the best-performing hedge funds I follow include Bridgewater Associates, Duquesne Family Office, and Elliott Investment Management.

You can track 13F filings via websites like WhaleWisdom.com.

How to Trade an IPO

One of the running themes of this section is *patience*. As we saw in the case study on Ferrari, the IPO was a failure...but only at first.

This is a pattern we often see with IPOs. For instance, Facebook also had a flop of an IPO in May 2012. While the company went public at a $100 billion valuation, that market capitalization was cut in half 6 months later.

As it turned out, just like Ferrari, Facebook roared back over the next few years and is now worth around $1 trillion. When you decide on the IPO you want to buy, the best action you can take is to *not* buy on IPO day. This is especially true with hyped IPOs like Ferrari and Facebook. Because when the initial euphoria wears off, you often get those huge pullbacks in the stock.

That's why I always wait 3–6 months after an IPO before investing. I also wait until after the lock-up period, as insiders who've held their positions for years will likely unload their shares. Once you've patiently waited for this lock-up period to pass, it's best to dollar-cost average into your position over a few weeks. If it's a business idea that you believe in very strongly, I'd go as far as making the position 5% of your portfolio.

However, since IPOs are almost always high-growth stocks, be prepared to ride out a lot of volatility.

Investing Quick-Start Guide:
INITIAL PUBLIC OFFERINGS (IPOs)

1. Devote no more than 3%–5% of your portfolio to an IPO no matter how bullish you are about the initial public offering.

2. Most importantly, wait for the early euphoria about the IPO to pass. After the initial excitement recedes, the IPO typically pulls back; this is the time to buy. Hint: Wait until the lock-up period is over (usually 3–6 months). Then you can start scaling into the IPO over the next couple of weeks, preferably using technical indicators for guidance. For example, add when the stock rises above its 50-day moving average.

3. Apply a 30% stop loss and sell when and if your losses hit that threshold. Never forget that the market is always right.

4. If the stock hits your target price, consider selling all or part of your position.

SPECIAL PURPOSE ACQUISITION COMPANIES (SPACS)

WHAT ARE SPECIAL PURPOSE ACQUISITION COMPANIES (SPACS)?

I've been creating financial content for most of my career. I like to think I have my finger on the pulse of what individual investors want to read and learn about. And I often learn what they're curious about by paying attention to what my fans are talking about in my videos' comment sections.

This could be anything from a stock people were interested in, to a specific trend my followers were keeping tabs on. But in April 2020 during the COVID-19 lockdowns, all anyone wanted to talk about was something called SPACs.

SPAC is short for "special purpose acquisition company." Also known as "blank-check companies," SPACs are an alternative way for private companies to go public. They are called blank-check companies because there is no business when the SPAC is formed. The SPAC is looking to merge with an existing business and bring that business public. In other words, they are waiting with a "blank check." Unlike the IPO process, which includes loads of regulatory red tape, SPACs are a quick and less expensive way to get your company on public markets.

Welcome to IPO 2.0

A SPAC is formed by a management team, often called a "sponsor." Once a sponsor establishes a SPAC, the blank-check company trades on public markets like a regular stock. Just like you can buy shares in Tesla, you can also buy shares in a SPAC.

The goal of a SPAC is to find a private company to "merge" with and go public. SPAC sponsors typically have 18–24 months after forming to find a target company before the blank-check company is liquidated. When a SPAC forms, it typically trades at a "net asset value" of $10. This is the price floor for the SPAC. If a SPAC is trading at $10, it most likely means that the management team has yet to find a private company to merge with and the SPAC is a placeholder for investor cash.

How the SPAC Process Can Work

To better understand how the SPAC process works, let's look at an example. Imagine that an entrepreneur named Brian Cohen is looking to take his company public. Cohen's firm is called Flight and is considered the Uber for private jets. It's a very speculative business, which is one reason the company has found it difficult to bring the company public via an initial public offering. Most underwriters are scared off by the high-risk nature of the business, so Cohen looks to SPACs to take his company public.

Cohen gets in contact with a SPAC known as Venture Acquisition Corp (VTIC). The company is headed by Stan Lackman, one of the world's best hedge fund managers. Since Lackman's SPAC does not have a target business yet, the SPAC is trading near its net asset value of $10 per unit.

Lackman understands Cohen's vision for a world where private jets are more accessible. And since the two see eye-to-eye on the business's outlook, Cohen and Lackman decide to "merge" Flight and Venture Acquisition Corp. They issue a press release, which causes the unit price of the SPAC to surge to $20 per unit. In line with most SPACs, Venture Acquisition Corp. includes a "warrant" that allows investors to buy a common share of the newly formed company 1 year from the merger date.

The SPAC—under the ticker symbol VTIC—now trades as if it's Flight. While the SPAC does not technically represent an interest in Flight, investors are confident the merger will go through.

Within 6 months, VTIC has officially changed its ticker to FLY. The VTIC units are converted to shares of FLY, and investors now have a stake in Cohen's private jet company.

While often called the IPO 2.0, the SPAC process is much less intensive than the IPO process and bypasses many strict financial reporting requirements. Naturally, this means that some companies that aren't suited for public markets make it onto the market anyway.

And that can lead to some serious cases of fraud.

NIKOLA MOTORS AND THE LITTLE ENGINE THAT COULDN'T

One of the hottest stocks over the last decade has been electric vehicle giant Tesla. Headed by eccentric billionaire Elon Musk, the company's stock price returned an average of 65% per year between 2011 and 2021.

Naturally, Tesla spawned a lot of imitators. But none were as infamous as Trevor Milton and his electric truck company Nikola Motors (NKLA). Milton's stated goal was to create an 18-wheeler truck powered by electricity and hydrogen rather than diesel. Milton revealed a prototype of the truck in December 2016, spawning a flurry of investor interest.

No company—not even Tesla—had figured out how to build a semitruck that runs solely on electric power. With logistics companies like Amazon and United Parcel Service pledging to reduce their carbon footprint, Nikola Motors had potentially stumbled upon a gold mine.

Milton claimed that the truck was fully functioning, and that the company had generated $2.3 billion in presales in its first month. Over the next 12 months, Nikola claimed that they would soon manufacture a zero-emission semitruck. Not only that, management also said that cross-country infrastructure would be in place for these trucks in the European market by 2021. In early 2018, Nikola released a video of its semitruck cruising down a desert landscape, seemingly under its own power.

Nikola Motors Stock Is Off to the Races

Nikola Motors caught the attention of former General Motors vice chairman Steve Girsky, who had started a company called VectoIQ. The company had a SPAC, the VectoIQ Acquisition Corporation (VTIQ), and was looking to merge with a company. Seeing a natural fit between Nikola Motors' new technology and Girsky's auto industry knowledge, Nikola CEO Trevor Milton agreed to merge with the SPAC.

The market loved the partnership. Once the merger was announced on May 6, 2020, units of VTIQ surged more than 150%. Not long after, Nikola Motors was trading on the New York Stock Exchange under the ticker NKLA.

Electric vehicles and SPACs were a match made in heaven in the summer of 2020. Retail trading activity was booming, and investors wanted a piece of Nikola or—as some bloggers touted—"The Next Tesla." The SPAC boom was also giving investors access to these emerging technologies without having to go through the rigors of an initial public offering.

While some applauded the ease with which these companies could now go public, there is a reason why financial reporting requirements for initial public offerings are strict: Without these requirements, companies that have no business trading on public markets are free to potentially con retail investors out of their hard-earned money.

When the Tide Goes Out...

Not long after the SPAC merger, Nikola claimed that they would manufacture a class 8 battery-electric and hydrogen-powered truck for the European market by 2021. Investors cheered the news, sending Nikola's market capitalization to more than $30 billion. At the time, this was even bigger than the value of Ford Motor (F).

This announcement was followed by two major partnerships—waste management giant Republic Services and General Motors, with the latter taking an 11% ownership stake in Nikola.

Not long after, cracks started to show in Nikola's grand plans.

The first hammer to drop was a September 2020 report from short selling firm Hindenburg Research. The 67-page report detailed how Nikola was an "intricate fraud built on dozens of lies" with Trevor Milton as its ringleader.

One of the accusations was that the 2018 video of a company semitruck was faked. The report contended that Nikola had used camera tricks to make it seem as if the truck was driving down the road when, in fact, it was simply "rolling." Nikola soon released a statement saying they made no claim that the truck had been driving under a propulsion system.

This caught the attention of the Department of Justice, which soon launched an investigation into whether Nikola and founder Trevor Milton had misled investors. The following week, Milton resigned, sending the stock down 20%. By the end of 2020, the SPAC darling that had briefly had a market value greater than Ford saw its stock plummet 80% from its highs.

Warren Buffett famously said, "Only when the tide goes out do you discover who's been swimming naked." As it turned out, Nikola Motors, under the sharp glare of reality, was caught swimming naked. It clearly could not live up to the lofty expectations it had set out for investors.

SPECIAL PURPOSE ACQUISITION COMPANIES (SPACS)

SPACs often give companies that are extremely high-risk access to public markets. Here's how to make the most of that opportunity.

How to Identify a Good SPAC

Investing in companies that go public via SPACs is akin to investing in start-ups, which have a very high failure rate. Many investors learned this the hard way. For example, after booming in 2020, the Defiance Next Gen SPAC ETF (SPAK) lost 35% of its value by mid-2021.

If you follow these suggestions, you'll increase your odds of generating returns in the SPAC market.

1. Consider the Management Team

Before a SPAC has a target company, there are no fundamentals to analyze. You can't look at a business's sales growth, margins, or anything involved in traditional equity analysis. These are truly "blank-check" entities with no backing at this stage.

Premerger, investing in a SPAC really is an investment in its management team. That's why it's very important to take a close look at who's managing the SPAC. You can do this by reading through the track record and biographies of those on the SPAC's management roster. You'll want to find management teams with lots of experience managing public companies and with long track records in public markets.

You can find names of every member of a management team in a SPAC's S-1 filing. From there, you will want to conduct an Internet search of all the names of all the key players managing the SPAC. Note: You can find S-1's on the SEC's EDGAR database or on the company's website under company disclosures.

2. Wait Until a Deal Is Announced

You can avoid a lot of headaches by simply waiting for the SPAC sponsor to announce a merger. Plus, there's data that shows that returns post-merger are actually better than gambling on which company a management team will close on. For instance, in 2021, only 15% of SPACs outperformed the S&P 500 before a merger was announced. That's compared to 46% for SPACs that announced a merger.

3. Keep an Eye on the SPAC's Price

New investors are always harping on the price of a stock. They think that a stock may be overvalued or undervalued simply because the share price is high or low. Investors should ignore the share price and focus on valuation metrics like price-to-sales, price-to-earnings growth, and other data points.

But that's not the case with SPACs. All blank-check companies go public at $10 per share. At that price, the SPAC has enough cash to acquire a private company based on the number of shares outstanding. But once a SPAC announces a deal—and even sometimes before, if it's a well-known management team—the "premium" over $10 will continue to swell. At that point, shares no longer represent a blank-check company and instead reflect the value of the company the SPAC acquired.

The higher the share price, the higher the premium at which you're paying for the SPAC. That can cut into your potential upside down the road. For that reason, it's a good idea to stay away from SPACs with high share prices because much of the upside is already factored into the shares.

How to Trade a SPAC

Once you've found a management team that you're comfortable investing in or a SPAC that's announced a merger, it's time to open a position. Keep your position small, as it's important to remember that SPACs—like all the assets in this book—are very high risk. That's why I limit my SPAC investments to around 1% of my investment portfolio.

I prefer to dollar-cost average into this position over 2–3 weeks. This will smooth out the entry price and reduce the negative impacts of any short-term volatility. That's key with SPACs, as the share price of these new companies tends to be quite volatile.

After a SPAC merger is announced and the SPAC trades with its new ticker, use the same analysis discussed in the high-growth stock section earlier in this chapter. That includes assessing the total addressable market, sales growth, and company management team. From there, you'll simply want to hold the position unless something changes with your investment thesis. As a general rule, I will cut any position that falls 35% or more. In investing, it's okay to be wrong but not okay to stay wrong. And if your position is down 35%, the odds of a turnaround are probably quite low.

Investing Quick-Start Guide:
SPECIAL PURPOSE ACQUISITION COMPANIES (SPACs)

1. Wait until the merger is announced between the SPAC management team and the target company. You want to know which company the sponsor is merging with before investing your full position. You can open a small position if you want to test the waters.

2. Compared to IPOs and high-growth stocks, SPACs are riskier. Allocate no more than 1%–2% of your portfolio to an individual SPAC. Think about this: SPACs are going public because they cannot raise enough money through traditional methods such as venture capital. That makes them risky businesses.

3. Once the SPAC merger is announced, scale into the position.

4. When the company goes "live," you will automatically get the shares.

5. Watch the company and see how it performs. As with other high-risk investments, maintain a stop loss of 30%, and sell if your losses meet that percentage.

6. SPACs can potentially double or triple if all goes right. If something goes wrong, your stop loss means the most you will lose is 30%. Basically, you are risking 30% for the potential to make 200% or more. As long as you keep your investment small, the risk-reward ratio should be reasonable (but that is a decision only you can make, as everyone's risk-reward comfort zone is different). The key is sizing the position correctly.

WHAT ARE DEEP VALUE STOCKS?

As I mentioned in the section on high-growth stocks, there are two ends of the investing spectrum: growth and value.

Generally, growth investors focus on companies with fast-growing revenues and earnings. On the other hand, value investors focus on companies trading below their *intrinsic value* (which we'll discuss in more depth shortly). Just as growth investors have high-growth stocks at the furthest end of their spectrum, value investors have *deep value* stocks at the fringes of their spectrum.

Deep value investing is just like value investing except these stocks are trading *far* below their intrinsic value. Pioneered by famed investor Benjamin Graham, the concept is all about figuring out what the company is worth. Graham—who was Warren Buffett's mentor—determined that stocks trading at low "valuation multiples" tend to outperform the market on a long-term basis.

By this, Graham was referring to stocks trading at a price-to-book ratio below 1.0 and a price-to-earnings ratio below 10. In Graham's view, investors were getting a lot of bang for their buck buying these stocks. After all, when you buy a stock, what you're really buying is a piece of that company's future earnings. The higher the earnings multiple, the more you're paying for that piece of a company's profit.

The rub with using this approach is that intrinsic value is based on assumptions. Actually, any financial model is completely assumption-based and is not an exact science. For instance, analysts must forecast what a company's earnings growth and trading multiple will be in the future to create a financial model. Since these are based on an unknowable future, they cannot be fully trusted.

I'm fond of saying that a financial model is simply a tool in an analyst's toolbox rather than the end-all-be-all for an analysis. But when used properly, models can help identify deep value opportunities that many have overlooked.

How to Calculate Intrinsic Value

There are a few ways to find a company's intrinsic value. The most common valuation technique is known as "discounted cash flow" (DCF) analysis. This approach estimates how much cash a company will earn in the future, calculates the "present value" of these cash flows, and adds them all up to formulate a stock's intrinsic value.

Another popular method is looking at a company's financial metrics like price-to-earnings (PE) multiples. To find the future intrinsic value of a stock, you would multiply the current earnings per share (EPS) by (1 + growth rate), then multiply that by the price-to-earnings ratio.

Let's use an example to illustrate this method. Say Coca-Cola has a current earnings per share of $1.87, an earnings growth rate of 4%, and a price-to-earnings ratio of 25. Both the earnings per share and price-to-earnings ratio are taken from Coca-Cola's current financials, while the earnings growth rate is an assumption used to forecast where the company's earnings may be headed. If we plug these figures into the equation described earlier, we get [1.87 × (1+.04) × 25], which means that Coca-Cola has an intrinsic value of $48.62.

Now, this is where the value versus deep value comes into play. If Coca-Cola is trading at $45 in this situation, that would constitute a value investment, as shares are trading a mere 8% discount to its intrinsic value.

Let's pretend there was a strike at a Coca-Cola plant in Cleveland, Ohio (my hometown). The news sent Coca-Cola shares down from $45 to $25. While earnings might take a short-term hit, a deep value investor would know that the company would likely bounce back soon and return to future earnings growth. In fact, the deep value investor uses the same financial metric approach to figure out Coca-Cola's future value and comes to the same $45 conclusion.

That means that Coca-Cola shares would theoretically have upside of 80% from current prices!

CHEAP STOCKS ARE OFTEN CHEAP FOR A REASON

Warren Buffett is fond of saying, "It's far better to buy a wonderful company at a fair price than a fair company at a wonderful price." All prospective deep value investors should keep this quote in mind before diving headfirst into this strategy.

Bottom Fishing versus Dumpster Diving

One of my early investing mentors was Tony Sagami. My first junior analyst position was at an investment research company called Mauldin Economics; Tony was the editor of a dividend investing newsletter there. As his analyst, I was given a crash course in finding undervalued dividend-paying stocks and—you guessed it—deep value. Tony would often refer to deep value investing as "dumpster diving" in unloved industries, with the implication being that most of these companies were trash.

And he wasn't wrong: Many of the companies that entice deep value investors operate in industries that are dying. Some of the most popular deep value plays today are in industries in secular decline like tobacco, shopping mall REITs, and landline phone companies. While there are certainly "cheap" stocks in these sectors, the deep value investor's job is to figure out if they are trading below their intrinsic value. Even if the stock is trading near Benjamin Graham's recommended low price-to-earnings and price-to-book ratios (see earlier in this chapter), you must make sure that these stocks aren't simply cheap because the business is eroding.

Keep in mind there is a difference between "bottom fishing" and "dumpster diving." That's why investors really need to do their homework (i.e., due diligence) when it comes to deep value investing.

And as I'm about to show you, the payoff can be huge when this strategy is used correctly.

CASE STUDY:
DAVID TEPPER AND THE BIG BANKS

David Tepper is one of the world's most famous hedge fund managers. He runs a fund, Appaloosa Management, that holds more than $13 billion in assets under management. Tepper made a name for himself in the financial community as a distressed debt investor in the early 2000s. However, he became famous for shrewd trades he made during the global financial crisis.

In 2008, the global economy was going through one of its worst financial panics in history. For years, US banks had been underwriting loans for people who could not possibly pay them back. These "predatory loans" targeted low-income homebuyers, and when the housing bubble burst in 2007, many people's mortgages were greater than what their homes were worth.

These same mortgages had been packaged and sold as something called "mortgage-backed securities" (MBS) by many of the big banks. Since real estate loans made up a significant amount of the assets on US bank balance sheets, many banks struggled during this period. In fact, two of the largest US investment banks—Lehman Brothers and Bear Stearns—collapsed during this period, with Lehman going bankrupt and Bear Stearns being sold to JPMorgan Chase for a fraction of its pre-crisis valuation.

A Deep Value Savant

The global financial crisis led to a collapse in the S&P 500, as the index fell 52% between October 2007 and February 2009. The crash was led by the big banks, with shares of some banks falling as much as 70%. In fact, many were now trading well below their book value.

Even though the bank stocks were cheap, most investors wanted nothing to do with them. David Tepper, however, is not most investors. He'd spent his career analyzing the stocks and bonds of distressed companies. While most hedge funds were struggling during this period—with 16% closing their doors—Tepper viewed the chaos as an opportunity.

Tepper had made billions buying out-of-favor investments. For instance, he'd bought loads of Korean stocks during the Asian financial crisis in 1997. A few years later, when these stocks rebounded, he was sitting on hundreds of millions in gains. He'd done the same with junk bonds, steel, and other commodities in the early 2000s.

Tepper clearly has an eye for deep value. And in 2009, he saw a ton of value in US bank stocks.

David Goes "Dumpster Diving" with the Big Banks

Tepper's fund was coming off a rough year in 2008. A big wager on auto parts company Delphi had gone south, which contributed to a 25% decline for his fund in 2008.

While he was cautious going into 2009, Tepper soon turned bullish on the big banks. The prevailing narrative at the time was that major US banks were beyond repair after the housing crisis and would likely have to be purchased by the government, or "nationalized." In this event, shareholders would be wiped out.

After reading the Treasury Department's Financial Stability Plan, Tepper grew bullish on the big banks. At the time, Bank of America (BAC) shares traded at $2.50 while Citigroup (C) traded as low as $0.97. Sensing an opportunity, Tepper ordered his traders to buy bank stocks and debt like mad, investing more than $1 billion of the fund's capital in the beaten-down sector.

It wouldn't take long for Tepper to be vindicated. Three months later, shares of Bank of America and Citigroup had tripled. And when all was said and done, Tepper had earned a grand total of $7 billion in profit.

DEEP VALUE STOCKS

Finding a deep value investment is one of the most difficult strategies introduced in this book. It has nothing to do with finding the relevant information, as all the financial information needed is readily available online at no cost. But you need some instinct, like Tepper has.

How to Identify a Good Deep Value Investment

Not everyone has a nose for deep value like Tepper. He'd spent his entire career finding beaten-down investments and zigging when others were zagging. When it came to the large banks, he was simply the first to do it—and he backed his thesis by betting big.

This trade could have easily gone against him. Tepper admitted in interviews years later that he thought there was a 20% chance the US would nationalize the banks. In that event, he would have vaporized more than a billion dollars of client money and may have had to close his fund.

The trick with deep value is finding a stock that's beaten down *temporarily*. For Tepper, he expected the pullback in big banks to wane after the Financial Stability Plan kicked in. He saw a way for the banks to navigate out of an incredible crisis, and he bet big as a result.

That said, it doesn't always work out like this. Sometimes these seemingly deep value stocks are really *value traps*. That means that a stock appears to be priced cheaply based on price-to-earnings and price-to-book ratios, but the stock never recovers. Deep value investors often encounter this scenario, which can lead to major losses.

Using the following three metrics can help you avoid these value traps.

1. Avoid Companies in Secular Decline

Many of the stocks that end up being value traps are industries in *secular* decline. This means that there are structural issues with the industry that are working against the company and the stock.

When looking for a deep value play, you want to focus on companies with a short-term problem. For David Tepper, the temporary issue was the collapse of the housing market and risk of nationalization.

On the other hand, value traps are often industries where the core product or service offered is declining. The tobacco industry is a great example, as the stocks have been cheap based on price-to-earnings and price-to-book for years. On the other hand, tobacco stocks are cheap because there isn't much growth in the industry. When looking for deep value plays, it's best to avoid these types of companies.

2. Look for Low Valuation Multiples

As we've touched on numerous times, a stock is only considered deep value if the shares are trading at a cheap valuation. The best way to determine this is to compile a list of a stock's key valuation multiples and compare them over many years.

The four multiples I look at are:

- Forward price-to-earnings
- Forward price-to-book
- Forward price-to-sales
- Forward price-to-free cash flow

You'll want to compile a list to make sure that shares are cheap based on the stock's history. If that turns out to be the case, you may have found yourself a deep value candidate.

3. Avoid Value Traps

There are a few factors you should look for to determine whether a stock is a value trap. The first is whether there are multiple classes of stock. You can find out if a stock has multiple classes if you search the ticker symbol. It will tell if it is "Class A," "Class B," and in some cases maybe even "Class C" shares. While not one-size-fits-all, companies with multiple share classes tacitly imply that one tier is preferred over another. This can include voting rights and other perks. With a company that's already struggling, you want to make sure management is laser focused on improving shareholder returns.

Next is the stock's float. One of the major drivers of stock returns is institutional buying. Much of this buying comes from pension funds, mutual funds, and other highly regulated asset managers. Many of these funds are restricted from buying shares of companies trading below $10 or less than $1 billion in market capitalization. To tip the scales in your favor, make sure to only focus on stocks that trade above $10 and over $1 billion in market capitalization.

Lastly, companies with high "insider ownership" are far less likely to be value traps. When managers have an ownership stake in the company, they have an incentive to try to drive the stock higher, which means that the interest of the shareholders and management are aligned. Therefore, if insiders are selling their shares like mad, it's likely the stock is a value trap and should be avoided.

How to Trade a Deep Value Stock

I put a lot of emphasis on figuring out whether a stock is a value trap or actual deep value opportunity. When it comes to trading a deep value stock, you must have a lot of patience. The position could take many months or years to come to fruition, so you want to make sure you aren't doing yourself a disservice by buying cheap stocks. After all, many stocks are cheap for a reason!

Once you've found a stock that meets the criteria laid out in this section, you want to dollar-cost average into the position. Because there's a chance this position is a value trap, don't bet too much. In fact, I would not allocate more than 3%–5% of my portfolio to a deep value position.

After you acquire your position, you simply wait. In the case study, David Tepper was rewarded rather fast with his big bet on US banks. However, many deep value plays require some sort of catalyst or event to send the stock higher. Waiting for this catalyst can take time, so any investor looking to use a deep value approach should be willing to wait months or years for the trade to pay off.

Investing Quick-Start Guide:
DEEP VALUE STOCKS

1. Once you have identified a deep value stock and determine why it has been cursed with a temporary "dark cloud," the key is to buy before the cloud lifts.

2. Allocate no more than 3%–5% of your portfolio to a deep value position. As mentioned earlier, the stock could be cheap for a reason (i.e., it could be a value trap).

3. Once you find the stock that meets your criteria, scale into it over a few weeks (don't wait too long because you want to buy low).

4. Once you have a position, watch the stock closely. Maintain a 30% stop loss (i.e., if share price sheds 30% or more, sell).

5. If the stock hits your target price, consider scaling out of the position.

CHAPTER 4

Exchange-Traded Funds

An exchange-traded fund (ETF) is a type of investment vehicle that tracks everything from stock indexes to commodities and other assets. These unique investments can be traded just like stocks on all major stock exchanges.

While many people use simple ETFs that track the S&P 500 or Nasdaq indexes, there are many exotic ETFs like thematic, leveraged, and volatility that can offer high-risk, high-reward opportunities.

Like any ambitious investor, I've long had an affinity for Warren Buffett, an investor who has compiled slices of many different companies under one holding company, delivering market-beating returns over the last 40 years. While this is often considered "basic" in the investment community, there's a reason why Buffett is often considered the G.O.A.T. (greatest of all time) investor. Buffett has said that individual investors should not try and beat the market by picking stocks. Rather, he says that nonprofessionals should focus on owning a "cross section of businesses that in aggregate are bound to do well."

That's what Buffett has attempted to do with his holding company Berkshire Hathaway (BRK). The company owns stakes in everything from technology companies like Apple Inc. (AAPL) to US banks including Bank of America (BAC). That's in addition to positions in payment processors, beverage makers, telecommunication companies, and a host of other businesses.

This approach works. In fact, Berkshire Hathaway shares returned a 20% annualized gain between 1965 and 2020. That's nearly double the S&P 500 return over the same period. By owning a cross section of growing industries curated by him and his team, Buffett gives his shareholders access to multiple growing sectors at once. If one sector starts to slow, he can rebalance his portfolio until it hits its optimal weighting.

Berkshire Hathaway is organized as a holding company. However, this same concept of owning many slices of different sectors has been adopted by a growing asset class known as "exchange-traded funds" (ETFs). While ETFs started by mirroring these diversified holding companies, a new crop of ETF products offers investors high-risk, high-reward opportunities.

THEMATIC EXCHANGE-TRADED FUNDS (ETFS)

WHAT ARE THEMATIC EXCHANGE-TRADED FUNDS (ETFS)?

ETFs are one of the most popular investment vehicles in today's markets. At its most basic level, an ETF pools investor funds into investments like stocks, bonds, or other assets. In return, investors receive a stake in the investment pool. This makes it much easier for investors to buy a diversified range of stocks. The most popular ETFs track the major stock exchanges, like the S&P 500, but there are hundreds of other ETF offerings.

The world's largest ETF is the SPDR S&P 500 ETF Trust (SPY). This ETF tracks the S&P 500, which is made up of 500 of the largest US public companies. Although ETFs didn't exist until 1993, the asset class has grown to a $5 trillion market over the last 30 years.

Prior to ETFs, investors had to rely on less liquid mutual funds, like the Vanguard 500 Index Fund. The problem was you could buy and sell shares only once per day at the market close, making it ill-suited for traders. With the advent of ETFs, investors can now buy securities at will.

As I have mentioned, even investors employing the high-risk, high-reward strategies in this book should have a hefty exposure to low-risk index funds (and blue-chip stocks). Not only do these index funds automatically rebalance; their fees for doing so are very low. In fact, the average *expense ratio*—or annual fee taken to rebalance passive ETFs—was a mere 0.13% in 2019. That's compared to an average fee of 0.66% for actively managed mutual funds. That means that passive investors are paying a mere $1.30 for every $1,000 invested, compared to $6.60 for actively managed funds. And since passive ETFs are tax advantaged, they lower your tax bill when compared to mutual funds. (Note: Speak to a tax professional or financial adviser for specific advice about your situation.)

While most ETFs are used for low-risk investing strategies, there are many that fit our high-risk, high-reward mandate.

Thematic ETFs

The most popular ETFs are those that track major stock indexes like the S&P 500 or Nasdaq. These include ETFs like the SPDR S&P 500 ETF Trust (SPY) and Invesco QQQ Trust (QQQ), which have a combined $600 billion in assets. These index ETFs should make up a large part of any investor's portfolio, as they give you exposure to the long-term growth of the world's top companies. But while they should be a core facet of a well-rounded portfolio, these funds are far from high-risk, high-reward opportunities.

Investors looking for high-risk, high-reward opportunities should consider looking at something called "thematic ETFs."

Unlike SPY and QQQ, which have holdings in many different sectors, a thematic ETF focuses on a niche market to allow investors to capitalize on a particular trend, region, or industry, for example. While it's true these thematic ETFs include low-risk funds like consumer staples and even grocery stores, there are many that offer investors exposure to high-growth, and potentially high-risk, industries like e-commerce, cloud computing, and space travel.

The Secular Trend Is Your Friend

One of my favorite ways to invest is to find secular growth trends. These are markets or industries that will unfold over many years and are therefore not influenced by short-term factors.

For instance, one of my favorite investing trends is e-commerce. As a millennial, I order well over 90% of my goods online. Whether it's groceries near my apartment in Los Angeles, loose-leaf tea from New Orleans, or birthday gifts for my family, most of my spending is done online.

Younger generations are accustomed to using e-commerce platforms like Amazon (AMZN), Alibaba Group Holding (BABA), and MercadoLibre (MELI). However, this isn't the norm. Research from the United Nations shows that fewer than one in five people used e-commerce platforms in 2020. While globally, e-commerce as a percentage of total retail sales increased from 16% to

19% from 2019 to 2020, most of the world's population still is *not* using e-commerce platforms.

As an investor, this tells me e-commerce platforms have a long runway for growth, also known as a "secular trend." And while I could buy a basket of e-commerce stocks, I could also profit off the long-term growth in e-commerce adoption by using a thematic ETF like the ProShares Online Retail ETF (ONLN).

When you buy shares of ONLN, you're buying a sliver of e-commerce companies like Amazon, Alibaba, and eBay. While Buffett's Berkshire Hathaway gives investors exposure to a cross section of growing industries, ONLN gives investors a cross section of the e-commerce industry.

While an e-commerce ETF is a solid risk-reward bet, I want to tell you about another industry that fits within our high-risk, high-reward environment.

CASE STUDY:
FROM THE LOWER EAST SIDE TO THE MOON

In the summer of 2019, I was in New York City shooting a promotional video for the investment research company I was working for. While I was in town, one of my colleagues was hosting a party on the Lower East Side at the Hotel Chantelle.

My colleague is well known in financial circles, as he'd published a best-selling investing book a few years prior. As a result, the party was a fantastic networking event. While at the bar ordering a drink, I struck up a conversation with a thirtysomething guy named Andrew Chanin.

Chanin was the cofounder of a company called Procure ETFs. While he'd started out creating ETF products for a host of large institutions in the precious metals space, he'd left gold and silver behind to start Procure after seeing the long-term growth in the ETF market. And at that time, his company only had one ETF: the Procure Space ETF (UFO).

Let's Go to Space

The UFO ETF is just what it sounds like: The fund was created to invest 80% of the ETF's assets into companies that generated more than 50% of their sales from space-related businesses or activities. This includes satellite manufacturers, aerospace, launch systems, and many other space-related firms.

Chanin explained that after NASA's budget was slashed in 2013, US space missions grew dependent on the Russian space program. In fact, the US was paying up to $80 million per seat to send US astronauts to space.

But that trend was starting to reverse. Frigid geopolitical relations with the Russians had created a market opportunity for private sector space companies like Elon Musk's SpaceX. In fact, Musk had secured $2.6 billion from NASA to send US astronauts to space via his private space company.

And while the space industry had short-term tailwinds, it certainly fell into the secular growth basket as well. According to a study from Morgan Stanley, spending on the global space economy was expected to grow from $350 million in 2019 to over $1 trillion annually in 2035. Bank of America was even more bullish, expecting the space industry to be a $2.7 trillion industry by 2040.

After Chanin launched Procure Space ETF (UFO) in April 2019, his ETF continued to trade sideways. That was, until the COVID-19 pandemic knocked the ETF off course.

This Space ETF Is Cleared for Takeoff

Ten months after the UFO ETF debuted on global markets, the COVID-19 pandemic ripped through the global economy. While stocks crashed across the board, the space industry was disproportionately affected. This made sense, as the US government had diverted trillions of dollars to stimulus checks. That meant there would likely be less money for defense and space companies. This cratered the UFO ETF, sending its shares down 45% in less than a month.

But Chanin was not deterred. In interviews during this period, he made it clear that many of the companies in the ETF would benefit from the *trend acceleration* we saw during COVID-19. This included proliferation of broadband Internet, cloud computing, and the Internet of things that surged in demand during the lockdowns.

Investors who followed Chanin's line of thinking would be handsomely rewarded. While it was high risk at the time, those who believed in the underlying trends fueling the space industry and held course with the fund reaped a return of 110% between March 2020 and September 2021, crushing the S&P 500 return of 80% over the same period.

THEMATIC EXCHANGE-TRADED FUNDS

When used correctly, the chance of making money with thematic ETFs is high. But that's not to say all thematic ETFs or secular trends are created equal. Investors need to keep close tabs on industry dynamics to determine if the trend they're investing in has staying power.

How to Identify a Good Thematic Exchange-Traded Fund

When I first started my career, one of the hottest sectors was 3-D printing stocks. Much like the cryptocurrency craze that would follow, any stock that was related to 3-D printing went parabolic in a short time period. The thesis was that 3-D printing would revolutionize the way we live our lives. Need a hammer? You can 3-D print one. Need a semiconductor? Just 3-D print it in your home.

Unfortunately, this was not a sustainable trend. After 3-D printing stocks like 3D Systems (DDD) shot up in 2013, they soon crashed, never again coming close to a new all-time high. When looking for a thematic ETF, make sure the trend isn't a flash in the pan like 3-D printing, in addition to assessing the other factors outlined next.

1. Find a Secular Trend

While this chapter is technically on thematic ETFs, the ETFs are simply a vehicle to profit off long-term growth in secular trends. As I mentioned earlier in the chapter, secular growth trends are markets that are highly likely to keep growing over the long term. These markets are said to have "tailwinds" that will keep generating more sales for the companies that dominate these industries.

One of the best ways to play these trends is by using actively managed thematic ETFs. Some of the secular growth trends I'm currently investing in are:

- E-commerce
- Cloud computing
- Payment processors
- Gaming
- Electric vehicles
- Streaming

Investors looking to add thematic ETFs to their portfolios would be wise to focus on these sectors.

2. Look Into Portfolio Holdings

Once you've found the secular trend, you want to determine which companies make up the ETF's holdings.

For instance, for those looking to profit from the long-term growth in e-commerce, two of the biggest ETFs in the space are ProShares Online Retail ETF (ONLN) and Global X E-commerce ETF (EBIZ). To reiterate, just as Buffett's Berkshire Hathaway is made up of many different companies, these thematic ETFs are composed of slivers of different companies. While both focus on the e-commerce market, the allocations for each company are vastly different. That's in addition to which companies are included.

To see which stocks make up each ETF, go to the ETF's website and view the fund's holdings. Some thematic ETFs focus on larger, more established companies in the e-commerce space.

For instance, ONLN holds only large e-commerce companies, such as Amazon (AMZN), Alibaba (BABA), and MercadoLibre (MELI). On the other hand, other ETFs may hold smaller, more speculative e-commerce companies. A good example of that is EBIZ, which holds niche e-commerce players like Etsy (ETSY), Williams-Sonoma (WSM), and Shopify (SHOP).

You can now choose which type you're comfortable with. But those looking for higher-risk ETFs should opt for thematic ETFs with smaller companies, while those looking for lower-risk ETFs should hold thematic ETFs with a higher allocation to large-capitalization stocks.

3. Choose Low Expense Ratios

An expense ratio is what an investor must pay each year for the management of the thematic ETF. Think of it as the price of admission for using the product. For instance, if you invested $1,000 in an ETF with an expense ratio of 1%, that means that you would pay $10 every year you hold that ETF. While it sounds small, those fees can add up over time. That's why investors who plan to hold an ETF for many years should consider thematic ETFs with low expense ratios.

To determine if an expense ratio is low, look up the expense ratio for each ETF for a particular theme. From there you can see which ETFs have the lowest expense ratios. You can find this information on free websites such as *Yahoo! Finance* and *Finviz*.

How to Trade a Thematic ETF

The hard part about deciding on a thematic ETF isn't so much how to trade it. Rather, it's about finding the right secular trend and holding the position as that trend unfolds.

Once you have found the right ETF, dollar-cost average into your position over 2–3 weeks. This will smooth out your entry price, ensuring you aren't deploying all your cash before a potential pullback.

While investing in thematic ETFs can deliver high returns, these returns will likely come steadily over many years. That means thematic ETFs should be a long-term, core portfolio position. Since they're relatively low risk, feel free to allocate a sizeable portion of your portfolio to thematic ETFs. Those with a diversified portfolio should feel comfortable allocating up to 10% of their investable assets to this high-risk, high-reward strategy.

Investing Quick-Start Guide:
THEMATIC EXCHANGE-TRADED FUNDS (ETFs)

1. Your broker should have a large variety of ETFs to suggest, including thematic ETFs, which should be established as a long-term position.

2. Once you have identified the right trend and the right ETF, dollar-cost average into that position over a 1-month period.

3. The thematic ETF can make up as much as 10% of your portfolio.

4. After buying, hold on to the position for years, letting the secular trend unfold over the long term.

5. If successful, the underlying companies' higher earnings will translate into a higher ETF price.

LEVERAGED EXCHANGE-TRADED FUNDS (ETFS)

WHAT ARE LEVERAGED EXCHANGE-TRADED FUNDS (ETFS)?

Most ETFs you read about give investors slices of different sectors of the stock market. That means when one sector begins to struggle, another sector picks up the slack. This diversified approach to investing is a tried-and-true strategy I employ in my personal portfolio.

But some investors want more risk (and more potential reward). They are not satisfied with buying and holding positions long-term and prefer to enhance their returns by using complex financial products. That's exactly what investors do with something called "leveraged ETFs."

First introduced by ProShares, a leveraged ETF is a financial instrument that uses derivatives such as options or futures to amplify the return of an underlying index. This means investors can now get 2, 3, or even higher times the returns on an underlying index such as the S&P 500. Let's see how this works with an example.

My ETF Goes Up to "11"

One of the most popular leveraged ETFs is the ProShares Ultra S&P 500 ETF (SSO). Traditional ETFs like the SPDR S&P 500 ETF (SPY) are designed to track an index like the S&P 500. But with SSO, this *leveraged* ETF is constructed to deliver twice the S&P 500 return over the same period.

For example, let's say you're an investor who wants to add the S&P 500 to your portfolio. You can buy something like the SPY, which will directly track the S&P 500 index. When the S&P 500 index rises 2% in a day, SPY perfectly mirrors the underlying index and rises 2%. On the other hand, a leveraged ETF like SSO allows you to add *leveraged* exposure to the S&P 500, returning 2 times the underlying index. So if the S&P 500 index rises 2%, SSO rises 4%!

But you have to remember, this dynamic cuts both ways. For example, let's say the S&P 500 falls 5% in a day. If you're holding SPY, your position will also fall 5%. But if you hold SSO, your position will fall 10%. Ouch!

There's Always a Catch

One of my core investing principals is that stocks tend to rise over the long term. Therefore, even if we saw that 5% decline in the previous example, an investor would be wise to hang on to that position since it will likely recover over the long haul.

If that's the case, wouldn't it make sense for me to hold *only* leveraged ETFs rather than regular index ETFs? Like most things that sound too good to be true, it's not quite that simple. Leveraged ETFs are underpinned by a complex array of options that amplify the fund's returns. Unlike stocks, options contracts have an expiration date and thus decline in value over time.

LEVERAGED ETFS CARRY HIGHER EXPENSE RATIOS

While the leveraged ETF you're buying is amplifying the return, the plumbing of the ETF is much more complex. These options must be managed closely, which is why leveraged ETFs often sport expense ratios of 1% or higher. That means for every $10,000 you invest, you're automatically losing $100 per year over the lifetime of your holding period. This is to cover both the management of the ETF and the option premiums that need to be paid for the ETF to function.

Although leveraged ETFs are a high-risk, high-reward vehicle, investors who pick the right ETF at the right time can amplify their returns.

CASE STUDY:

I BOUGHT THE DIP (WITH A LEVERAGED ETF) AND I LIKED IT

I'd seen bouts of market volatility during my time as the senior equity analyst for an investment research company. However, neither I nor any of my colleagues had seen anything like the COVID-19 crash. The S&P 500 had fallen 36% in only a few weeks on fears that businesses would be shut down with no end in sight. The prevailing narrative was that with so many people out of work due to the fear of catching a virus we didn't yet understand, the very idea of a globally linked economy would be put to the test.

While everyone was running around with their hair on fire, I decided to face the chaos head-on.

A Famous Adage Rings True

If you go back and read my writings from this period, you can tell I was doing my best to keep my audience calm. People were rightfully freaked out by how fast the virus had spread and the death toll it left in its wake.

Social implications aside, people were also convinced that the market might never be the same. Stocks that we had bought even a month earlier were now sitting on 30% losses. People were both angry and scared, which is a terrible combination for market sentiment.

But I knew I'd trained my entire career for this moment. That's why I kept revisiting the old Warren Buffett quote: "Be greedy when others are fearful." At the time, I wrote to my audience that the S&P 500 had crashed many times before. And in each crash, it was always a buying opportunity, as the S&P 500 had always come back to hit new all-time highs.

I'm not one to think "this time is different." The US had been through much more dire circumstances, whether it was World War II, the Great Depression, or 9/11. Every time, the country bounced back—along with its stock market.

Following my belief that all the fear and anger were temporary, I started researching the best way to play a rebound in US stocks. And that's when I came across a leveraged ETF called ProShares Ultra S&P 500 ETF (SSO).

Seriously, Don't Fight the Fed

After determining that this leveraged ETF was one that had minimal "contango" due to its structure (more on that in the next section), I started to build a position in SSO. This was despite the market falling in dramatic fashion.

Then, like a sign from the heavens, came Federal Reserve Chairman Jerome Powell. In a speech on March 23, 2020, Powell announced the central bank would use "unlimited bond purchases" to support the economy.

In a phone call soon after, I kept ruminating with a colleague on what "unlimited" entailed. We were both economists and knew that central bank policy had a dramatic impact on asset prices. As a rule, the more bonds the Federal Reserve purchased, the higher asset prices should go.

If the Federal Reserve would buy an *unlimited* amount of bonds, it followed that asset prices—like stocks—should surge. And despite the market selling off after the announcement, I decided to double down on my SSO position.

It would turn out to be one of the greatest investments of my career. March 23, 2020, turned out to be the cycle low for the S&P 500. While the index rose 77% over the next year, my giant SSO position surged to a spectacular 193% return over the same period.

INVESTMENT STRATEGY:
LEVERAGED ETFS

The story of SSO—like many of the trades in this book—has a lot to do with timing. If you don't get the timing of your trade correct, it doesn't matter which strategy you use. This section will help you make the most of timing to invest in leveraged ETFs.

How to Identify a Good Leveraged ETF

To use the strategies in this book successfully, you must mentally train yourself to think differently. If you simply follow the crowd and buy the same stocks everyone else is buying, you will generate the same returns as everyone else.

And if you plan to use a leveraged ETF to express a trading idea, make sure to follow these three guidelines.

1. Make Sure the ETF Does Not Suffer from Contango

In my years of being a public investor, I've had many people—unfortunately—select leveraged ETF products with lots of "contango." Contango is simply the difference between the expected price and the execution price. This means that while the ETF may magnify the return of the underlying index by 2 or 3 times in a short time period (i.e., 2–3 days), it will significantly begin to lag the index after this 3-day period and eventually separate from the underlying index.

Straightforward leveraged ETFs experience lots of contango. This is due to the options that make up the ETF amplifying the returns losing value over time. One way to tell if a leveraged ETF suffers from contango is to look at its 3-year chart. If the ETF shows a 99% loss over this period, it means the ETF suffers from contango and is not worth holding for longer than a few days.

2. Choose Low Management Fees

Trying to amplify your returns always comes at a cost. Whether you plan to trade your position on margin (i.e., borrowing from your broker) or shorting (as we'll cover in Chapter 10), you must pay a fee. For margin and shorting, you're paying a broker or market maker to borrow either cash or underlying securities.

Generally, you want to choose the leveraged ETF with the lowest management fees.

3. Look for Liquidity

One of the most important factors when choosing a leveraged ETF is whether it's liquid. Generally, liquidity is a measure of how easy it is to buy or sell something. For instance, a share of Microsoft (MSFT) stock is highly liquid, as there's always a buyer or seller for a share of blue-chip stocks. On the other hand, a car is a less liquid asset, as there are fewer buyers and sellers in that market.

The same concept applies to leveraged ETFs. Low-volume ETFs should be avoided, as you want to be able to close your leveraged ETF position easily. For that reason, only invest in leveraged ETFs that trade more than 500,000 shares per day. You can find this "average daily volume" on free websites like *Yahoo! Finance* and *Finviz*.

How to Trade a Leveraged ETF

Once you've checked all three criteria and determined the timing is right, it's time to open your position.

For a leveraged ETF that suffers from contango, don't hold your position for long. These ETFs are meant to only mimic the underlying index on a 2–3 day time horizon. If you choose to use one of these riskier ETFs, make sure to not hold for more than a week.

For a leveraged ETF that does not suffer from contango, you can hold the position in your portfolio like any other ETF. Set a stop loss to automatically sell your position if it falls more than 30%. This is to ensure that your loss doesn't turn into an insurmountable loss. After a 30% loss, the math is no longer in your favor and it's a good time to cut your losses and reallocate elsewhere.

Investing Quick-Start Guide:
LEVERAGED ETFs

1. Your brokerage firm will have a long list of leveraged ETFs that can be purchased.

2. Unlike many strategies in this book, do not dollar-cost average into leveraged ETFs, as most leveraged ETFs—not including ProShares Ultra ETF (SSO)—are meant to be held short-term.

3. Allocate no more than 1% or 2% of your portfolio to this product.

4. When your target price has been reached, scale out of the position.

5. Hint: If a leveraged ETF makes an extreme move, and your profits are substantial, sell most or all of your position.

VOLATILITY EXCHANGE-TRADED NOTES (ETNS)

WHAT ARE VOLATILITY EXCHANGE-TRADED NOTES (ETNS)?

Volatility exchange-traded notes are investment vehicles that track the CBOE Volatility Index (VIX) over short time periods and often move inversely to the S&P 500. To understand how volatility ETNs work, it helps to think about some of the reasons the market is volatile in the first place. One reason is that sometimes humans act based on fear.

Fear is one of the most natural emotions in nature. When you see something threatening, like a snake or a bear, your brain triggers a response that releases stress hormones. It also causes a surge in adrenaline, which leads to increased heart rate, shortness of breath, and "butterflies" in your stomach. When people have a fear response, they often act impulsively. We make decisions that may make us feel better in the short term but set us back in the long term.

This response isn't limited to antiquated scenarios like seeing a bear outside your hut. In fact, controlling your emotions—both fear and greed—is one of the keys to investing success, especially when considering volatility ETNs.

But this process is easier said than done. For instance, let's say that you just bought shares in the insurance company Allstate Corp. (ALL). After doing your due diligence on the company, you know that if there was a natural disaster the business would likely struggle in the short term. And since Allstate has been around for decades and always bounced back from such short-term hiccups, you also know that the underlying business is built on a solid foundation.

Not long after you opened your position, your resolve is put to the test. A major hurricane comes barreling into the southern United States, decimating many areas where Allstate earns huge insurance premiums. When this happens, Allstate naturally must pay up on the flood insurance policies that make up much of their bottom line.

That fact weighed negatively on its share price. In the 3 months since you opened your Allstate position, your shares are down 15%. To add insult to injury, the S&P 500 is up almost 10% over this same period.

But your position keeps tumbling even after the initial 15% decline. The hurricane continues on through the US and spurs massive flooding on the East Coast, another key hub for Allstate. This collateral damage sends shares down another 10% in a single day! At this point, your fear levels are surging. You simply want to sell your stake so you don't have to think about insurance or hurricanes anymore.

This is, in fact, the worst time to sell. Instead of panic selling your position, you should revisit your original investing thesis to see if anything has changed. After all—as you originally outlined—Allstate has always bounced back from other natural disasters and put in new all-time highs.

While this is a microcosm of a single fear scenario in the stock market, there's an even broader way to measure investor fear.

Looking at the "Fear Index"

The best way to see how fearful investors are about the stock market is to check the CBOE Volatility Index, also known as the VIX or "fear index."

The VIX is the best measure of how investors feel about the markets (i.e., fear or greed). When the VIX is low (i.e., under 15), investors are not as worried about the broader economy or stock market. When the VIX spikes (i.e., over 40)—such as during the COVID-19 pandemic or global financial crisis—investors are worried about the near-term future for the stock market and economy. Note: When the VIX spikes above 40, it's statistically one of the best times to buy stocks.

VIX AND THE OPTIONS MARKET

The VIX is also a very important component of the options market. When the VIX is high, the premiums paid for a call or put option are also higher. The opposite is true when the VIX is low, as investors can buy options cheaply to hedge their positions. We'll dive deeper into these concepts in Chapter 7.

The VIX cannot be bought or sold directly like a stock. Rather, investors use ETFs or ETNs—exchange-traded *notes*—to trade and invest in volatility. The difference between an ETF and an ETN is that ETFs are a basket of financial assets traded on an exchange, while ETNs are a basket of underlying securities combined by fund developers. And for VIX ETNs, the securities are VIX futures contracts.

However, much like leveraged ETFs, volatility ETNs also suffer from contango.

Short-Term Trading Only

The VIX is defined by periods of low volatility and sporadic surges in volatility. As a result, many new investors recognize this pattern and think they should simply buy popular VIX ETNs like the iPath S&P 500 VIX Short-Term Futures ETN (VXX) during these lull periods and sell during VIX spikes. After all, there will always be events in the future that kick market fears into high gear and send the VIX surging.

This is a classic mistake. For instance, if you look at a long-term chart of VXX you'll notice that the stock has gone from a split-adjusted price—the price prior to all option contracts being rolled over—of over $120,000 to the low teens. This is because VXX does not track the VIX index. Rather, it is underpinned by VIX futures contracts that must be periodically rolled over. The reason VXX is constantly losing value is that futures contracts expire and must be replaced by new contracts.

As you can see on sites like VIXCentral.com, VIX futures have a "term structure" (i.e., these are the dates when the near-term VIX option contracts expire) that includes where investors believe the index will be during the next 6 months.

Once the closest month contract expires, it is replaced by the following month. This cycle continues over and over, with the nearest month contract expiring (and its price converging with the VIX index) and a new month becoming the largest holding in the VIX ETN.

While this may seem a little confusing, it's important to understand how these products work before investing in them. Because as we saw in February 2018, people who didn't understand how this worked were shocked when an inverse VIX ETN known as the VelocityShares Daily Inverse VIX Short-Term ETN (XIV) crashed to $0. Yes—to $0.

This is one of the risks when investing in these products, as many learned the hard way.

A PRELUDE TO "VOLMAGEDDON"

There's a popular saying on online investing message boards that goes: "Buy the dip, short the VIX." That's because over the last 10 years, there has been a ripping bull market plus a rapid decline in market volatility.

For instance, between 2009 and 2020, the S&P 500 embarked on its longest bull market in history. While there were certainly bouts of volatility along the way—like the "taper tantrum" and European debt crisis—the VIX index was near its lowest levels in history. After hitting a then-high of 62 during the height of the global financial crisis, the VIX had been on a steady downtrend. By the start of the new year in 2018, the VIX was at an all-time low of 12.4. This naturally brought a lot of individual investors onto the "short the VIX" bandwagon, including a retail investor named Seth Golden.

Golden was the quintessential retail investing success story. The former Target manager had made millions betting that volatility would keep falling. Whether it was threats of nuclear war from North Korea or terrorist attacks from the Islamic State causing a spike in the VIX, Golden continued to take the other side of that bet and short the VIX.

Golden wasn't alone; according to FactSet, these "short VIX" ETNs like the VelocityShares Daily Inverse VIX Short-Term ETN (XIV) had attracted more than $14 billion in investor cash between 2012 and 2018. Now there were more than thirty different VIX-themed products to choose from, making them some of the most actively traded products on the market.

There's No Such Thing As a Free Lunch

Investors like Golden were making cash hand over fist shorting the VIX. At a certain point, it seemed like these investors couldn't miss.

That's typically the worst time to bet heavily on a specific strategy. When all investors are thinking one way—such as shorting the VIX—that usually leads to calamitous distortions in the market. After all, if those investors turn out to be wrong about the move in the VIX—and those products shorting the VIX—the end result could be catastrophic.

Many investors do not understand how these sophisticated VIX products work. In early 2018, even Robert Whaley—known as the "father of the VIX"—told the Securities and Exchange Commission that products like the VelocityShares Daily Inverse VIX Short-Term ETN aren't suitable for retail investors. But with the "short VIX" trade working for so long, it kept attracting new investors seeking to make easy money in the market.

While Golden may have been correct that volatility would continue to decline for many years after 2018, he didn't pay attention to the vehicle—XIV—that he'd used to initiate this trade.

A Sea of Red Drowns XIV

Swiss bank Credit Suisse introduced the VelocityShares Daily Inverse VIX Short-Term ETN (XIV) in 2010. The product did exactly what Golden and other betting against the VIX needed: It rose in value when the VIX index fell.

As the bank made clear in its prospectus, XIV was not meant to be held for the long term. In its 197-page filing, Credit Suisse stated the ETN was designed "to go to zero" and that those holding XIV as a long-term investment would "likely lose all of [their] investment." Most retail investors like Golden were not aware of these risks. They simply knew the ETN rose when the VIX fell and that they could make a lot of money employing this strategy. And regrettably, what Credit Suisse warned about in its prospectus came to fruition.

In early 2018, investors grew concerned that the Federal Reserve would raise interest rates. These fears culminated with the Dow Jones Industrial Average falling 6.5%, shaving a thousand points off the index. At the time, it was the largest single-day point drop in history—a whopping 1,100 points!

This massive pullback in stocks caused an enormous spike in the VIX on February 5, 2018, sending the "fear index" up over 200% in a few days. As the VIX spiked, its inverse ETN counterpart XIV plummeted more than 95%. And the following day, Credit Suisse announced that it was liquidating its leveraged VIX products, leaving those investors who bought XIV with nothing.

Although Golden survived "Volmageddon," he and many others who shorted the VIX will probably think twice about using volatility strategies in the future.

<hr/>

INVESTMENT STRATEGY:

VOLATILITY EXCHANGE-TRADED NOTES (ETNS)

You may be wondering why anyone would want to trade such a strange product. After all, if the ETN loses value by design (like the iPath S&P 500 VIX Short-Term Futures ETN [VXX]) and can potentially go belly-up during stretches of high volatility (like the VelocityShares Daily Inverse VIX Short-Term ETN [XIV]), it doesn't seem like a stable product.

That's until you realize that VXX is a great vehicle for hedging your portfolio *in the short term*. Like leveraged ETFs, these products are not meant to be held long-term like a blue-chip stock. Rather, they are meant for short-term trading. While I don't condone day trading, I've personally used VXX to hedge my portfolio during times of high market stress.

How to Identify a Good Volatility ETN

Trading the right volatility ETN can help you cash in on market crashes—and the subsequent volatility spike—along with general bouts of volatility. Volatility also has a low correlation to the stock market, which means that your portfolio of "long" positions falls as your volatility positions increase in value.

This can be very important for the stability of your portfolio during times of uncertainty. But it's paramount that you fully understand the risks associated with volatility ETNs. As we saw with XIV, those who did not understand what they were buying were left holding the bag when the index collapsed.

But if you use the following three factors when deciding on which ETN to use, you will have much better luck trading volatility.

1. Look for High Liquidity

Liquidity is a measure of how easy it is to trade into and out of an asset. For instance, a share of Apple Inc. (AAPL) stock is highly liquid, as you can easily buy or sell its shares. On the other hand, your rare book collection is illiquid because there are only a few interested buyers.

The same concept applies to volatility ETNs. The higher the volume in the ETN, the easier it is to buy or sell your position. This is important to remember: When the VIX rises rapidly or falls rapidly, it may be difficult to buy or sell your position.

The most liquid volatility ETN is the iPath S&P 500 VIX Short-Term Futures ETN (VXX), which trades on average more than 27 million shares per day. When looking for a volatility ETN, make sure that the volume is a minimum of 1 million shares per day.

2. Set Your Time Horizon

As I've repeatedly written in this chapter, VIX ETNs are not meant to be held for more than a few days. As the VIX option contracts that underpin these ETNs are rolled over, the ETNs will gradually grind toward zero.

Therefore, before you even select an ETN, set out a time frame for your trade. Investors should avoid holding these products for more than 3 days, as by that point your position will start feeling the effects of contango.

You can see how much contango affects your ETN by looking at a 3-year chart of the ETN's price. If the ETN is down 95% over that period, you've confirmed the ETN suffers from contango and should only be held short-term.

3. Choose a Lower Expense Ratio

An expense ratio is a fee that users of an ETF or ETN are assessed for management of the investment vehicle. The ratio is expressed on an annual basis. For instance, if you have an expense ratio of 1%, it means if you invest $1,000 and hold the position for a year, you pay $10.

We've already established that you shouldn't hold a volatility ETN for more than a few days. But if you are frequently trading volatility products, you want to make sure you are not paying relatively high expense ratios.

As a rule, you should look for the best liquidity and expense ratios, and your expense ratio should never be higher than 1%.

How to Trade a Volatility ETN

Once you've found the right volatility ETN, it's time to open your position. You will buy shares of your volatility ETN like you would a share of a stock. In this case, I would not allocate more than 1% of your portfolio to volatility ETNs. Unless there are serious extenuating circumstances—perhaps we're experiencing another COVID-19 crash or financial crisis—it's best to keep your short-term bets small.

There are a few reasons for this. One is that investors will have to pay short-term capital gains taxes on any profits they make trading volatility ETNs. This can sometimes be as high as 40% (consult your tax professional for guidance on your situation). In addition, you want to make sure you're not assuming too much risk when trading these products.

Second, while volatility spikes do happen, they often occur before you can position yourself to profit. By the time the VIX spikes, you may have missed your shot to profit. Instead of trading a volatility ETN, you'd have much better luck buying stocks during this spike. In fact, S&P 500 returns are 55% higher when bought when the VIX is above 40.

That said, if you are positioned to profit from a VIX spike with your volatility ETN, you want to watch closely where to take profits. Historically, spikes in the VIX are short-lived. Between June 2020 and July 2021, the VIX had eight spikes of 30% or more for an average increase of 61%. This was in line with historical averages for VIX spikes.

It follows that investors who are positioned for a spike would be well served to scale out of their positions after the VIX rises more than 50%. Once the VIX starts to decline, sell the rest of your position to protect profits. You can track the VIX on free websites like *Yahoo! Finance* and *MarketWatch*.

Investing Quick-Start Guide:
VOLATILITY EXCHANGE-TRADED NOTES (ETNs)

1. Your brokerage firm will have a list of volatility ETNs that can be purchased.

2. Volatility ETNs are designed to be held for no more than a few days.

3. Allocate no more than 1% or 2% of your portfolio to these volatile products. As the VIX rises, so do your profits (i.e., you are "long" the VIX).

4. Once the VIX rises above 30, scale out of the position. If the VIX keeps rising, close out your position.

5. If the VIX suddenly drops, cut your entire position.

CHAPTER 5

Special Situations: Short Squeezes, Meme Stocks, and Bankrupt Stocks

In finance, "special situations" are when a stock's price movements are caused by unusual factors independent of the market as a whole. The phrase comes from Benjamin Graham, mentor to Warren Buffett and author of the classic investing book *Security Analysis*. Graham describes a "special situation" as follows:

> A situation in which a particular development is counted upon to yield a satisfactory profit in the security even though the general market does not advance.

He was referring to complex deals like mergers, recapitalizations, and legal proceedings, which are almost exclusively reserved for hedge funds and institutions. A more modern definition of special situations would include investments like short squeezes, meme stocks, and bankrupt stocks. All three are unique situations that—if you know where to look—can return massive profits in a short time period.

Investing is all about finding an edge. Having an investing edge means you have unique knowledge that can help you beat the market.

And that's especially true when you look to profit from investing in "special situations" such as the ones discussed in this chapter. And as I'm about to show you, spotting these opportunities before the wider investment community does can be the difference between a potential 1,600% gain in 2 weeks and perhaps nothing.

This is a complex topic, so make sure to read this chapter carefully before diving into any of these high-risk, high-reward opportunities.

SHORT SQUEEZES

WHAT IS A SHORT SQUEEZE?

Most investors go "long" stocks. This means they buy a stock and expect to make money when the price rises. But there's another side to that coin; investors can also make money when a stock price falls. This is known as "shorting," or "selling short." When you short a stock, you first sell the stock (that you don't even technically own), with a plan to buy it back at a lower price. For those unfamiliar with the concept, shorting might seem counterintuitive. In fact, expecting to make money when a stock price goes *down* might even sound unethical, but the strategy is perfectly legal and can potentially be a useful high-risk, high-reward opportunity.

Shorting is a sophisticated strategy that allows you to make money on weak stocks that are having a bad day or a bad year, or on stocks that are simply overvalued. While investors like Jim Chanos have made *billions* shorting stocks, it can be really risky for a simple reason: Your potential losses are infinite.

Here's an example to illustrate short selling, both what can go right and what can go wrong: Let's say you short 100 shares of Ford at $10 per share. First you borrow 100 shares of Ford (F) from your broker at $10 per share. The cost is $1,000 (100 shares × $10 per share). For every dollar that Ford *falls*, you make $100. If Ford falls to $5 per share, your *unrealized gain* is $500. If Ford actually fell to $0 (very unlikely but always possible if a company goes bankrupt), you would make the maximum gain of $10,000. In summary, for a $1,000 short sale, you booked a profit of $10,000.

The risky part about shorting is what can happen if you are wrong. In the example, you shorted 100 shares of Ford at $10 per share. Since Ford is an excellent company with popular trucks, it's a risky bet to expect that share price will fall. Let's say that instead of Ford falling lower, which you hoped would happen, the price of Ford instead moved higher.

Let's say shares of Ford went from $10 to $11 to $15. For every dollar that Ford rises, you lose $100. If Ford tripled to $30, instead of the profits you dreamed of, your *unrealized losses* are $2,000 ($20 × 100 shares).

How much higher can shares of Ford go? The answer: an infinite amount! The higher that Ford goes, the more money you lose. This dynamic makes short sellers nervous. If the investing community finds out you are short a stock and are intentionally bidding up its price, you will be forced to cover your short at a loss.

And that's where a special situation called a "short squeeze" comes into play. The short squeeze is a new strategy that can help you make the most of these situations.

The Great Fidget Spinner Short Squeeze

Here's an example: Imagine a friend of yours collects rare fidget spinners. You're convinced fidget spinners are going to go down in value because—let's face it—nobody uses fidget spinners anymore. To "short" fidget spinners, you would call your friend and say, "Hey, I need to borrow one of your rare fidget spinners."

Let's say he agrees to let you borrow his most expensive fidget spinner— valued at $100—for a small fee. Once you have the fidget spinner in your possession, you immediately sell it for $100.

A few days after you sell the fidget spinner, news leaks that this model of fidget spinner was coated in lead paint. Since lead paint is poisonous, the market collapses for this type of fidget spinner. In fact, the fidget spinner you borrowed and sold for $100 is now worth a mere $10.

Seeing an opportunity, you buy back the fidget spinner for $10 and pocket the difference in price ($100 – $10 = $90). You then return the fidget spinner to your friend, paying him a small fee for letting you borrow his toy.

People do the exact same thing with stocks. If an investor thinks a company's business model is collapsing, he can "borrow" shares from a broker and sell them. If the value of the stock falls, he can buy those shares back and pocket the difference between where he "sold" and where he "bought back." He then pays a broker a small fee for permission to borrow the stock.

But when lots of people are short a stock and that stock starts to rise rapidly, they may suffer the infamous short squeeze.

Squeezing the Shorts

Let's go back to the fidget spinner example. Let's say you once again borrowed the rare fidget spinner and sold it for $100, thinking the price would go even lower.

But this time there was renewed interest in fidget spinners. In fact, Elon Musk started tweeting about how he's collecting rare fidget spinners! That caused the price of rare fidget spinners to skyrocket. Now that fidget spinner you sold for $100 is worth $120.

You've now *lost* $20 on that investment. And since Musk won't stop tweeting about fidget spinners, you think you could lose even more. You then decide to close your trade and buy back that rare fidget spinner for $120.

But you aren't alone: Many other investors who were "short" fidget spinners are also buying them back at the same time. That's in addition to people who are buying fidget spinners because of Elon Musk.

That means both the investors who were "short" fidget spinners *and* the investors who now love fidget spinners are feverishly buying them. In short, there is a wave of buying in the fidget spinner market.

And when there is lots of buying and little to no selling, supply and demand kicks in and the price shoots higher...some might say, "to the moon."

CASE STUDY:
GAMESTOP AND WALLSTREETBETS

"I'm making so much money off GameStop."

I get nervous when friends message me about stocks. When novice investors suddenly start texting me about the markets and bragging about quick profits, it usually means a stock market "top" is near.

The GME Short

It was clear why investors were shorting GameStop stock: Very few people buy video games in person since the advent of e-commerce platforms like Amazon and direct-to-consumer gaming distribution from Microsoft and Sony.

But not everyone agreed with this thesis...many of whom resided on a popular *Reddit* board called WallStreetBets.

Keith Gill was an active member of WallStreetBets. He disagreed with the "short" GameStop thesis and frequently made posts claiming GameStop was a good long-term investment.

In December 2020, Keith's idea started to gain traction. News broke that GameStop added someone named Ryan Cohen to its board of directors. Gill and other investors thought Cohen—the former CEO of Chewy Inc., a multibillion-dollar pet food e-commerce company—was the perfect person to revitalize GameStop. Because if Cohen could figure out how to sell pet food online, why not video games?

This resonated with lots of amateur investors on WallStreetBets, who then started buying GameStop stock and pushing up its price. And that was bad news for the hedge funds who were short GameStop stock.

The GME Squeeze

After WallStreetBets and Keith Gill started accumulating GameStop stock (and pushing up its price), investors who were "short" GameStop started losing tons of money. This included a hedge fund called Melvin Capital, which lost more than $4 billion shorting GameStop in January 2020.

To stop the financial bleeding and make sure they didn't lose any more billions, Melvin Capital and others had to buy back *tons* of GameStop stock. With both WallStreetBets and these hedge funds purchasing the stock all at once, there was a buying frenzy.

This frenzy led to a textbook short squeeze. And it's why we saw GameStop stock rise 1,600% in 2 weeks.

INVESTMENT STRATEGY:

SHORT SQUEEZES

Short squeezes are one of the most popular high-risk, high-reward investment strategies. This section will help you implement this strategy as safely as possible.

How to Identify a Good Short Squeeze

The GameStop short squeeze turned an entire generation onto the strategy that's been around for well over 100 years. While social media played a major role in the GameStop short squeeze, the concept was known long before *Facebook* and *Twitter*. Companies ranging from grocery stores like Piggly Wiggly to automakers like Volkswagen were short squeeze targets well before the social media age. But while these companies were in different industries and operated decades apart, they shared similar features that can help you find the next short squeeze.

Savvy investors now troll the Internet for short squeeze opportunities. While counterintuitive, they often buy shares in these highly shorted companies not because it's a strong business, but to coordinate a short squeeze with other people on the Internet.

And if you can follow the breadcrumbs left by these Internet renegades, you can reap rewards similar to what we saw with GameStop. The following guidelines can help you.

1. Look at Short Interest As a Percentage of Float

The first step in finding a short squeeze is to look at "short interest."

Short interest is the total number of shares "sold short" for a stock. The metric shows how many shares are actively being bet against by investors.

The other side of the equation is a stock's "float," or number of shares traded for a stock.

Those looking for short squeezes should look at the number of shares sold short divided by the float. This shows you what *percentage* of outstanding shares are currently sold short. Compiling a list of companies with a short interest as a percentage of float over 30% is a great way to start your research.

2. Assess the Market Capitalization

A company's market capitalization is the total value of the company's outstanding stock. Also known as "market cap," this data point tells you how large or small a company is.

Smaller is always better when it comes to short squeezes. When researching short squeezes, make sure to limit your search to stocks under $2 billion in market capitalization. With a smaller market cap, fewer traders know about it, which is an ideal scenario for short squeezes.

3. Figure Out the "Days to Cover" Number

Days to cover shows you the number of days it will take those short a stock to "cover" or "close" their short position. This metric is calculated by dividing a stock's short interest by its average daily volume.

As a rule, the higher a stock's days to cover, the more likely a short squeeze is imminent. So, look for a higher days-to-cover number.

How to Trade a Short Squeeze

After finding your short squeeze, you want to dollar-cost average into your position over 2 weeks. You also want to keep your investment small (less than 1% of your portfolio), as there's a chance your target will keep falling in price for months and never get "squeezed."

Track the short interest reporting on your target stock to see if the number of shorted shares is rising or falling (rising is better for a short squeeze). The bimonthly reports can be found on FINRA.com and FINVIZ.com.

If your short squeeze thesis works, you want to watch the stock's volume. The squeezed stock's daily volume will double and triple in the early stages of the squeeze as the stock rockets higher. Once volume peaks and starts to decline, it's time to sell.

Investing Quick-Start Guide:
SHORT SQUEEZE

1. Go on FINVIZ.com and compile a list of the companies that have a high short interest as a percentage of float.

2. Look for stocks that have a market cap of under $2 billion. Typically, you will find no more than 20 stocks that have both high short interest and a market cap under $2 billion.

3. Find "days to cover." You are looking for small-cap stocks with a high days-to-cover number. These are the best short squeeze candidates.

4. Open a small position (no more than 1% of your portfolio). Then dollar-cost average into the position.

5. Hold as long as necessary. If the stock loses value, consider selling all or half of the position. I cut my losses at 30% and sell the entire position. Don't forget that managing risk is essential when buying a short squeeze (or when using any of the strategies in this book).

6. After 6 months, if the stock hasn't moved, sell it all.

7. Other sell signals: If there is a huge surge in volume (double or triple), and if the stock suddenly spikes and peaks, sell. Don't get greedy: Sell when you have a huge-enough profit.

WHAT ARE MEME STOCKS?

Psychologist Frank Durgin coined the term "the Tinkerbell effect" for things that can exist only because people think they do. It comes from the play *Peter Pan*, where the audience is asked to clap if they believe in the fairy Tinker Bell. The louder the claps get, the faster Tinker Bell reveals herself.

We see this same phenomenon in financial markets in the form of speculative bubbles. The most famous example is the tulip mania of the 17th century, where the price of tulips rose thousands of percent over a few years. Nothing had changed with the tulips, but the value of the bulbs kept rising because more and more people *believed* they had more value.

We now have the modern take on this age-old concept: meme stocks. Meme stocks are stocks that see sudden and dramatic surges in price and volume thanks to social media activity. They often have poor underlying businesses, with their share price typically falling for years prior to being "pumped" by social media forums. These stocks "go viral" on the Internet in the same manner as a video of a cute cat or sports clip. And while it may start out as just a few people buying the stock from a particular forum, the buying can often surge until the stock's price balloons to the stratosphere.

Here's an example of how it works. Let's say someone with the username RoaringDoggy posts on *Reddit*'s WallStreetBets forum about a small video game equipment manufacturer called Corsair Gaming (CRSR). RoaringDoggy believes that Corsair Gaming has great long-term prospects due to its exposure to gaming and because of growth in the streaming industry. And based on his discounted cash flow analysis, he believes that Corsair—which is currently trading at $30 per share—is worth closer to $50 per share.

RoaringDoggy writes a full analysis on Corsair Gaming and posts it to WallStreetBets. While he does get twenty upvotes on his post, it doesn't seem like many people are interested in his deep dive on this small company. And that's reflected in Corsair's share price, which hasn't budged since he posted. Nobody is commenting on his post, and little buzz is created. Therefore, his post has no impact on Corsair Gaming's share price.

But what would happen if RoaringDoggy's post instead got 100,000 upvotes and made it to the top of *Reddit*'s WallStreetBets? That would mean potentially hundreds of thousands of people would not only read about Corsair Gaming;

they might also possibly buy the stock! And since 10 million people subscribe to WallStreetBets, it means that they could easily move Corsair Gaming's stock. After all, the stock only trades 1 million shares per day.

If that came to pass, Corsair Gaming would leap from being just a stock to being a meme stock.

Who Needs Fundamentals When You Have Memes?

Traditional stock analysis typically focuses on two main topics: fundamentals and valuation. The stock's fundamentals—like profit margins, earnings growth, and debt levels—help you understand how strong a business is, while the valuation tells you how much you're paying for those fundamentals.

For example, a company that consistently grows its earnings at a high clip would always be preferred to a similar company with consistently lower earnings growth. And if a stock with higher earnings growth is trading at a cheaper valuation than a stock with lower earnings growth, it usually means there is a market inefficiency that you can exploit. (If you can buy more of a better stock for less money, it's typically a good idea.)

Meme stocks throw this analysis by the wayside. These assets typically rise based on what economist John Maynard Keynes called the "animal spirits" of the market. When there is a lot of euphoria—such as when the Federal Reserve surprises investors with an interest rate cut—investors are more likely to chase riskier assets like meme stocks. This phenomenon is seen in the market for cryptocurrencies as well.

Earnings growth, valuation, and other traditional fundamental factors also carry little weight with meme stocks. As we'll discuss later in this section, returns on meme stocks are driven more by short seller activity, options volume, and general market momentum. And one of the best ways to assess a meme stock investment is to keep a close eye on social media activity.

Tracking the Buzz on Social Media

Meme stocks are a modern iteration of "sentiment investing." Investors have always paid close attention to how people are feeling about the market. The more investors *feel* the market (or a meme stock) will rise, often the more likely it is to actually increase in value.

This market sentiment can be very useful for finding meme stocks. There is even an index known as the BUZZ NextGen AI US Sentiment Leaders Index, which tracks the seventy-five US stocks that are seeing the most positive social media activity. That's in addition to the MEME ETF (MEME), which is specifically designed to help investors profit off meme stocks. There are even entire websites (such as *YoloStocks*) dedicated to tracking which stocks are being discussed on websites like *Reddit* and *Twitter*.

This tracking is important because if you can pinpoint which stock will be the next to "meme" on *Reddit* or *Twitter*, you can make loads of money. (You can lose money too; we'll discuss that later.)

CASE STUDY:
AMC ENTERTAINMENT HOLDINGS (AMC)

I have a large social media following, with roughly 500,000 followers among all my accounts. During the GameStop short squeeze, I'd have dozens of people commenting on my videos that the next short squeeze target was struggling movie theater stock AMC Entertainment Holdings (AMC).

The company had been one of the worst-performing stocks in the market during my decade-long career as a stock analyst. While the S&P 500 had risen 90% between 2014 and 2019, AMC had fallen 50%.

AMC's struggles all came back to changing consumer preferences. Home movie theater costs had fallen, while streaming technology advanced rapidly. That meant people could pay $20 per month for unlimited Netflix movies as opposed to paying $20 to watch a film in a movie theater.

But then I had an epiphany: AMC Holdings really was just like GameStop. Both were based on outdated business models but had the nostalgia factor that resonated with the mostly millennial crowd frequenting WallStreetBets. And while it didn't have quite as high a short interest as a percentage of float as GameStop, the underlying narrative was the same.

Before I knew it, AMC was off to the races.

The "Apes" Have Taken Over the Zoo

While AMC shares did surge along with GameStop in January 2021, they quickly fell back down to earth. But that didn't stop the "apes"—as those buying AMC stock called themselves—from invading my comments every time I posted a new video. (They call themselves "apes" in reference to the film *Planet of the*

Apes, in which the apes say they are stronger together.) Their claims revolved around one of two themes:

- AMC stock was undervalued and should be bought.
- AMC stock is being depressed by short sellers and should be bought to "squeeze the shorts."

And buy they did...but not only *shares* of AMC. In fact, the "apes" were loading up on call options on AMC stock. Call options are contracts that give the buyers the right to buy a stock at a certain date and price, generating a profit for the buyers if the underlying shares increase in value.

A rise in call options activity may compel some institutional market participants to buy the stock, like a short squeeze. But instead of cornering those bearish investors betting against the stock, increasing call options activity pushes market makers to buy the stock to *hedge* their positions. That's because the sellers of the call options are required to deliver those shares if the contracts are ever executed.

In late May, traders spent $11.6 billion on options tied to AMC. That was more than traders spent on the S&P 500 and Nasdaq indexes *combined* over the same period. This would set into motion a "gamma squeeze" and send AMC on one of the most incredible runs I've witnessed in my career.

A "Gamma Squeeze" Sends AMC to the Moon

In options trading, "gamma" is the rate of change in an option's delta per a single move in the underlying asset. (The terms *gamma* and *delta* will be discussed later in this book.) Gamma is often called the "change of the change" and is a pivotal gauge when stock prices move by large amounts.

A gamma squeeze is exactly what happened with AMC. Institutional market makers who sold options had to deliver the underlying stock they lost on the trade. To hedge these positions, they also had to buy AMC call options. This meant that both retail "apes" *and* institutional market makers were buying AMC options. And when AMC shares started to rise, it meant that those market makers had to buy even *more* options.

Much like GameStop's short squeeze, this "gamma squeeze" caused AMC shares to surge 700% in a matter of days.

MEME STOCKS

Meme stocks are a rapidly evolving asset class that only became "a thing" in January 2020. That was when GameStop, AMC Holdings, and others first started to surge based solely on activity from *Reddit*'s WallStreetBets. This section will show you how to invest in these stocks safely and effectively.

How to Identify a Good Meme Stock

It makes sense that the renegade GameStop and AMC traders have such influence. For one, the stocks they're targeting are small and can be influenced by WallStreetBets' 10 million users. Because even if these users have an average brokerage account of $1,000, that means they can effectively manage $10 billion worth of assets.

If you keep track of where that $10 billion is headed next, you, too, can profit from meme stock mania.

1. Study Website Crawlers

Many retail investors pore over WallStreetBets trying to figure out which stock will be the next to catch *Reddit*'s eye. While this strategy works, it can be time-consuming. To make the most efficient use of your time, look for a WallStreetBets "crawler."

Crawlers are websites that aggregate data from other websites. They rank which stocks are being discussed on WallStreetBets from 1 to 25 based on how many times the ticker is mentioned on the forum.

While there are numerous crawlers, the most popular is www.yolostocks .live. (*YOLO* stands for "you only live once," a fitting acronym for a high-risk trading strategy.) This site allows you to see which stocks have been mentioned most on WallStreetBets in the last 24 hours, 14 days, or 100 days. The stocks most likely to surge higher are consistently in the top 10 in the last 24 hours.

2. Look at Unusual Option Activity

Once you've identified which stocks are trending on WallStreetBets, it is important to keep track of changes related to *short-dated* call options for those stocks, or contracts that expire within 2 weeks.

Most retail investors are piling into these risky contracts to profit off short-term movements in the stock. You can see when retail investors start buying these contracts en masse by looking at the "open interest" for these short-dated contracts. Look for that information at your broker's website or on Nasdaq.com.

When you see open interest for a particular short-dated contract quadruple or quintuple in a few days, that's your signal that WallStreetBets and institutional funds are positioning for a meme stock frenzy.

3. Calculate the Short Interest As a Percentage of Float

The WallStreetBets community enjoys "sticking it to the shorts." This means that—as what happened with GameStop (GME)—they want to force short squeezes on institutional investors.

Most meme stocks will have a relatively high short interest as a percentage of float. As a rule, any stock with a short interest as a percentage of float greater than 20% is a good meme stock candidate.

How to Invest In Meme Stocks

Once you've found your meme stock, dollar-cost average into your position over several days. This ensures you get into your position at the best possible price.

Since this is a very risky strategy, I recommend allocating not more than 1% of your capital to meme stocks. Meme stocks could either surge 1,000% or plummet to zero. By using a small amount of your portfolio, you're risking $1 to potentially make $10 or lose that $1.

After building out your position over a few days, wait for the gamma squeeze. There's a good chance the squeeze never materializes, but if it does, you should see your meme stock position skyrocket in value.

This is when you'll want to look at two things: volume and implied volatility.

1. In the early stages of a squeeze, the *volume* in the stock will increase dramatically, perhaps four- or fivefold. This is because institutional investors will be both buying and selling options to hedge the flurry of activity from retail investors. That's on top of retail buying from forums like WallStreetBets. Once you see volume surge, it's likely that the top is near and you want to sell.

2. The second factor is *implied volatility*. This is a measure of the future volatility of the underlying stock based on options activity. While unusual in "normal" stocks, meme stocks undergoing a gamma squeeze typically see their implied volatility increase hundreds of percent in a matter of days. When the implied volatility of your meme stock rises over 250% and volume has tripled, for example, it's a good time to take profits.

Investing Quick-Start Guide:
MEME STOCKS

1. Find a meme stock by searching website crawlers such as www.yolostocks.live.

2. Be on the lookout for unusual option activity, especially "open interest."

3. Also, look for short interest as a percentage of float that is higher than 20%.

4. Once you find your target, dollar-cost average into the position over several days.

5. Wait for a "gamma squeeze," which will cause implied volatility to skyrocket (by over 250% in some cases).

6. Wait for volume to explode.

7. If the trade is successful, take profits quickly. This is not the time to be greedy.

BANKRUPT STOCKS

WHAT ARE BANKRUPT STOCKS?

Investors typically want to avoid any stock associated with bankruptcy. And for good reason; bankruptcy is a legal proceeding for companies that can't meet their debt obligations. Declaring bankruptcy is confirmation that your business model doesn't work and you need to liquidate your assets.

And if you're a shareholder of a company that's gone bankrupt, you will likely get the proverbial short end of the stick when it comes to asset liquidation. When a company files for Chapter 11 bankruptcy, the assets of the business are distributed in the following order:

- **Secured creditors:** usually banks, who are always paid first
- **Unsecured creditors:** banks, suppliers, and bondholders
- **Stockholders:** owners of the company who have the last claim to any assets until the previous two are fully paid off

That means stockholders get whatever is left over after banks and bondholders are completely paid off. In most cases, stockholders get nothing.

Here's an example. Let's say you bought 100 shares of JCPenney for $10 per share. The department store had recently added a key executive from a large tech company who plans to turn the company into an e-commerce giant. But as months turn into years, the strategy does not yield any higher sales. In fact, all the extra money spent on marketing the new strategy has pushed the company deep into debt.

This higher debt load and weak sales cause JCPenney's stock to keep falling (along with the value of your 100 shares). Eventually JCPenney can no longer meet its debt payments and files for Chapter 11 bankruptcy protection.

JCPenney goes to court and sells off its remaining assets to the tune of $100 million; $75 million goes to the banks that financed the loans, and the remaining $25 million goes to pension funds that invested in JCPenney's debt. Unfortunately for you and other shareholders, there is no money left over after these asset sales, so you have lost 100% of your $1,000 investment.

This is how 99.9% of bankruptcy proceedings go for shareholders. But there is that 0.1% of the time where you can "buy the dip" on the bankrupt company.

And if you time it right, you can make a lot of money.

Betting on a Bankrupt Company

Let's go back to our JCPenney example. Let's say the shares you bought for $10 have fallen to $0.50, and your attorney says you will likely not get anything from the asset liquidation since you're only a stockholder.

But then something unusual happens—a private equity group who specializes in retail turnarounds is interested in buying JCPenney's assets. There is also buzz online related to JCPenney branded clothing. According to the kids on social media, JCPenney-related clothes are now "vintage," and prices for anything connected to the brand have skyrocketed on secondary markets.

You had ignored your attorney's advice about selling your shares for $0.50. And you were rewarded, as the stock has shot up to $3. In fact, if the package mentioned in the bankruptcy proceedings comes to pass, your shares could be worth $15!

While doing this might seem counterintuitive, you were rewarded for holding stock in a bankrupt company.

Bankrupt Investing Isn't Anything New

In 2004, JPMorgan Chase looked at 100 companies that had declared bankruptcy over the prior 15 years. The research showed that these stocks beat the S&P 500 by 84% in their first year out of bankruptcy. These formerly bankrupt companies were some of the best-performing stocks that year. This makes sense, as the companies often had great underlying businesses; they simply had too much debt to service. The stocks included stalwarts like Kmart, Six Flags, and Charter Communications.

But there is an important distinction between these companies and the trade we're covering in this chapter. When those three companies declared bankruptcy, their rulings stipulated that equity holders would not receive any compensation when the company emerged from Chapter 11 bankruptcy. So while stocks coming out of bankruptcy tended to outperform, you would have wanted to wait until *after* the company was relisted on the stock market before buying.

The real high-risk, high-reward strategy is finding a company that's declared bankruptcy but rewards shareholders who stuck around through the proceedings.

HERTZ AND THE COVID-19 PANDEMIC

The COVID-19 pandemic was unkind to many businesses. Whether you were a brick-and-mortar store with little e-commerce presence or a restaurant dependent on foot traffic, your customers instantly dried up in early 2020. But no industry was hit harder than travel. Airlines, hotels, and other travel-related companies saw their sales disappear overnight. And no company typified this struggle more than rental car agency Hertz Global Holdings (HTZ).

Hertz is the oldest rental car agency in the United States. But the business was struggling even before the global pandemic. In fact, the company had lost money for 4 consecutive years, including a $58 million loss in 2019.

COVID-19 rang a death knell for the company. With most of the world cooped up in their homes, nobody was traveling, let alone renting cars. The lockdowns pushed Hertz's struggling business to the brink and its stock down 82%. The company held $19 billion in debt, and nearly its entire 700,000 fleet was idle due to the pandemic. With no end in sight, Hertz management filed for bankruptcy on May 22, 2020.

But this was far from the end of Hertz's story.

Hertz Comes Back from the Dead

When a company files Chapter 11 bankruptcy, a 60-day clock starts. During this period, secured lenders like banks and pension funds must wait before they can foreclose on a company's assets (in this case, Hertz's 700,000 used cars).

But something unusual happened during Hertz's 60-day period. While most traditional investors would be scared off by a company declaring bankruptcy, a new crop of retail traders were less risk averse.

The number of people opening brokerage accounts on apps like Robinhood skyrocketed during the COVID-19 lockdowns. In fact, retail investors opened a record 10 million new brokerage accounts in 2020. These fearless traders knew about America's largest rental car agency. So when they saw the stock trading for pennies, some started to buy. Since there were so few people trading the stock, Hertz shares started to surge higher. In fact, the post-bankruptcy Hertz stock rose nearly 1,000%!

This was a *highly* unusual event. The financial media were flabbergasted by the surge in shares of bankrupt stocks like Hertz, Whiting Petroleum (WLL), and others. Hertz even attempted to capitalize by issuing millions in stock to shore up its weak financials.

To the surprise of many, the "Robinhood traders" had been right to buy the dip.

Vindication for the Robinhood Traders

While Hertz shares were officially delisted from the New York Stock Exchange in October 2020 (as is the procedure if the stock price closes under $1 for 30 consecutive days), the stock still traded "over the counter." This meant that those who believed the company would eventually emerge from bankruptcy could hang on to their shares.

By early 2021, COVID-19 vaccines were being distributed, and much of the world geared up for a busy summer travel season. Plus, the price of used cars—Hertz's main asset—had surged 25% over the last year. This dynamic created a bidding war for Hertz's assets while it was still in bankruptcy court.

The best offer came from private equity firm Knighthead Capital Management. Like in any bankruptcy deal, the group agreed to pay off Hertz's secured and unsecured debt. But the final deal also included a distribution of $8 per share to the company's current shareholders. That meant that all those Robinhood traders would get at least $8 for the shares they might have bought for as low as $0.30.

This unusual deal proved lucrative for these traders, as many sat on gains as high as 2,566%.

INVESTMENT STRATEGY:

BANKRUPT STOCKS

Bankruptcy is typically not great news for any company. No manager wants to tell his employees that the company has run into trouble and needs to reorganize operations. Or, in worst-case scenarios, completely shut down the business.

But from an investment standpoint, you can make money by identifying bankrupt companies that could emerge from bankruptcy better than before and—like Hertz—compensate shareholders who stuck with the company.

How to Identify a Good Bankrupt Stock

Of all the high-risk, high-reward special situations in this chapter, trying to make money off bankrupt companies is by far the riskiest strategy. There is only a slim chance that a stock emerges from bankruptcy and—if it does— rarely do stock investors reap any benefits.

And unlike some of the other strategies in this book, you lose 100% of your investment if you're wrong about the company. But if you want to delve into this strategy, these three steps will help manage the risk associated with investing in bankrupt companies.

1. Compile a List of Bankrupt Stocks

Your first step in this process is to compile a list of companies that have recently filed for Chapter 11 bankruptcy. The easiest way to find this information is to search on *Wikipedia* for "Companies that filed for Chapter 11 bankruptcy."

This page will give you a long list of companies (both public and private) that have filed for Chapter 11 bankruptcy. Once you have a list of those with publicly traded stock, you can move on to the next step.

2. Assess the Company's Brand Value

Companies that emerge from Chapter 11 bankruptcy typically have a very strong brand. Hertz is a great example. These companies have also made the transition from bankrupt to legitimate company:

- General Motors
- Chrysler
- Marvel Entertainment
- Six Flags
- Sbarro

What all these businesses have in common is their strong brand. To find how valuable a company's brand is, you'll want to pull up the company's balance sheet. You can find this information for free on company websites or *Yahoo! Finance*.

Once you have the balance sheet, look under "Net Intangible Assets" and see how much of their asset base is from Trademarks and Patents. If the figure is over $1 billion, it's safe to say the company has a strong brand and is a good candidate.

3. Define Reasons the Company Went Bankrupt

Companies can go bankrupt for a variety of reasons. Some businesses like Blockbuster or Sam Goody saw their core business go into secular decline due to technological advancements. But others enter bankruptcy for more temporary reasons. For Hertz, a global pandemic temporarily brought the global travel industry to a halt. Once vaccines became widely available, the market returned to normal.

If a company on your list has a strong brand *and* went bankrupt only due to a temporarily weak market environment, it may be a good idea to take a small position in the stock.

How to Trade a Bankrupt Stock

Once you've identified a bankrupt stock worth a high-risk trade, you can start dollar-cost averaging into your position. This is to make sure you enter your position at the best possible price.

Buying stock in a bankrupt company is a very risky strategy. As such, you want to keep your position very small in case stockholders get wiped out in Chapter 11 bankruptcy proceedings. That's why I wouldn't allocate more than 0.5%–1% of my portfolio to companies going through Chapter 11 bankruptcy. While your position could potentially rise 2,500% (like Hertz), it could also fall 100%, thus wiping out your entire investment.

Once you've opened your position, you will want to keep a close eye on news related to the bankruptcy proceedings. This includes following any press releases for the company in addition to reporters covering the story.

If you're lucky enough to see your bankrupt stock come out of Chapter 11, your position should skyrocket in value. At this point you would want to take profits on the position, as even though this special situation yielded strong results, the business will likely still struggle.

Investing Quick-Start Guide:
BANKRUPT STOCKS

1. Find bankrupt stocks on *Wikipedia* (under "Companies that filed for Chapter 11 bankruptcy").

2. Look for companies with a strong brand (in the balance sheet, look for "Net Intangible Assets"). A company with more than $1 billion in trademarks and patents is a good candidate.

3. Evaluate why the company went bankrupt. If it's a temporary setback, consider buying.

4. Warning: Buying bankrupt stocks is extremely risky, so dollar-cost average into the stock with a small position (less than 1% of your portfolio).

5. After buying, follow the news. If the bankrupt company comes out of Chapter 11, the stock may skyrocket. As always, take profits if trade is successful.

CHAPTER 6

Over-the-Counter (OTC) Stocks

Over-the-counter stocks are tiny stocks—usually trading under $1—that do not trade on major exchanges. Instead, OTC securities trade via a "dealer network," which tracks each transaction and displays prices. OTC stocks offer some of the highest upside of any asset in this book. However, the asset class is rife with scams, so make sure to read this chapter carefully before investing.

Whether in life or in investing, one of the best ways to get ahead is to do things other people aren't willing to do. When most people begin their investing journey, they want to take the easy route by hiring financial advisers or—for the younger generation—robo-advisers.

Most of these advisers (especially those of the human variety) are not financial analysts. They don't use financial modeling or independent research to figure out which company is the best investment. Rather, financial advisers are often salespeople trying to convince you to buy their company's financial products.

It also means many do not understand the financial products they're selling. These companies have large research departments that do that legwork for them. But even in the research firms, most default to the "consensus" analyst opinions when deciding whether to recommend buying or selling a security.

Consensus is a powerful thing. When dozens of analysts consult their financial models, and they agree with each other's research on stocks, consumers, and trends, there is consensus. That sounds good, until you remember what happens when everyone rushes to the same side of the boat—it tips over! Those who invest based on consensus should be content with average returns; they will likely follow the whims of the market (for better or worse).

Some financial markets don't have a consensus. While companies like Apple, Tesla, and Microsoft have thousands of analysts covering their stock, there are hundreds of thousands of small companies that have zero analyst coverage. These are known as "over-the-counter" stocks. If you know how to pick the right ones, you can generate out-of-consensus returns.

MICROCAP STOCKS

WHAT ARE MICROCAP STOCKS?

Most of the stocks discussed so far in the book—such as growth stocks, IPOs, etc.—fall into the "small-cap" or "mid-cap" section. This is loosely defined as companies with a market capitalization between $300 million and $10 billion. Here is a list of types of stocks by market capitalization amount:

- Large-cap stocks: $20 billion or more
- Mid-cap stocks: $2 billion to $20 billion
- Small-cap stocks: $300 million to $2 billion
- Microcap stocks: $50 million to $300 million
- Nano-cap stocks: $50 million or less

But while the small- and mid-cap stocks are the companies you have heard most about so far in this book, there is an entire universe of stocks known as "microcaps" that can yield high-risk, high-reward returns. Microcap stocks are companies with a market capitalization between $50 million and $300 million. Because of their small size, they are typically much riskier than their large- and mid-cap peers. Microcap stocks are also less likely to have much of a public presence, as they do not have the funds to allocate to promotional content. They also typically trade at or below $5 per share.

Smaller Can Often Be Better (in the Stock Market)

While they carry much more risk, microcap stocks can often outperform their large-cap peers. For instance, let's look at two hypothetical companies: Large Cap Enterprises and Small Cap Inc.

Large Cap Enterprises has been in the enterprise software industry for over 30 years. The $50 billion market cap company is well established in this industry with many long-term contracts. They have high profit margins, a rock-solid balance sheet, and are growing sales by 10% per year. Due to their wide coverage by sell-side analysts, the stock is also a favorite of institutional investors, who own more than 80% of the company's outstanding shares. Large Cap Enterprises management—headed by a founder who is one of the most respected CEOs in the industry—even introduced a dividend and share buyback plan last quarter to reward its investors.

On the other hand, Small Cap Inc. was founded a mere 6 years ago. The $100 million market cap company has had some success in its short time as a publicly traded company. However, its financial performance has been mixed, with sales growing in the high double digits last year but falling into negative territory in the latest year. While the average annual sales growth over the last 5 years is 30%, there have been huge swings in the company's financial performance and thus its stock price.

The company has only one analyst covering its stock and—since it's so small—the firm has no institutional ownership. Information on Small Cap Inc. is also hard to find, as the company is not even on the Securities and Exchange Commission website. And while there are a few *YouTube* videos with the company's management team, the CEO is largely unknown.

Large Cap Enterprises is clearly a less risky bet than Small Cap Inc. The former is an established name in an industry with long-term growth potential. And since it is well covered by the financial media, you can be sure that the company has real products and isn't a scam.

On the other hand, the fact that Large Cap Enterprises is so well known means that its overall returns will likely be lower. Since institutional ownership is so high, much of the gains in the stock have already been realized.

That is not the case with Small Cap Inc., which is flying under most investors' radars. This information asymmetry works in the favor of Small Cap Inc., as investors in the company are getting in before a potential flood of interest from institutional buyers and the investing public. This means that Small Cap Inc. has significantly higher upside if management is able to capitalize on its market opportunity.

While Large Cap Enterprises is a fine stock to hold, it will not have nearly as much upside as Small Cap Inc. But that also means Small Cap Inc. carries much more risk.

It Can Pay to Be Small

As I mentioned, one reason why microcap stocks have more upside is because they have little institutional adoption. The hedge funds, pension funds, and other "smart money" cannot invest in microcap stocks for a few reasons.

1. First, microcap stocks are extremely risky. Pension funds like CalPERS and New York State Common Retirement Fund with billions in assets cannot risk investing their clients' money in risky microcap stocks. Many are required to invest in companies within certain limits, such as a bond rating higher than AA.
2. Second, institutional clients typically purchase millions of dollars' worth of shares at one time. This means they cannot invest in microcaps with any meaningful returns. Even if they bought every outstanding share and the company performed well, the overall impact on their portfolio would be minimal.

Individual investors are not restricted by any of these issues. While it shouldn't come as a surprise, managing a $10,000 portfolio is much different than managing a $10,000,000,000 portfolio. That creates opportunities for individual investors, as they can get in early on microcap stocks before institutional money comes into play.

But as I'm about to show you, some money managers have made boatloads of money investing in microcap stocks.

GENEVIEVE AND THE ARIZONA WATER UTILITY

In the 2000s, there was a major housing boom in the US. Enabled by government programs encouraging home ownership, banks were giving out loans to many people who had no business taking on such high debt loads. When the global economy began to slow and people could not make their loan payments, a major crisis unfolded known as the "subprime mortgage crisis."

This housing crisis soon spiraled into a banking crisis. By the end of 2008, many of the world's largest investment banks (like Lehman Brothers and Bear Stearns) were bankrupt or on shaky ground. Investors had lost faith in the banking system, which caused credit markets to seize up.

Very few businesses were spared during this period, including traditionally safe industries like utilities. Utilities are the companies that deliver power, water, and other essential services to homes and businesses. Since people always need to turn on their lights, faucets, and showers, these businesses are very stable. A global financial crisis didn't change these basic facts of the utilities market. Nevertheless, these great businesses were trading at their cheapest valuation in years.

Former fund manager Genevieve Roch-Decter saw an opportunity during this chaos. While she currently runs a popular financial media and education company called Grit Capital (which you can find online at GritCap.io), she was managing a $100 million portfolio in the early 2010s. She saw a major opportunity in a water utility called Global Water Resources (GWRS).

The Blue Gold Rush in the Desert

Global Water Resources operates a water, wastewater, and water utility service in Phoenix, Arizona. The US water sector has long been a steady source of returns for investors, largely due to its favorable demographics and industry dynamics. For instance, there are currently 333 million people living in the United States. By 2050, the US population is projected to climb as high as 440 million. That means the US government will likely continue to invest heavily in water infrastructure to meet the upcoming surge in demand.

Roch-Decter recognized that the demographics alone supported the long-term thesis. Add in the high barriers to entry associated with owning and operating a water utility, which ensured that new competitors would not be popping up any time soon, and there was a compelling investment case.

In the lead-up to the subprime mortgage crisis, there was a huge home-building boom as well. While companies like Global Water Resources had built up their inventory to meet this surge in demand, the housing market bust meant many of these homes were empty.

And when the demand for housing dried up, so did Global Water Resources' revenue sources. This tanked the company's shares, which were trading as low at $4.45 in 2014.

Letting the Profits Flow

Roch-Decter recognized that the housing crisis in the US would eventually pass and demand for water in these empty houses would increase once they were inhabited. Since the infrastructure—which is very expensive to build—was the latest technology, Global Water Resources could maintain their systems while they waited for demand to recover.

Seeing the writing on the wall, Roch-Decter started buying shares like mad. She assumed that once people moved into these homes and were locked into continuous rate increases for water services, the earnings—and a rise in the share price—would come eventually.

She was right on the money. While she initially opened her position at $4.45 per share, shares have since returned over 600%.

INVESTMENT STRATEGY:
MICROCAP STOCKS

As Roch-Decter's story shows, investing in microcap stocks can be very rewarding. The 600% return on her investment is nearly quadruple the S&P 500 return over the same period. However, as any microcap investor will tell you, not every investment will be profitable. In fact, you will more than likely lose out on most of your microcap stock investments. This section will help you minimize losses.

How to Identify a Good Microcap Stock

Investing in microcap stocks is truly a high-risk, high-reward strategy. Nevertheless, if you use the following three metrics, you should increase your chances of making money in this lucrative market.

1. Dig for Reliable Information

As we reviewed in the Large Cap Enterprises example, microcap investors are at an information disadvantage compared to their larger peers. The CEOs of microcap stocks rarely speak at conferences, go on CNBC, or host earnings calls.

Microcap stocks also don't have dozens of analysts covering their stock, and many don't have information on the Securities and Exchange Commission website. This means microcap investors must be far more diligent than their large-cap or mid-cap peers.

As a rule, if you can't find much information on a microcap stock, you should move on to another company. The microcap space is rife with fraud and scams, so if you can't find reliable data on the stock, it's best to avoid it. If possible, set up a call with the company's investor relations department to get a full rundown of the company.

2. Invest Only in Secular Growth Industries

Many of the companies in the microcap space are tiny pharmaceutical companies or mining companies (both of which we'll cover in this chapter). These companies have a host of industry-specific risk.

For other sectors, focus on industries with high rates of growth. Microcap stocks are extremely high risk, so you only want to invest in companies that can compensate you via high returns—think 1,000%—for taking on such high risk.

For instance, microcap investors should focus on "next generation" industries. This includes high-growth markets like blockchain, e-sports, cannabis, sports betting, and financial technology. By buying microcaps only in these industries, you will drastically increase your odds of generating above-average returns in this challenging market.

3. Assess the Dilution Risk

All the sections in this chapter will talk about something called "dilution risk." This refers to a company's need to raise funding to finance its operations. The problem is that many companies sell stock to finance their operations, thus "diluting" the pool of stocks owned by current shareholders and leading to wild swings in its share price.

One way to see if a company will need to dilute its shares is to look at its cash and cash equivalents relative to its annual operating expenses. (You can find cash and cash equivalents on the company's balance sheet, while annual operating expenses will be on the income statement.) Divide the cash and cash equivalents by annual operating expenses to see how much capital the company has on hand to finance its operations.

If this figure is greater than 1.5, it means the company has sufficient cash to finance its business for 18 months. As a rule, the higher this figure, the better. On the other hand, if the figure is below 1.0, it means the firm will likely need to dilute its shares to raise funding in the near term. Those companies should be avoided, as share dilution can eat into your long-term investment returns.

How to Trade a Microcap Stock

One thing to remember about investing in microcap stocks is that you will lose much more than you will win. These stocks are extremely high risk, and many of these companies have low share prices because the underlying business is weak. Therefore, it is likely that many microcap stocks will go bankrupt, and you will lose 100% of your investment.

Knowing that, it's important to diversify your microcap investment between 10–15 positions. While individual investors who can handle volatility can put up to 10% of their investable assets in microcap stocks, you want to make sure that no position accounts for more than 1% of your portfolio. Again, many of your microcap stock investments will fail. But since the gains reaped on these investments can be 500% or more, you will potentially make up for those weak positions with big gains.

Once you've found your microcap stock investments, sit and wait. I would approach microcap investing with a medium-term time horizon. You also need to learn to manage the risks associated with these investments. For instance, if one of my microcap stock investments falls 35%, I close the position. This is to avoid having a bad loss turn into an insurmountable loss.

If you hit it big on a microcap stock investment, you should "de-risk" the position. For instance, if you invest $1,000 at $5 per share in a microcap stock and shares rise to $10, your position is now worth $2,000. Sell enough shares to cover that initial $1,000 investment so only your profits are at risk. As long as nothing changed with your underlying thesis, you can sit on that position for years and let your gains compound.

Investing Quick-Start Guide:
MICROCAP STOCKS

1. Find a broker that allows you to buy microcap (i.e., over-the-counter) stocks. Not every broker does, so ask to make sure.

2. Once you find an over-the-counter stock you want to own, buy the number of shares you want. Be sure the position size is correct (preferably no more than 1% of your portfolio) before you purchase.

3. Monitor the position closely and be sure to use hard stop losses (i.e., sell if your position drops more than 35%).

4. Have a target price for selling. Most importantly, obey your rules.

5. When your target price is reached, sell your position.

SMALL-CAPITALIZATION BIOTECH STOCKS

WHAT ARE SMALL-CAPITALIZATION BIOTECH STOCKS?

Most people reading this are familiar with biotechnology stocks. These are companies such as Gilead Sciences (GILD), Merck & Co. (MRK), and Moderna (MRNA) that make everything from COVID-19 vaccines to cold medicine.

These companies are the kind that your robo-adviser would recommend buying. That's because most large-capitalization biotech stocks (or "large-cap" for short) offer predictable cash flows and steady returns for their investors. Part of the reason these companies are so reliable is they've been around for many years and are established in the biotechnology industry.

For instance, let's look at Pfizer Inc. (PFE). The company primarily develops and produces oncology (cancer) and immunology (immune systems) medicines. It also has a significant presence in the global vaccines market and—as I'm sure many of you have heard—was the first company to release a COVID-19 vaccine in 2020. The company sells its products in more than 125 countries, giving Pfizer access to some of the fastest-growing pharmaceutical markets on the planet.

Pfizer also has traits of what's known as a "wide economic moat." This concept—popularized by Warren Buffett—refers to a business's ability to maintain an advantage over its peers. This protects the long-term prospects of the business and prevents competitors from taking market share. Pfizer has a wide economic moat because of its vast patent portfolio. This gives the company strong pricing power in key markets like oncology and immunology. These cash-cow businesses give Pfizer the ability to invest heavily in research and development, allowing the company to make new drugs and—ideally—more patents to solidify its economic moat.

One feature of "wide moat" companies is strong fundamentals. This includes high gross profit margins, strong free cash flow growth, and low debt. Since these are mature companies, they also often trade at reasonable price-to-earnings (P/E) and price-to-sales (P/S) valuation multiples. Many even pay large dividends and buy back a lot of their own stock. And since they have strong patent portfolios, they can easily raise financing in public markets by selling debt or equity without issue. Like most giant companies, their shares can be easily bought or sold on major exchanges; your retirement account probably includes large-cap biotech stocks.

Almost all large-cap biotechnology companies look like this from a bird's-eye view. At that level, you're less concerned with how their new up-and-coming drugs will perform and more concerned with how they will protect their intellectual property.

However, all these large-cap companies started out as small biotechnology companies.

Money Talks in the Small-Cap Biotech Market

On the other end of the biotech spectrum are small-capitalization, or "small-cap," biotech stocks. Unlike large-cap companies, small-cap biotech stocks—loosely defined as biotech companies under $100 million valuation—do not offer predictable cash flows or steady investment returns. They don't have an economic moat to protect their market share because—in most cases—they don't have *any* market share. That's because many don't have a working or marketable drug. For the most part, traditional financial analysis techniques will not help you when analyzing small-cap biotech stocks.

There are a few small-cap biotech factors investors should keep an eye on. For instance, all biotech companies go through a process called clinical trials. These are the steps a company must take to get their drug approved by regulatory bodies such as the Food and Drug Administration (FDA). Typically, results from these clinical trials—whether positive or negative—will have a significant impact on a small-cap biotech stock's share price.

To make sure the company has enough funding to survive these clinical trials, investors should look at the company's cash position relative to operating expenses. For example, let's say a small biotech company called Small-Cap Sciences has a promising new drug candidate we'll call glaxomectin. They have made it through the first clinical trial, which shareholders cheered by sending the stock up 50%.

In the US, drugs must complete three clinical trials before they can be brought to market. That means that while Small-Cap Sciences' glaxomectin made it through its first trial, it still needs to finish two more trials before it can begin earning any revenue. To finalize those two additional clinical trials, the company needs enough funding to bring the drug across the finish line.

One way to tell if Small-Cap Sciences has enough money to conduct its upcoming clinical trials is to look at its cash position relative to its average operating expenses. A company's cash position can be found on its balance sheet under "Cash and Cash Equivalents."

Small-Cap Sciences currently has $10 million in cash on its balance sheet. To determine if they have enough cash on hand to fund clinical trials, you want to look at Small Cap Sciences' income statement to calculate its average operating expenses. For Small Cap Sciences, annual expenses are approximately $2 million. That means that Small Cap Sciences would have roughly 5 years' worth of funding ($10 million / $2 million) on its balance sheet.

Let's look at one of Small-Cap Sciences' competitors, Bio Pharmaceuticals. While they also have $10 million in cash on their balance sheet, their annual expenses are $8 million per year. That means the company has 1.25 years of cash to fund clinical trials...but those trials can last for many years.

The Biggest Risk with Small-Cap Biotechs

Bio Pharmaceuticals, unfortunately, doesn't have enough cash on their balance sheet to make it through clinical trials. That means that they *must* raise cash to fund these trials.

Businesses have two ways to raise capital: issuing debt or selling equity. With small-cap biotech stocks, very few banks are willing to underwrite a debt offering since there is no collateral to put up. That means that most small-cap biotech companies must issue stock to fund operations.

For example, let's say Bio Pharmaceuticals has 600,000 shares outstanding on its income statement. To raise cash to fund clinical trials, Bio needs to issue another 150,000 shares at $15 per share, which raises $2.25 million in funding.

While that's good for Bio Pharmaceuticals, as they can now fund their clinical trials, it's bad for investors who had already invested in the company. That's because Bio "diluted" its shares by 25% to raise capital. When Bio announced the share offering, share price of the company fell 25% to account for this dilution.

This is extremely common with small-cap biotech stocks. That's a key reason why you want to make sure any small-cap biotech stock you invest in has plenty of cash on its balance sheet. Because if a company continually dilutes its shares, it also dilutes your initial investment.

While small-cap biotech investors can improve their odds by making sure the company is well capitalized, there are certain risks in this sector that are completely out of your control.

THE GREAT BEAR RAID

In 2015, I was working as a small-cap biotech analyst for an investment research company. At the time, I was paired with a biotechnology expert and economist named Patrick Cox. Patrick was an independent biotechnology veteran with 30 years of experience. He'd spent much of his career researching and writing on cutting-edge biotech projects, speaking at conferences, and sitting on the boards of small-cap biotech companies.

However, Patrick was not interested in the investing side of the biotech market. That's why my company asked me to issue recommendations and trades based on Patrick's outlook on the hard science behind the companies he was bullish on.

We had a lot of success in our years working together. But while his scientific acumen and my financial analysis skills made for a great pairing, there were certain things neither of us could control—one of which was something called "bear raids."

The Bears Have Taken Over the Asylum

Patrick and I were bullish on a company called Applied DNA Sciences (APDN). The company used molecular technologies to enhance supply chain security and anti-theft technology. For example, when a company sent goods from point A to point B, they would be fitted with a microchip to ensure the goods got to their destination. The company had a large addressable market, and even had contracts with the US Department of Defense.

It was one of our highest-conviction ideas in the portfolio. While the firm had dilution risk, the upside outweighed that risk. That's especially true since APDN's management included many of the original members of the team who developed and marketed radio-frequency identification (RFID). (Have you ever scanned an item at the grocery store? That's RFID.) For that reason, we spent a lot of time writing about APDN and the outlook for the company.

The problem with these small companies is that they have a small "float," meaning there are not many shares traded per day. So when someone issues a buy or sell recommendation, it can move the share price dramatically. And if someone writes a piece saying APDN is a fraudulent company, the selling can pick up quickly.

"The Pump Stopper" Sends His Regards

On the morning of October 29, 2015, I awoke to a flurry of emails from both Patrick and our subscribers. APDN shares had cratered by 45% that morning seemingly out of nowhere. I did several Google searches and quickly discovered what had happened: a "bear raid" by someone called "The Pump Stopper."

WHAT IS A BEAR RAID?

Bear raids are an illegal practice whereby an investor opens a short position in a company then spreads false information about it to force down the stock price. The raiders typically target small, illiquid companies—like APDN and other small-cap biotechs—as they can be easily influenced due to their low volumes.

"The Pump Stopper" posted a 10,000-word article on the investing website *Seeking Alpha*, stating that APDN was a fraud. They even mentioned Patrick by name, stating that he was being paid by APDN to promote the stock.

While none of this was true, the article spread like wildfire across the investment community, causing many investors to panic. By the end of the day, APDN shares were down more than 60%. While the company is still around today, the shares never came close to putting in a new all-time high.

All small-cap biotech investors should keep in mind the APDN example; even if the underlying technology and management team are sound, these high-risk investments are susceptible to issues such as bear raids and other unique risk factors.

INVESTMENT STRATEGY:
SMALL-CAP BIOTECH STOCKS

Investing in the small-cap biotech market is like walking through a minefield. Instead of looking at revenue and cash flow projections, small-cap biotech investors try to figure out which company will develop the drugs of the future. Unless you have a science background, it's hard to gain an edge in this market.

How to Identify a Good Small-Cap Biotech Stock

Even if a small-cap biotech company has an amazing product, there's no guarantee it will make it through the rigorous clinical trial process. And even if the company makes it to the final round of trials, early investors will have their shares diluted so much at that point the returns will be minimal. Meanwhile, anyone with a laptop and an Internet connection can upload fraudulent information to investing websites, potentially causing your position to tank.

This makes small-cap biotech an extremely difficult market to invest in. But if you use the following parameters, you should increase your odds of making money in this market.

1. Evaluate the Management Team

An overarching theme in this book is that management teams are extremely important to a company's success. When it comes to small-cap biotech, there is no factor more important than management.

A top biotech management team should include seasoned industry veterans who have helped bring biotechnology products to market. These managers understand the regulatory framework necessary to achieve bringing a product from the lab to patients.

They are also savvy in raising funds and securing partnerships. You can find information related to small-cap biotech managers on the company's website and on each manager's *LinkedIn* page. Look for managers who have brought other products to market and successfully managed other small-cap biotech companies.

2. Assess the Dilution Risk

As we discussed in the Bio Pharmaceuticals example, dilution risk can weigh heavily on a small-cap biotech's stock. Since these companies have no choice but to dilute their shares to raise funding, it's simply the nature of the beast.

Your goal shouldn't be to completely avoid dilution, as basically every company in this industry needs to dilute their shares at some point. Rather, you want to find companies that need to dilute less often so your investment doesn't lose value.

The best way to do this is to see which biotech companies have the highest cash and cash equivalents relative to annual operating expenses. Generally, a company with less than 1 year of cash financing is due for a dilution and should be avoided. On the other hand, companies with more than 3 years' worth of financing can likely fund operations through multiple clinical trials. You can find both cash and cash equivalents and annual operating expenses in the company's financial statements for free on *Yahoo! Finance* and *Finviz.*

3. Check Out the Market Opportunity

People typically want to invest in a small-cap biotech company because of one individual drug. However, the best way to invest in this market is to take a wider view, and see the full pipeline of drugs for a specific company.

Most small-cap biotech companies have many drugs in their pipeline. Each one has been developed to treat a specific disease. When determining which small-cap biotech stock to invest in, you want to see the market potential for each of these drugs. This can be as simple as looking up how many people have a particular disease and how many treatments there are for it.

Companies focusing on diseases that have no current treatment are often the best bets, as they will enter a market with little to no competition. On the other hand, investors would be wise to avoid small-cap biotech companies targeting diseases where large players already hold market share.

How to Trade a Small-Capitalization Biotech Stock

Once you've found a small-cap biotechnology stock that meets these criteria, you want to decide how much to invest. Small-cap biotech stocks offer significant upside (i.e., potential gains); however, it is an extremely risky market. Therefore, I would not allocate more than 1% of your investment portfolio to any small-cap biotech company.

Small-cap biotech stocks are famously volatile. That's why you want to scale into your position over many weeks or months. Ideally, wait for shares to have a steep pullback before opening your first position. That allows you to take advantage of any near-term weakness in the share price.

Once you've opened your position, wait for an upcoming catalyst. This will typically be the results of a clinical trial, which will weigh heavily on the stock's performance (for better or worse).

If your small-cap biotech reports positive news and surges, it's a good idea to take some capital off the table. Whenever one of my small-cap biotech positions crosses over a 100% gain, I take my initial investment off the table. This is known as a "free ride" and makes it so only your profits are at risk.

On the flip side, let's say clinical trials come in poorly and shares fall. I'm a fan of cutting any position that's down 35% and moving on. When it comes to high-risk, high-reward investing, it is essential that you manage the risk. If a stock falls more than 50%, it will have to more than double in order for you to just break even. Instead of riding shares lower, it's best to cut positions that aren't working and move on.

Investing Quick-Start Guide:
SMALL-CAPITALIZATION BIOTECH STOCKS

1. If you want to trade an over-the-counter biotech stock, be sure to find a broker that offers over-the-counter securities. Call them if you are not sure.

2. Be sure to do your due diligence before buying into this sector. One idea is to use your broker's scanning software program to narrow the search.

3. Once you find a small-cap biotech stock you want to own, buy the number of shares you want. Be sure your position size is reasonable (1% of your portfolio or less).

4. Monitor the position closely and be sure to use hard stop losses.

5. Have a target price for selling. Never forget to follow your rules.

6. When your target price is reached, sell your position.

JUNIOR MINING STOCKS

WHAT ARE JUNIOR MINING STOCKS?

One of the higher-risk, higher-reward asset classes in this book is something known as "small-cap mining stocks." Sometimes referred to as "junior miners," these companies—usually with a market capitalization between $25 million and $300 million—are at the forefront of the mining industry. This includes companies mining everything from precious metals (i.e., gold, silver, etc.) to radioactive materials like uranium.

There are two sides of the mining industry: major miners and junior miners. The "majors" are companies like Barrick Gold Corp. (GOLD) and Newmont Corporation (NEM), which are among the largest gold miners in the world. These companies mine millions of ounces of gold every year and have operations all over the world.

"Majors" have been around for decades and have proven methods for exploration and production. This leads to consistent mining and cash flows, which leads to steady (and often growing) stock prices. They also have huge teams of geologists and other mining specialists helping the company find new deposits and—if all goes well—mine them as efficiently as possible.

Junior miners are on the other end of that spectrum. Unlike a "major" mining operation, junior miners often do not yet have a single functioning mine. They have likely only been around for a few years and simply own a piece of land that may or may not have mineable precious metals or oil beneath its surface. Although they likely have a geologist on staff, they certainly don't have a team working around the clock looking for new opportunities.

Unfortunately, these junior miners may end up never mining anything at all! That makes the sector extremely high risk.

You Want the Wind at Your Back

There's a famous phrase in investing that goes: "A rising tide lifts all boats." This is due to the fact that if the broader market is in a bull market, that will benefit all stocks, not just a handful of players.

That's also the case with junior miners. Before investing in this sector, you want to make sure the market for the commodity you're targeting is also in a bull market. Whether it's gold, oil, or uranium, the share price of your junior miner will languish if the underlying commodity is not rising.

For example, let's say we have a miner called Loumont Gold (not a real company). Loumont is headed by a seasoned management team that has taken multiple mining operations from nothing but a hole in the ground to a fully operational and profitable mine. They also have a top-notch team of geologists on their staff that has discovered a potentially lucrative gold deposit.

Loumont Gold's management team successfully raises a lot of capital to fund the mine. However, while the mining is in progress, news comes out that central banks around the world have started to sell their gold holdings for bitcoin. Since central banks are some of the largest holders of gold in the world, this tells the market that central banks are bearish on the metal and expect prices to fall. This causes the gold price to fall from $1,700 per ounce to $1,000 per ounce.

While Loumont Gold has one of the best management teams in the world and top-notch geologists and miners, none of it matters if the price of the commodity they are mining plummets in value.

Remember: This dynamic cuts both ways. Let's say that while Loumont Gold's top-tier mining team is digging, China announces that they will now go on the gold standard. This implies that the Chinese—one of the largest economies in the world—will be buying tons of gold for their coffers. Since the demand for gold is rising while supply remains the same, this means that gold prices rise.

This kicks off a major bull market in gold, sending the price from $1,700 per ounce to $2,500 per ounce. Since Loumont Gold is mining gold, that means the price of their commodity has risen, thus making their mining operation much more valuable.

It's Always Darkest Before the Dawn for Junior Miners

Most bull and bear markets in a commodity will not be as obvious as in the previous examples. There's only a small chance that China would ever go on the gold standard, nor is it likely that a central bank will begin dumping its gold reserves.

But there are a few ways to tell if a bull market in a commodity—and thus a surge in junior mining share prices—is on the way. As we've discussed in other chapters, one of the best times to buy any asset is when no one is talking about it. You want to buy heavily in markets when they are out of favor, and one way to measure this is to look at sources like Google Trends. This shows you how many people are using gold-related search terms. When you start to see search activity rising for gold, silver, or another commodity, it's usually a good sign a bull market is coming.

Investors can also tell when the "bottom" is in for junior miners when times are the toughest. This is known as "capitulation" in the mining industry. It means that many of the junior mining companies are going bankrupt or merging with other companies. After many of the weaker players fold or merge with other firms, the only companies left are the strongest firms that can withstand a downturn. These are the companies that will lead the next leg of the bull run higher.

Another way to identify potentially successful mining companies is if you see rising interest in the riskiest junior mining stocks. Many mining analysts will have a large watchlist of junior mining stocks ranked from least risky to most risky. When you see the share prices of the riskiest junior miners perk up, it usually means there is a lot of money flowing into the sector. You'll also see the junior miners outperforming the major miners—like Barrick Gold and Newmont Corporation—as investors position themselves for a bull run.

Even if you have the wind at your back in the bull market, you still need to make sure the management team is top notch. After all, if management isn't aligned with investors' goals, you can lose a lot of money—and that's what happens in the following case study.

CASE STUDY:
TRAVELING TO SEE A HOLE IN THE GROUND

E.B. Tucker is a pioneer in the junior mining space. I met E.B. while we were working at an investment research company called Casey Research; he's since gone on to write a bestselling book on investing in the gold market called *Why Gold? Why Now?: The War Against Your Wealth and How to Win It*. That's in addition to starting a precious metals royalty and streaming company, Metalla Royalty & Streaming.

E.B. has had many years of success investing in the junior mining market. That means he's made tremendous gains on some of his positions, but he has also incurred massive losses on others. One of those losses involved a trip he and his team made to Mexico.

In 2012, E.B. was running an asset management company. He and his team analyzed a host of junior mining companies, and if their analysis worked out, he would invest on behalf of his clients. Part of this type of research involves visiting the mines in person. When investing in this sector, it's often important to have "boots on the ground," as there are many things that can go wrong when investing in the junior mining space.

To get a glimpse of the mine and meet with management, E.B. and his team took a flight to Mazatlán, Mexico, a Mexican resort town in the state of Sinaloa.

Let the Games Begin

In the junior mining space, you often have people called "promoters." Much like the promoters for a concert, these financial promoters curry interest in a small company so as many people as possible hear about the good things the miner is doing. The companies involved in the space are so small that they actively need people to go around and tell them about it.

After a flight to Mazatlán and subsequent 6-hour truck ride through the desert, E.B. and his team arrived at the mining operation. The team was on its way to see a mine that had been shut down. While this may not sound like a reason to travel halfway around the world, this mine was producing 50,000 ounces of gold back in the 1990s.

If that doesn't *sound* like something to travel for, after they arrived, it didn't *look* like it either! When E.B. and his team went to the mine, all they saw was a giant hole in the ground that was half full of water. The owners of the mine claimed they were going to drain the water, as they believed there was another 50,000 ounces of gold underneath. Considering that gold was trading at $1,700 per ounce, this would be worth $88 million.

The Gold Miner Wears No Clothes

The miners had already raised $30 million to restart the mine. This funding came from many sources, including private investors and asset management companies like the one owned by E.B. This $30 million was intended to fund the reopening, exploration, and production of the mine. If the operation was successful, these early investors would own a piece of the cash flow and profits from the $88 million worth of gold in the ground.

However, E.B. and his team soon realized that—while the mine was real—the management team behind the mine was not very serious. The people E.B. met with spent every penny of the capital they raised on helicopter rides, fine foods, and translators. They'd even bought drilling rigs that they turned around and leased to other mining companies! The management company found every legal—although unethical—way to spend investor money.

While E.B. and his team realized how unscrupulous these miners were, most of the investors had no clue. They had simply been buying shares of the junior miner after positive press releases, interviews, and promotional videos.

Behind the glossy finish on top of the junior miner, in the end it remained a dirty hole in the ground in the middle of a Mexican desert.

Not surprisingly, a few years later the company went out of business and all investor money was lost.

INVESTMENT STRATEGY:

JUNIOR MINING STOCKS

Again, investors in this sector must make sure the market is strong for the underlying commodity. This is important because if there isn't a bull market in the target commodity, there will be little activity in the smaller junior mining stocks.

How to Identify a Good Junior Mining Stock

Junior mining stocks can yield some of the greatest gains you can possibly imagine. But it's a sector rife with scams, which is why you need to really do your homework before making an investment. While not many of you will take trips to visit the mines, there are other ways you can mitigate the risks of a poor management team.

This truly is a high-risk, high-reward investment. If you follow these steps, however, you will vastly increase the odds of making money in this lucrative market.

1. Make Sure You're in a Bull Market

While you can do research on a junior miner until you're blue in the face, the fact is that none of that will matter if the broader environment is weak. Often, even the worst junior mining stocks will rally if the broader market for the underlying commodity is hot.

On the other hand, if you're years away from a bull market, the junior miner will need to keep raising money to keep the lights on. That means the miners will have to dilute their shares. Just like diluting sugar and water, the more water you add—in this case, shares of the mining company—the less sugary—or valuable—the water tastes. Dilution can take a major bite out of your investment, so you want to make sure the timing is right when investing in a junior miner.

That way if the company does catch lightning in a bottle, the odds of the benefits flowing to you are much higher. Otherwise, investing in the junior mining market will be akin to riding your bike into the wind.

2. Vet the Management Team

As we saw in the case study, the mine that E.B. and his team visited was all smoke and no fire. While the company had raised millions in financing from multiple sources, the mine was still just a water-filled hole and stayed that way until the capital had been spent and the mine went belly-up.

Many junior mining firms hire public relations companies to promote their companies. They issue press releases and promotional videos to drum up interest in the project. This approach is fine as long as it's paired with a proficient mining operation.

While not everyone can fly to an actual mine, one action you can take is to contact management via a junior miner's investor relations department. You'll want to get on the phone with someone from the team and ask them questions about progress with the mine. Find out if they are slated to hit the goals described in each press release. If the manager is dodgy and won't answer your questions directly, it's safe to assume something is amiss.

3. Check the Balance Sheet Strength

Like any small company that is pre-revenue, junior miners must raise funds via debt or equity markets to finance their operations. Since it's notoriously difficult to convince a loan underwriter to give miners bank loans, most opt to issue stock to fund operations.

While this is a necessary evil of the sector, you must be wary about committing too much of your capital at once, as it's possible your position will get diluted to zero if you're forced to hold for many years.

One way to tell if a company needs to raise cash is by looking at its balance sheet. Look for the line item "cash and cash equivalents." From there, look at the income statement to see what the company's average operating expenses are. Divide the cash and cash equivalents by the operating expenses. Ideally, a company will have enough cash on its balance sheet to finance operations for more than 1.5 years. However, if that figure is less than 1 year, there is serious risk of dilution, and you should avoid that junior miner.

How to Trade a Junior Mining Stock

Junior mining stocks typify the high-risk, high-reward ethos of this book. But like all high-risk investments, in addition to the possibility of big payouts, the odds of losing all of your money in a junior mining investment are high.

First, you need to learn whether the underlying commodity is in a bull market. Without this, the tide will not "lift all boats," and your position will be diluted as you wait for the tide to turn.

Second, once the bull market begins, allocate only 1% of your portfolio to junior miners. Your goal is to take 1% of your portfolio and spread it among 5–10 high-quality junior mining stocks. There is a good chance that most of those positions will fail. But if you hit the jackpot on even one of those companies, you may realize 500%–1,000% gains on your investment. Since you're only risking a small amount of your capital, you will not blow up your brokerage account even if you miss on all ten positions.

If you do end up nailing a junior mining investment, I recommend selling off your initial investment as soon as possible. For instance, if you invest $1,000 at $5 per share in a junior mining stock and shares rise to $10, your position is now worth $2,000. I would sell enough shares to cover that initial $1,000 investment so only your profits are at risk. Once you have "de-risked" your investment, you can sit on the profits until the bull market in the commodity starts to fade. At that point, you should sell the remainder of your position and reallocate elsewhere.

Investing Quick-Start Guide:
JUNIOR MINING STOCKS

1. When buying junior mining stocks, be sure to find an established broker that allows trading in junior mining stocks. Several brokerages do not let retail investors buy these high-risk, high-reward securities, so find one that does.

2. Keep in mind that these stocks are less liquid, so they may be easy to buy but not always easy to sell.

3. Be sure to do your due diligence before buying one of these stocks.

4. Once you find a junior mining stock that you want to own, buy the number of shares you want. Be sure your position size is reasonable (1% of your portfolio or less).

5. Monitor the position closely and be sure to use hard stop losses or mental stop losses.

6. Have a target price for selling, and never forget to follow your rules.

7. When your target price is reached, sell your position.

CHAPTER 7

High-Risk Options

A stock option is a financial derivative that gives the buyer the right—but not the obligation—to buy or sell an asset at a stated price within a specific period. Options are great tools to amplify your returns.

However, if used incorrectly (as we'll discuss in the case studies), you can also lose money quickly. Make sure to read this section thoroughly before delving into the high-risk, high-reward world of the options market.

A few years ago, I was meeting with a former colleague. During our visit, he mentioned he founded a company called Blue Zone. Seeing the bewildered look on my face, he quickly explained that the name comes from certain regions of the world called—as you may have guessed—"blue zones."

Data showed people living in blue zones live surprisingly longer than the general population. According to the research, common traits among the "blue zone" population contributed to these people living longer and healthier lives.

The traits these regions share include:

- Isolated populations
- Consistent physical activity
- High social engagement
- No smoking
- Plant-based diets

Blue zones are found in four countries: Japan, Costa Rica, Italy, and the United States (specifically, Loma Linda, California).

Just as there are blue zones where human longevity is enhanced, there are blue zones in investing that can enhance the longevity (and returns) of your portfolio. For instance, one of the most underrated stock traders of all time is a man named Ed Seykota.

While not often lumped into the investing pantheon that includes people like Warren Buffett and Peter Lynch, Seykota is just as influential. He was one of the first investors to introduce something known as "systems trading." His goal was to systemize investing so that human error was no longer a factor.

He's also famous for the following adage: "There are old traders and there are bold traders, but there are very few old, bold traders."

This quote is the very definition of an investing "blue zone," in that it can enhance your investing strategy. Seykota is saying that taking on too much risk in the markets (i.e., trading too boldly) is a recipe for disaster. In other words, bold traders don't typically have much longevity in investing. It can work from time to time, but in the long run those taking on too much risk will eventually blow up their accounts.

In my experience, the method most commonly used recklessly and incorrectly by "bold" traders—especially newly minted traders—is options strategies.

CALL OPTIONS

WHAT ARE CALL OPTIONS?

An option is a contract that grants the option buyer the right—but not the obligation—to buy or sell a specific underlying security, at a specific price, on or before a specific date. As with any transaction, an option contract involves two parties: the buyer and the seller.

An option contract has three basic parts:

- **Calls and puts:** The option is either a call or a put. A call option gives the holder the right to *buy* an underlying security at a specified price. A put option gives the holder the right to *sell* an underlying security at a specified price.
- **The strike price:** The price at which the holder can sell the underlying stock.
- **The expiration date:** The date the contract expires, stated as either a month, week, or day. Most stock options expire on the third Friday of the stated month.

A buyer is said to be exercising his right to buy or sell if he elects to act. A seller collects the money paid by the buyer—known as a "premium." In exchange, the seller is obligated to buy (if it's a put) or sell (if it's a call) the underlying stock at a specified price if the option is exercised.

Lastly, most option contracts represent 100 underlying shares of stock. This last point is extremely important, as it means options contracts employ "leverage." This means that options buyers can pay a relatively small "premium" for an option contract but realize large percentage swings in the price of the contract.

In this section, we're going to focus on "call options." A call option buyer speculates that the stock will see a substantial price increase before the option expires. This is similar to holding a long position on a stock.

The following story should help you understand how options work.

Buying Calls on Elon Musk

Let's say that you expect Tesla shares to rise in the near term. Elon Musk is hosting the company's annual Battery Day—the day they announce new battery technology—on September 17, and you think shares will surge on a big announcement.

To capitalize on this idea, you decide to buy one call option on Tesla (TSLA). Shares of the electric vehicle maker are trading at $700 per share. After the announcement, you believe shares will trade up to $750 per share. To profit from your thesis, you decide to buy one September 17 TSLA call option with a strike price of $750. As outlined earlier in the chapter, you now have the three components of an options trade: a specific stock, a date (the expiration date), and a price (the strike price). Lastly, you paid a $500 *premium* to open this position.

There are a few things that can happen from here. In the first scenario, let's say that the Tesla CEO announces a rare breakthrough in battery technology. Since Tesla is the only company with this technology, the market cheers the response and sends shares above your strike price of $750. If you'd only bought one share of Tesla, you would be sitting on a $50 gain ($750 – $700 = $50).

Remember that each option contract represents 100 shares of the underlying security. In this case, that means your gains are amplified significantly. Instead of earning a modest $50 gain, you earned a $5,000 gain (your profit = $50 × 100)! The huge potential gains are the main reason why options are so popular with speculators.

As you probably guessed, this is the ideal scenario. When it comes to options, however, things can get much messier.

What If Things Take a Turn for the Worse on Battery Day?

Let's look at some other scenarios for your Battery Day trade. All the parameters are the same as in the previous example, except in this case the news announced on Battery Day is *not* positive.

Instead of announcing a new battery technology, Elon Musk announces that he's going to be on the next manned mission to Mars and is stepping down as CEO of Tesla! This sends shockwaves through the financial markets, and Tesla stock falls more than 10% to $630 per share on the news.

This is bad news for your options contract. Since options contracts expire at a certain date—in this case September 17—there's a chance you will lose your entire investment ($500) when speculating on options. That's exactly what happens in this situation, as Tesla shares trade well below the $750 strike at expiration, and your contract expires worthless.

Many new investors want to dive headfirst into the options market because they're looking to make a quick buck. They see posts on forums like WallStreet-Bets and *Twitter* showing the massive gains others have made in options and think it's a layup. I've seen countless ads on social media saying investors can make steady income from buying calls.

This couldn't be further from the truth. For one, the odds are against you from the beginning in the options market, as most options expire worthless. This is precisely why I prefer to *sell* options, which we will cover in the next section.

But for now, I want to share a story with you from one of my subscribers.

IVAN AND THE COVID-19 VACCINES

I've run subscription investing services for much of my career. Many of these are options-based, where I show individual investors how to use options strategies responsibly. During my time running these services, I've heard my fair share of horror stories. For instance, in March 2021, one of my new subscribers (who we will call "Ivan") messaged me not long after he signed up.

Back then, there was a lot of enthusiasm over COVID-19 vaccines. Five months earlier, biotechnology companies Pfizer, Moderna, and Johnson & Johnson collectively announced that they had successfully synthesized COVID-19 vaccines. This was a major relief for the global economy, as lockdowns around the world had crippled many industries. Soon after, we saw a furious rally in stocks that had been hit by COVID-19 lockdowns.

Ivan Thinks He's Found a Great Opportunity

In the mind of many investors, it seems all but certain that these biotechnology companies would profit handsomely from COVID-19 vaccines. After all, if there are 7 billion people on Earth and each requires two doses of the vaccine, that means there will be a minimum of 14 billion shots.

To the layman investor, that seemed to guarantee massive gains for the biotechnology companies manufacturing and selling the vaccines. Since these companies would have a new source of revenue, their earnings should increase. And at the very least, other people would pile into these stocks and drive up their prices.

Acting on this idea, Ivan bought call options on Pfizer. At the time, shares were trading at $35 per share, and he believed upside in the stock was significant. That's why he picked a strike price of $45 on the stock along with an expiration date of January 2021 (3 months out).

At first, Ivan's trade started to work in his favor. Feeling more emboldened that his idea was right, he sold most of his safer investments and plowed his capital into more Pfizer options.

Buy the Rumor, Sell the News

There's a famous saying in investing that goes: "Buy the rumor, sell the news." This means long-awaited news about a stock or other asset that should seemingly be positive has the opposite effect. This can be chalked up to investors already anticipating the news and buying shares before the announcement (i.e., buying the rumor). Since the announcement comes, investors often sell to lock in their profits (i.e., selling the news).

This is what happened with Pfizer. Between the month before the successful COVID-19 vaccine announcement and the month afterward, Pfizer shares surged 26%. Then something unexpected happened: Shares started to fall. It seemed as if investors had "sold the news" on the vaccine announcement.

Unfortunately for Ivan, he had never heard this expression. He also didn't know that—unlike stocks—options expire. When I explained this concept to him, it was already too late. As his option contracts kept declining in value as they approached expiration, Ivan continued to double down on his losing trade. By the time he contacted me, he had lost more than 90% of his brokerage account, or roughly $30,000.

INVESTMENT STRATEGY:

CALL OPTIONS

While it may be easy to buy options, it's extremely difficult to *consistently* make money trading call options. Many people—like Ivan—start out in the options market thinking they can make a quick buck, and end up losing big.

As the case study shows, buying call options can be a very risky and costly endeavor if you don't fully understand the negative ramifications. Unlike with stocks where you can buy and hold for decades, the clock is always ticking when you buy options. It's the looming expiration date that causes many option traders to lose money even when they choose the right underlying stock. To make money buying calls, you need to be right about the timing, direction of the security, and entering the trade at a decent price.

How to Identify a Good Call Option

I often say that buying stocks is like shooting a bow and arrow at a target. While this is difficult enough, options trading is like shooting a bow and arrow while riding a horse. The timing factor makes things even more difficult.

That said, I have taught thousands of investors how to speculate on options responsibly. And if you use these three guidelines, you, too, might have success in the options market.

1. Find Your Catalyst

In the Tesla example earlier in the chapter, there was a specific event that the investor was trying to exploit. In the investor's mind, this event had yet to be priced into the market. To capitalize on this trade, the investor decided to buy a call option on the stock to amplify his return.

This is known as a "stock-specific" event. When laying out your investment thesis for a trade, you want to make sure there is some sort of catalyst that will move the stock price up or down. Common stock-specific events are earnings releases, product launches, and spin-offs.

In addition to stock-specific events, you have "market-wide" events. While these announcements are not directly related to the underlying stock, they still will materially affect the share price. Examples of market-wide events are economic data releases, Federal Reserve policy announcements, and other government-related announcements.

2. Pick the Right Strike Price

Once you've found your catalyst to move the stock, you want to figure out how much the stock will move on the event. This depends on how certain you are about your investment thesis.

For instance, the amount of risk you want to assume for a trade depends on whether you buy an in-the-money (ITM), at-the-money (ATM), or out-of-the-money (OTM) call. Here's what each one is:

- **In-the-money (ITM):** A call option is in the money when the underlying stock is above its strike price.

- **At-the-money (ATM):** A call option is at the money when the underlying stock is the same as the strike price.
- **Out-of-the-money (OTM):** A call option is out of the money when the underlying stock is below its strike price.

The highest risk option you could buy is an ITM call, as these contracts have a high "delta" (we will cover this concept in the next section). This means that the more the underlying stock moves, the more the option contract moves. On the other hand, an OTM call has a relatively low delta. This means that the option contract won't move as much when the underlying security moves.

If a stock price rises, the ITM contract would rise much more than an ATM or OTM call option. But if the stock price falls, the higher-delta ITM contract would fall more than an ATM or OTM contract. As a general rule, those looking to assume more risk should opt for ITM calls, while those looking for less risk should focus on OTM calls. However, please note that OTM calls can be very risky when bought at or near expiration.

Note: While these are general guidelines, there are exceptions to all of the previous trading ideas. Some experienced traders may buy ITM calls because they consider them less risky, while others consider OTM options as long shots. The only way to know what works for you is to take the time to study options thoroughly and practice trading before buying with real money.

3. Pay Close Attention to Implied Volatility

One factor that all option traders need to understand is *implied volatility*. This is a data point used by investors to approximate future changes in a security's price. Implied volatility is different than the CBOE Volatility Index (VIX) we covered in Chapter 4, as the VIX can be measured exactly. Instead, implied volatility is a constantly changing indicator that shows how much investors are willing to pay for an option contract.

Financial writer and investor Michael Sincere described implied volatility in his classic book *Understanding Options* as the "feeling of urgency traders have about options." When implied volatility is relatively high, traders are expecting a strong move in the stock price. For those looking to profit off an upcoming earnings release or other stock-specific event, investors may want to avoid contracts with high implied volatility. That's because many investors have already "priced in" the earnings move, meaning the contracts are expensive.

However, this concept cuts both ways. A contract with low implied volatility implies that traders do not expect much movement in the underlying security. If your thesis conflicts with this outlook, that option contract may be mispriced. That is a trade you may consider.

How to Trade a Call Option

Once you've developed a strategy and decided to open your options position, allocate no more than 1% of your investable assets to a call option position. There is a good chance you may lose your entire investment, so allocating only 1% means you will not blow up your brokerage account if your thesis is incorrect.

To illustrate how you should handle a call option trade, let's look at an example with different scenarios. Let's say you buy a call option on Apple Inc. with a strike price of $90 and a $300 premium. In addition, the contract has a 2-month time horizon (i.e., expiration date). The current stock price is $92, and you expect Apple to announce a new product at its upcoming product release that will send the stock higher.

For one example scenario, let's say Apple delays their presentation because of a global chip shortage. The market reacts negatively to this news and thus pushes Apple shares down below $90. Since the stock is now below the strike price, the price of your option contract has been crushed. It is down 75%. Since option contracts decline in value the closer they get to expiration, your losses are accelerating. You have already lost most of your principal, so you have little to lose by holding the position longer since there is a chance positive news could send the contract higher before expiration.

For a second sample scenario, imagine Apple releases a new iPhone, which is what the market expected. Therefore, the share price is little changed from where you bought the contract. This is a bad situation, as option contracts steadily lose value if the underlying position remains constant. Because shares in the underlying stock are not moving, you are down 25% on your position. Since the catalyst you expected did not move the share price upward, the best course of action is to cut your position for a small loss and move on.

In the last example scenario, let's say Apple announces the release of the Apple Car. This blows the market away, and thus sends the shares up above the $92 strike price. You're thrilled, as that means your option contract is up over $200 [($92 – $90) × 100 shares = $200]. Since your thesis proved correct, your best bet is to take profits on your position.

Investing Quick-Start Guide:
BUY CALL OPTIONS

1. Contact your broker and let them know you want to trade options. It's your choice whether to open a margin account (i.e., when you borrow money from the broker to buy securities with a promise to pay it back). If you're using basic option strategies, a margin account is not required. You must also fill out an options agreement. Make sure that you download the options disclosure document, *Characteristics and Risks of Standardized Options*, which can be found on the Options Clearing Corporation website (www.theocc.com).

2. After being approved, look for a stock that has the potential to move higher in a short time period.

3. Look at the *option chain* on your broker's software to find the bid and ask price, expiration date, and strike price.

4. After choosing an appropriate underlying stock, select "Buy to Open."

5. If this is your first option trade, buy only one call option. The key to success in buying calls is trading small. Use a limit order (not a market order). A limit order guarantees your trade is filled at or better than the predetermined price level. A market order, on the other hand, is filled quickly but may not be at a price that is good for you.

6. Set a target price for the position. Also, be sure to have a mental stop loss if your guesses area wrong, perhaps selling after a 20% or 30% loss.

7. If the target price is attained, or if you have a decent profit (an amount that will be different for each trader), sell the entire position.

8. Note: I do not recommend that you hold the call option until the expiration date. Because options are so volatile, it's important to book profits soon, especially when speculating with call options. In addition, I suggest that you sell profitable options and not exercise the option. However, this is a personal choice.

9. To sell the call option, select "Sell to Close" on your trading screen.

PUT OPTIONS

WHAT ARE PUT OPTIONS?

If the call option is the yin, then the put option is the yang. A put option contract gives the holder the right to sell a stock at a certain price on or before a certain date. A put option buyer thinks the stock will have a price decline before the option expires. This is similar to taking a short position in a stock.

A put option has the same parameters as a call option. This includes the strike price, expiration, and premium. Each contract also represents 100 shares of the underlying stock, meaning put option contracts also employ leverage. The biggest difference is that when you buy calls, you are bullish on the underlying stock. When you buy puts, you are bearish. Therefore, the reason you buy puts is the opposite of why you would buy calls.

Here's how you can make (or lose) money buying a put option.

Buying Puts on Alibaba Holdings

Let's say you are bearish on Chinese e-commerce giant Alibaba (BABA). You expect shares to fall in the near term, as the Chinese government has started to crack down on its tech sector. Since you believe that shares have not fully "priced in" the regulatory headache that is coming toward Alibaba, you are certain that shares will fall in the next 2 months.

To trade on this idea, you decide to buy one put option on Alibaba. Shares of the e-commerce company are trading at $150 per share. However, after China announces further sanctions against the e-commerce giant, you think they will trade closer to $125 per share.

To profit from this scenario, you decide to buy one September 17 BABA put option with a strike price of $125. You now have the three components of an options trade: specific stock, expiration date, and strike price. Lastly, you paid a $300 *premium* to open this position.

Here are a few things that can happen. In one scenario, let's say Chinese president for life Xi Jinping announces Alibaba has grown too large and the company needs to be broken up. Since that is bad news for Alibaba shareholders, the stock price falls *below* your $125 strike price. Since each contract represents 100 shares of the underlying security, your gains are amplified. In fact, you earned $2,500 ($25 × 100 shares = $2,500) by buying that single option contract. (Don't forget, these are put contracts, which means that you profit when the underlying stock falls.)

Let's take a look at another scenario for the Chinese e-commerce giant. All of the parameters are the same as the previous example, except in this case the news from Xi Jinping is *positive* for Alibaba.

Instead of Xi Jinping announcing the breakup of Alibaba, he announces that he's granting the company a monopoly over e-commerce in China. This means Alibaba will take all the market share from competitors like JD.com and generate much more earnings for their shareholders.

Investors cheer the announcement, sending Alibaba shares from $150 to $175. However, since you were betting Alibaba shares would *decline*, your options contract has fallen dramatically. Your option position is now down by 90%. Since option contracts expire at a certain date—in this case September 17—it looks like you will lose your entire $300 investment (what you paid in premium). That is the risk of trading call and put options. When you are wrong about the direction or the timing of the underlying stock, you can incur severe losses.

Using Put Options to Hedge

Put options are generally frowned upon by individual investors. Since US stocks have tended to rise over the long term, "going long" put options contracts have not been great investments. And since shorting implies investors are thinking negatively about a stock, many investors generally avoid them.

However, this is a simplistic view of put options. One of the best ways to use these unique securities is to *hedge* your portfolio. Hedging is an investment that gives your portfolio downside protection. While your portfolio declines in value, these assets actually increase in value.

While there are multiple ways to hedge (such as holding cash, stocks, or other option positions), put options make it convenient to offset some of your portfolio's losses during a market pullback. In other words, think of put options as an insurance policy. For instance, let's piggyback on the Alibaba example and imagine that you own 100 shares of Alibaba. You believe in the company for the long term, so while you do worry whether Xi Jinping will crack down on the company, you don't want to sell your shares.

Instead of selling your position or riding the shares lower, you can pay a small fee—known as the "premium"—to hedge the position. If the stock ends up falling, part of your losses in the 100 shares you're long will be offset by the rising value of the put option. And if shares continue to rise, your gains still far outweigh your losses.

While hedging is a great strategy, sometimes you don't need it. One of my greatest put option trades showed that it's possible to invest in put options successfully.

THE ONLY GUY TO MAKE MONEY SHORTING TESLA

I was talking with a close friend—a highly successful tech entrepreneur—when he asked an odd question: Is Elon Musk a hero or a villain? Musk is one of those personalities who splits opinions of him into two sharply opposing camps.

The "hero" camp loves to praise the ideological goals of the eccentric, affable billionaire. They are captivated by his ideas of weaning the planet off fossil fuels, privatizing space travel, and colonizing Mars.

Then there's the "villain" camp. This group doesn't care about his big ideas. They see a guy who attacks short sellers, lashes out at analysts on conference calls, and blatantly violates Securities and Exchange Commission (SEC) regulations.

Back in February 2019, I wasn't sure which camp I fell into. But I did know that Tesla was about to have a serious issue with something known as "convertible bonds."

Shorting the Smartest Man in the World

A convertible bond is a unique type of bond. Before or when it matures, depending on the stipulated covenants, a couple of things can happen. The company can "convert" the bonds into a specified number of shares of common stock, or the company might have to pay investors the value of the bonds, plus interest.

For Tesla, the outcome depended on whether its shares traded at an average price of $359.87 through March 1. If the stock could do that, Tesla would be able to convert the bonds to stock. If not, the company would have to pay bondholders an agreed-upon $920 million. A payout like that would consume 30% of the company's cash, making it one of the biggest debt payments in company history.

At the time, shares needed a 15% rally for Tesla to avoid this debt payment. Since the company was on shaky financial footing, it was clear the company would be in deep trouble if this debt payment came due.

After doing my research, I noticed that Tesla put options had not "priced in" the possibility of this debt payment. On February 19, 2019, I sent an email to my subscribers recommending they "buy to open" a Tesla March 29, 2019, put option with a strike price of $305 for a cost of $1,600. This contract gave us the right to sell 100 shares of TSLA at $305 per share through March 29, 2019, or 38 days until expiration.

Musk Pays the Piper (and My Subscribers)

The deadline for Tesla's bond payment came and went, and shares did not trade above the required price at expiration. Therefore, Musk had to write a massive check to bondholders.

This came with a comedy of errors along the way. First came the news that Tesla's general counsel Dane Butswinkas was leaving the company. Normally this wouldn't be a big deal, but Butswinkas had only held the position for 2 months. He followed a herd of forty executives who had jumped ship in the previous 12 months. Among them was chief accounting officer Dave Morton, who left the company after just 1 month on the job.

Adding insult to injury, the SEC asked a federal judge to hold Elon Musk in contempt of court for making specious statements on his *Twitter* account.

This was bad news for Musk and Tesla shareholders. Because the stock had fallen more than 11% since I told readers to open a put option position, they were sitting on a gain of more than 100%. Knowing how quickly options can move against you, I issued a sell recommendation, thus doubling my subscribers' positions in under a month.

INVESTMENT STRATEGY:

PUT OPTIONS

Selecting the right options contracts is more of an art than a science. You could write an entire book on this topic alone. While I'm going to give you a few key tools to finding the right contracts, those who want to dive deeper into this concept should consider buying a copy of Michael Sincere's book *Understanding Options*.

How to Identify a Good Put Option

Finding the right put option is very similar to finding the right call option, as discussed in the previous section. It takes a lot of research to find these strategies;

however, as we learned in the case study, the rewards can be tremendous in a short time window.

If you follow these steps, you'll increase your odds of success on a put option contract.

1. Find Your Catalyst

In the Tesla case study, the entire investment thesis started with an upcoming event. While I was not necessarily bearish on Tesla's long-term prospects, I was confident the market had not yet "priced in" the prospect of the company paying this large convertible bond. When the news came to fruition—along with a stream of other bad news—the stock quickly tanked, which sent my put options up more than 100%.

This is known as a "stock-specific" event. This was not a bet on the broader market pulling back; rather, it was a trade based on something uniquely related to a company's financial position.

On the other hand, there are plenty of *market-wide* events investors can capitalize on. This is especially true for the hedging strategy we discussed. Since most investors hold long-term positions in their retirement accounts, some savvy investors may choose to hedge these long-term holdings with put options during times of market stress. Recent stress points include the COVID-19 pandemic, the SPAC bust, and the "taper tantrum." (You can look these up online for more information about each.)

2. Understand Your Strengths

One goal for new option traders is to evaluate your forecasting abilities. Some traders have a knack for using technical analysis to predict short-term market movements, returns of which can be enhanced with short-dated put options. On the other hand, other traders may have a keen eye for forensic accounting and thus have more success buying long-dated out-of-the-money put options.

Once you have a good grasp of your abilities, your next task is figuring out how to initiate these trades as effectively as possible.

3. Pick the Right Expiration

After you understand your strengths and weaknesses as an options trader, you want to figure out your time horizon for your trades. For instance, if you are a savvy technical trader adept at predicting short-term movements, you may want to use an expiration of 1 month or less. While these short-dated options are more volatile and expire in only a few weeks, they are also cheaper. If you have a great track record of predicting short-term market movements, this may be the strategy for you.

On the other hand, any forensic accountants who spot a long-term catalyst may want to use long-dated options. Specifically, you want the expiration date to be at least a few weeks after the expected catalyst. While these will be more expensive than their short-dated peers, it should pay off if your analysis comes to fruition.

How to Trade a Put Option

Once you've identified your strategy and upcoming catalyst, you want to allocate no more than 1% of your investable assets to your put option position. Your goal with this trade is to theoretically spend $10 to make $40, for example. The risk is that you lose your entire $10 premium in the process. There's a very high probability of this occurring, so you don't want to overallocate to a speculative options trade, as your thesis may be incorrect.

To illustrate how you should handle a put option trade, let's look at an example with a number of different scenarios. Let's say that you buy a put option on Pinterest (PINS) with a strike price of $50 for a premium of $300 ($3 per contract). The contract has a 2-month time horizon, and shares are currently trading at $55. You expect Congress to introduce legislation that would restrict social media access to minors in coming weeks, which would send the stock lower.

Note: Your break-even point is $47 per share, which equates to the $50 strike price *minus* the $3 premium you paid to purchase the put option.

In one scenario, let's say Congress delays its legislation because of a pressing budgetary issue that needs to be addressed. The market likes this news and pushes Pinterest shares up to $65. Since the stock is well above the strike price, the price of your option is down 75%. Since option contracts decline in value as they approach expiration, you begin to lose money daily on an accelerated basis. This process is known as "theta decay," or the daily decline of an option's value.

Since you have already lost most of your principal, you have little to lose by hanging on to your position (especially since legislation might be released before expiration). Nonetheless, you are advised to sell it and salvage what premium might be left over.

In another sample scenario, imagine Congress releases its legislation, but it's not nearly as far-reaching as you expected. Therefore, the share price has changed little from where it was when you bought the contract. This is not good for you either, as options contracts steadily lose value even when the underlying position remains constant (in this case, Pinterest's share price). By Pinterest shares staying flat at $55, your option contract has already lost 25% of its value. Since the catalyst you expected did not move the share price downward, the best course of action is to cut your position for a small loss and move on.

In the last scenario, Congress announces sweeping legislation against the social media industry. In fact, the bill names Pinterest directly as a company that's at odds with the government's interests. This sends shares tumbling to $45 (or $5 below your strike price). This is good news for you, as you've now earned a profit of over $500 [($55 − $50) × 100 shares = $500]. Since your thesis proved correct, your best bet is to take profits on your position.

Investing Quick-Start Guide:
BUY PUT OPTIONS

Buying put options is the same procedure as buying calls:

1. To review, after the broker approves you for trading options, look at the *option chain* on your broker's software to find the bid and ask price, expiration date, and strike price.

2. After selecting an appropriate underlying stock that you believe will fall in price, select "Buy to Open" on your screen.

3. To limit risk, buy only one put option. The key to success in buying puts is trading small. Use a limit order (not a market order).

4. Have a target price for the position. Be sure to have a mental stop loss if the price goes against you, and consider selling after a 20% or 30% loss.

5. If the target price is attained, or if you have a decent profit (an amount that will be different for each trader), sell the put position.

6. Note: I do not recommend that you hold the put option until the expiration date. In addition, I suggest that you sell profitable options and not exercise the option, especially put options. If you did exercise the option, it means you are converting your profitable put positions into a short position. This is not recommended.

7. To sell the put option, select "Sell to Close" on your trading screen.

WHAT ARE CASH-SECURED PUTS?

This chapter thus far has focused on strategies that involve *buying* options. What most new option traders don't realize is you can generate investment income by *selling* options. While you can sell both call options (i.e., "covered calls") and put options, the strategy I find most compelling is the latter.

Selling put options is known as "put writing" or selling "cash-secured puts." There are two main advantages in using this strategy:

- Buying stocks at a discount
- Earning income while waiting for shares to fall into your "buy range"

Selling cash-secured puts does require putting up enough capital to buy 100 shares of the underlying stock. While you can use this strategy without putting up collateral—known as "naked puts"—I do not recommend it. Most brokerages require that the put seller has enough cash in their brokerage account to buy the shares in the event they are "put" to them. This is why the strategy is known as selling cash-secured put options. The cash required to buy the shares must be "secure" (i.e., ready to be used) if shares are put to the person selling the contract.

Note: When a stock is "put" to you, it means you are assigned an exercise notice and you are obligated to buy the stock. You won't mind if you planned on buying the stock. However, if you had no intention of owning the stock that is moving lower, having this stock in your account will be an unwelcome surprise.

Buying Shares of Meta (at a Discount)

Let's say you want to own shares of Facebook's parent company Meta Platforms (MRVS). Shares are currently trading at $300. You are bullish on the company's long-term prospects, but you want to open a position at the best possible entry price. You think Meta shares will either remain flat or rise over the next 3 months, so you decide to sell a cash-secured put.

You have also noticed that shares get a lot of "support" at the $280 level. This means that Meta has willing buyers at that price. In fact, you observed that when Meta shares trade near or just below that level, they tend to quickly reverse. If you draw a line from $280 across the chart for the last 6 months, shares seem to "bounce" off this level every time Meta shares hit this price point.

You look at the options available for Meta and decide to sell a put option with a strike price of $280 for $8 per contract. Since each put option contract sold represents 100 shares of the underlying position, you immediately pocket $800 in premium. The premium is yours to keep no matter what happens. Do not forget, however, that the price of the option will most certainly fluctuate in value before the expiration date.

Note: Your break-even point is $272 per share, which equates to the $280 strike price *minus* the $8 premium you collected upon selling the put option.

You also must have $30,000 in your brokerage account if the 100 shares of Meta get put to you. Since the contract has an "option yield" of 2.6% ($8 / $280 = 2.85%), the income earned for locking up your shares is reasonable (option yield is discussed in more detail later in this chapter).

There are two scenarios that can play out from here. First, let's say that Meta shares close above $280 on the day your option expires. In this event, nothing else happens. Your obligation to buy the 100 shares of Meta expires. You pocket the $800 option premium and your trade is complete. That's an excellent ending to a well-executed trade.

In the second scenario, Meta shares trade below your $280 strike price on the expiration date. In this case, shares of Meta will be "put" to you. This means you are obligated to buy 100 shares of Meta at $280. Even if shares are trading below $280, you are still obligated to buy 100 shares at the agreed-upon price. However, since you are bullish on Meta's long-term prospects, you are happy to buy the shares.

A Win-Win Strategy

Selling cash-secured puts is truly one of the few win-win strategies in the options world. You will not only own the underlying shares; you will also earn a solid income—usually 2%–3% per contract sold—and acquire shares you'd like to own. And since the income lowers your average cost, you will be entering your long-term position at a better entry point.

While estimates vary, many statistics show that the vast majority— usually 30%–50%—of put option contracts expire worthless. Most are also closed before expiration, meaning the market is in the option *seller's* favor. This is one reason I am consistently selling options in my own portfolio to earn income.

Option sellers should also keep a close eye on the CBOE Volatility Index (VIX). As covered in Chapter 4, the VIX is the best measure of how investors are feeling about the markets. When the VIX is low, investors are not worried about the broader economy or stock market. But when the VIX spikes—as it did during the COVID-19 pandemic or the global financial crisis—investors are worried about the near-term future of the stock market and economy.

The VIX is also a very important component of the options market. When the VIX is high, the premiums paid for a call or put option are also higher. That means those investors *selling* options are getting more bang for their buck.

And during the COVID-19 crash in March 2020, I used this exact strategy to reap huge rewards.

CASE STUDY:

BOEING AND THE COVID-19 CRASH

I've always been a fan of businesses with wide economic moats, which we discussed in Chapter 6. This is a Warren Buffett concept that describes businesses with sustained competitive advantages. Basically, a business is considered to have a wide moat if the company has some sort of feature that other companies can't replicate. This often leads to higher gross margins and stronger free cash flow growth over the long term.

One company that always typified this trend was Boeing Co. It's one of two firms in the world—the other being Airbus—that manufacture large commercial airliners. Boeing also has heavy ties to the US government, as during times of war, governments need industrial capacity to pump out tanks, trucks, and—you guessed it—planes. That means it's *highly* unlikely the government will let this firm go bankrupt. This creates high barriers to entry in the aviation industry.

But though Boeing had always been a classic example of a company protected by a wide economic moat, the entire business looked to be in jeopardy in March 2020.

Boeing Shares Were in Freefall

The onset of the COVID-19 pandemic sent shockwaves through the financial markets. Global lockdown orders wreaked havoc on every industry imaginable. The industry that was adversely impacted the most was airlines.

While global travel never fully ceased during lockdowns, the number of people traveling collapsed. In fact, US travel volume fell from a 7-day average of 2.3 million in January 2020 to 100,000 by April 2020.

No industry is prepared for this type of collapse in demand. While the whole airline industry was struggling, Boeing fared the worst. Long-term demand for new planes quickly dried up as airlines were forced to cancel contracts with the company. While Boeing seemingly still had a wide economic moat, there wasn't much to protect if demand for the product dried up.

The news sent Boeing shares from $340 in February 2020 to $89 by March 2020, or a month-over-month decline of 74%. The CBOE Volatility Index was also surging, hitting its highest level ever. Nevertheless, as a trained options trader, I viewed this as a major buying opportunity.

Taking Advantage of the Chaos

Even though the situation was uncertain and was something I'd never seen, I was confident the government wouldn't let Boeing go bankrupt. After all, would the US government really start working with French Airbus on military defense technology?

Seeing that the worst of the selling was likely over, I decided to sell a 1-week cash-secured put on Boeing when the stock traded at $100 per share. The contract had a strike price of $90 and paid a comically high $1,350 ($13.50 per contract)—or an option yield of 15%—for a 5-day holding period. In this case, if Boeing shares traded below $90 on that Friday, I would be obligated to buy 100 shares of Boeing at $90 and keep the $1,350. But if shares traded above $90, I would keep the $1,350, and I wouldn't be obligated to buy the stock.

I had thought the selling had concluded, but I was mistaken. By Friday, shares of Boeing had closed at $87. This meant that I was required to buy 100 shares of Boeing. However, since I was a fan of the company's wide economic moat business, I was happy to acquire those shares. Since I was paid $1,350—or $13.50 per share—my entry price was technically $76.50 ($90 – $13.50).

Although I was a little nervous holding a sizeable position in a floundering company, the trade worked out perfectly. By March 2021, global air travel had normalized and Boeing shares had rebounded 209%. It was one of my best trades that year.

CASH-SECURED PUTS

Selling cash-secured puts is one way of acquiring a stock you want to own at a discount. For the privilege of waiting and seeing if the stock will trade below your selected strike price at expiration, you are paid a premium. If the stock is below the strike price when the contract expires, you are required to buy 100 shares of that stock at that strike price (this is known as being "assigned").

Since you wanted to own that stock anyway, you're happy to acquire shares at the lower price. If you initiate this trade during a time of high volatility—like I did with Boeing—you may earn a very large premium.

How to Identify Good Cash-Secured Puts

Of course, there are risks associated with selling cash-secured puts. For instance, in the Boeing example there was the possibility the company could have gone bankrupt. If this had happened between the time I opened the contract and the expiration date, and the shares fell to $0, I would have still been obligated to buy 100 shares of Boeing at $90 (or $9,000 worth). That means I would have basically lit $9,000 on fire.

But if you use the following three guidelines, you can drastically lower the odds of making a misstep when trading cash-secured puts.

1. Find a Stock You Want to Own

One of the main mistakes new option traders make when selling cash-secured puts is selling puts on companies they really don't want to own. This is a classic mistake, and it can lead to unfathomable losses.

For instance, some traders see that a stock is struggling. The *implied volatility* in the stock is rising, so they know they can earn a large premium for selling a cash-secured put. The options trader—thinking he can make a quick buck—sells the cash-secured put. Unbeknownst to the unseasoned trader, the implied volatility was high for a reason and the stock keeps falling. When expiration comes, the trader is forced to buy 100 shares of a stock he didn't want to own.

Instead of picking any old stock, focus on selling cash-secured puts on stocks you want to own.

Identifying which stock to sell cash-secured puts on is a similar strategy to finding stocks to buy. Whenever I begin my stock research, I always look for companies that have exposure to long-term secular growth trends. These are markets or industries that will unfold over many years and are therefore not unduly influenced by short-term factors. This is in addition to stocks with a wide economic moat (like in the Boeing example).

2. Determine the Stock's Technical Level of Support

Technical analysis involves finding investing opportunities in chart patterns and price trends. Entire books have been written on technical analysis, but I will do a brief overview of one of the best patterns for selling cash-secured puts: support levels.

A *support level* refers to a pattern whereby a stock's price does not fall below a certain price over a certain time period. These levels are created when a stock falls to a price level and a flood of buying enters into the stock and the demand for shares outstrips supply. Technical analysts draw trend lines on stock charts to see where these support levels reveal themselves.

Since support levels show where a stock is likely to stop falling, and possibly rebound, investors looking to sell cash-secured puts would be wise to set their strike price at or below support levels. This increases the odds that the trader will not have their shares "assigned," as it's unlikely the stock will fall and stay below that level. For those looking to generate income as opposed to acquiring the stock, setting your strike price below support levels is an ideal strategy.

3. Find a Stock with a High "Option Yield"

You want to get the best bang for your buck when selling cash-secured puts. One of my favorite methods to determine the yield on the contract is to look at what I call "option yield."

For instance, let's say it's September and your analysis shows Apple has a level of technical support at $140. While shares are trading at $145, you believe that shares won't close below $140 when the contract expires in 2 months, so you decide to sell a November 19 put option on Apple with a strike price of $140. You receive a premium of $4 (or $400 since it's 100 shares per contract). To calculate option yield, you take the *premium* divided by the *strike price*. In this example, the option yield is 2.86% ($4 / $140 = 0.02857).

Note: Your break-even point is $136 per share, which equates to the $140 strike price *minus* the $4 premium you collected upon selling the put option.

However, let's say you considered selling the at-the-money contract. In this scenario, shares are still trading at $145, but you decide to also set the strike price to $145. Since there is a higher likelihood that you will be assigned shares, you earn a higher premium of $6 (or $600). This means this riskier contract has an option yield of 4.13% ($6 / $145). The amount of money you earn on the contract is higher since the risk of being assigned is higher.

As a rule, you don't want to sell a cash-secured put if the yield is under 2%.

4. Take Advantage of "Theta Decay"

One rule that all prospective cash-secured put investors should know is that you should only sell contracts with a 30- to 60-day time horizon. As we've discussed, options lose value the closer they are to expiration. In fact, as outlined earlier, options lose value even faster as the expiration date approaches.

When selling cash-secured puts, you want to take advantage of this acceleration, also known as "theta decay." We will discuss the "option Greeks" in the next section; for now, remember to only sell cash-secured puts expiring within 30–60 days, as theta decay is strongest during this period.

How to Trade a Cash-Secured Put

Once you've found a stock you want to own, a proper level of support, and a decent option yield on your target company, you want to open your position (i.e., sell to open). I would recommend allocating not more than 10% of your portfolio to a cash-secured put position. While the rules I've laid out will mitigate the risks associated with this strategy, it's not wise to allocate more than 10% to any option position (even if you want to own the stock).

After you "sell to open" your position, you need to be patient. If the underlying stock rises or moves sideways, the value of the option contract is likely to fall. This is a good sign because we are "short" the put option contract.

If the trade is working in your favor, there are a few things you can do. The first is to lock in your gain by "buying to close" your position. I will do this on occasion if I'm sitting on a quick 40%–50% gain and I expect shares to fall after a great run. While you may lose some of your premium, it's often worth it to lock in the position to avoid being assigned.

However, you can also hold the position until expiration. You open yourself up to being assigned by using this strategy; however, you are compensated via securing the entire premium payment.

Lastly, if the stock keeps falling after you sell a cash-secured put and you are near expiration, you will likely be required to buy 100 shares of the stock. However, if you follow my instructions and only sell cash-secured puts on companies you want to own, this is a desirable outcome because you'll be acquiring 100 shares of a solid company.

Investing Quick-Start Guide:
SELL CASH-SECURED PUTS

1. Make sure that your broker has given you permission to sell cash-secured puts. You must have a margin account.

2. Find a stock that you want to buy at a discounted price.

3. Check that you have enough money in your account to buy the stock in case the stock is "put" to you.

4. To place this trade, select "Sell to Open" on your trading screen. Your broker will hold enough cash in your account as collateral in case you are assigned.

5. You receive a premium for selling the put, one of the advantages of using this strategy.

6. If the underlying stock rises or stays at the same price, the put option expires worthless. You keep the premium and do not have to buy the stock. Select "Buy to Close" on your trading screen.

7. If the underlying stock falls below the strike price at expiration, you are assigned an exercise notice and are obligated to buy the stock. Since you wanted to buy this stock, this is also a desirable outcome. You own the stock but at a discounted price.

LONG-TERM EQUITY ANTICIPATION SECURITIES (LEAPS)

WHAT ARE LONG-TERM EQUITY ANTICIPATION SECURITIES (LEAPS)?

Most new traders prefer to trade short-term options. They notice a pattern with a particular security and—thinking the pattern will hold—decide to buy a call or a put option to amplify the returns.

While the three other strategies discussed in this chapter—buying calls, buying puts, and cash-secured puts—involve short-term trading, there are high-risk, high-reward options strategies that involve longer-term trading; one of the most popular is known as "long-term equity anticipation securities," or LEAPS.

LEAPS are option contracts with expiration dates between 9 months and 3 years. They are identical to traditional call or put options; however, the time horizon is much longer. Seasoned option traders sometimes use LEAPS on long-term positions, as they can be an efficient use of a trader's capital.

Buying LEAPS versus Buying Shares

Many financial writers say buying LEAPS is simply a more cash-efficient way to enjoy the long-term upside in a stock. While this may be true, it's important to remember that LEAPS are still options, and therefore investors must pay a premium for using them.

Think of an option's premium as the price of admission for using the contract. And since LEAPS are long-dated options, you must pay higher premiums for using them. This is because the further out the expiration date for the contract, the more time the stock has to potentially make a sizable move. This is an example of the *time value of money*, which states money is worth more now than the same sum in the future.

For instance, one of the most popular stocks to buy LEAPS on is Etsy. The company occupies a niche market in the lucrative US e-commerce industry.

Let's say you have two investors: Jane and Andy. Both investors are bullish on Etsy stock over the next year, and each has $2,500 to invest. To act on this idea, Jane decides to buy 100 shares of Etsy at $250 apiece. Jane is bullish on Etsy's business and is happy to hold her position for 12 months at a minimum. Her target price for this trade is $370, or a return of 48%.

On the other hand, Andy recently heard about LEAPS and wants to give them a try. He also has $2,500 to invest and believes shares will hit a target price of $370 in the next 12 months. However, he's not sure he wants to tie up $2,500 in one position, as that will account for nearly 10% of his portfolio.

Instead of buying 100 shares like Jane, Andy finds a deep in-the-money LEAPS option contract that expires in 12 months. He selects the option contract with a strike price of $370, as he believes the stock will be above that price in 1 year. Andy pays $1,235 for his LEAPS contract ($12.35 × 100 shares), which provides him with potential upside if the shares do hit their strike price.

There Are a Few Ways This Cookie Can Crumble

Let's look at what may happen next. First, say in the 12 months after both investors open their positions, the US government decides to crack down on Etsy and break up the company for selling counterfeit goods (this is not a true story, just a hypothetical example). This sends shares of Etsy cratering to $150 per share. For Jane, this means that her 100 shares of Etsy have lost 40% of their value, or a dollar amount of $1,000. Her position is now worth $1,500.

However, Andy is not so lucky. Since his LEAPS look like they will expire well below the $370 strike price, his options have lost 99% of their value.

But that's not the only scenario. For instance, let's say Etsy shares stay flat for the 12-month holding period. Jane is upset that her thesis hasn't worked out, but she still has her full $2,500 investment. On the other hand, Andy's LEAPS haven't come close to hitting their $370 strike price. A year after opening his position, his options expire worthless and he takes a $1,235 loss.

For a final example, let's say that Etsy's business accelerates. There's a renewed interest in handmade goods, which has been a boon for Etsy's share price. In the 12 months since Jane and Andy opened their positions, the stock has surged to $400. Jane is ecstatic, as her shares have surged 60% and are now worth $4,000. But she's not nearly as excited as Andy. Since Andy's LEAPS have exceeded the $370 strike price, the value of his contracts surged 87%! That brings his total to $4,675.

As you can see, Andy was able to make more money with less investment than he would have made by simply buying shares outright. By using LEAPS, he was able to invest his capital as efficiently as possible.

In June 2020, I did something similar when I bought LEAPS on what I call the "greatest company in the history of companies."

THE GREATEST COMPANY IN THE HISTORY OF COMPANIES

In investing and in life, there are two main schools of thought: optimists and pessimists. In finance, the two types are called bulls and bears. A "bear" is a person who consistently believes that markets will fall. He or she typically invests heavily in things like gold stocks and other precious metals, claiming that there will soon be some sort of economic "collapse."

In the wake of the COVID-19 crash, these bears were out in full force. At the time, I was working for an investment research company that had a lot of bears. I had turned bullish on stocks in March 2020, after the Federal Reserve announced its massive monetary stimulus. Not only had I been buying high-quality stocks like Apple, Facebook (now Meta), and Alphabet after the crash; I was also telling readers of my subscription newsletters to buy them.

As you can imagine, this didn't sit well with the bears at my company. While my readers and I were sitting on solid gains from late March to June, many were claiming I should tell my audience to take profits since we were likely going to crash again.

This Is Bear-Hunting Country

I'm usually receptive to other people and their ideas. While I may not agree, I am still respectful of their views. However, this situation was slightly different. The bears were lambasting me on conference calls in front of our management team, saying I was setting our readers up to fail. Yet, the more fearful my colleagues got, the higher my conviction became in the long-term growth of the stock market.

My opinion was out of consensus at the time. There were many who viewed the post-COVID S&P 500 surge as a "dead cat bounce," or a short-term recovery that isn't really indicative of a trend reversal. I've never had an issue going against the consensus. After all, some of the greatest trades of all time were made by people who bucked the status quo.

Instead of selling off positions, I doubled down by recommending my readers buy LEAPS on one of my highest-conviction companies: Microsoft. The company had designed a formidable business model to thrive in the post-COVID world. After all, Microsoft is the second-largest cloud computing company on the planet, holding 16% market share. But Microsoft also had a stranglehold on the budding remote work market via its Microsoft Office, Skype, and Teams platforms.

...And the Bears Were Never Heard from Again

When my bearish colleagues caught wind of my idea to buy long-term options on what they saw as an "overvalued" tech company, they were floored. In their eyes, the $1.6 trillion market cap company was setting up for a crash rather than a surge higher. They were worried that by recommending this company I would tarnish our firm's reputation.

But I was undeterred. I was convinced that Microsoft's booming underlying businesses would continue to outperform. The global economy had fundamentally changed during the COVID-19 lockdowns, and the company—and its shareholders—would be a major beneficiary.

The LEAPS I recommended were 12-month contracts with a strike of $250. If Microsoft shares traded above $250 at expiration, I would make a handsome profit. This represented upside of 25% from where I opened the position in July 2020.

The trade took a few months to get going, as Microsoft stock went nowhere through the rest of 2020. However, in the final 6 months of the contract, shares rose as high as $275. When the contracts crossed the strike price, I recommended readers close their position for a massive gain.

INVESTMENT STRATEGY:

LEAPS

Using LEAPS can be a capital-efficient way to play the options market. As opposed to tying up lots of capital by buying shares, investors looking to amplify their returns can turn to the options market.

How to Find Good LEAPS

The great thing about LEAPS is the stock has more time to follow the trend that drives your bullishness. This contrasts with short-term options, where your trade needs to unfold quickly. The trade-off with LEAPS is that the premiums are much higher compared to regular options.

But if you use the following advice, you are apt to have much better odds of finding an attractively priced LEAPS contract.

1. Find a Stock You're Bullish On

Most investors use LEAPS for stocks they expect to rise over the next year. When looking for a company that supports your LEAPS opinion, make sure that the company has good potential to perform well over the period during which you will hold your contract.

For example, if you believe a stock will only have a short-term pop due to an earnings catalyst or technical pattern, use short-term options contracts instead. LEAPS are trades that take a minimum of 6 months to unfold, so you want to make sure the stock you select is poised to outperform.

One way to find stocks that will outperform is to look at analyst ratings. If a stock is trading well below its 12-month consensus analyst target price, there's a good chance that the stock is undervalued and primed for growth.

In addition, buying stocks with exposure to long-term secular growth trends—which we covered in Chapter 4—are preferred companies for which to buy LEAPS options.

2. Understand Your Option Contract

An option contract is said to be "in-the-money" when the underlying stock is above its strike price. For call options, the strike is lower than the price of the underlying stock.

Risk-averse LEAPS investors would be better served to buy in-the-money contracts. These are considered safer and more likely to retain their value. However, since they are lower risk, they also yield lower profits.

By contrast, out-of-the-money LEAPS are riskier. There is a far greater possibility that they will lose value compared to in-the-money contracts. However, if you are correct, your profits will tend to be much higher.

3. Keep an Eye on the Option's "Delta"

Every option contract has something known as "Greeks." These are different ways option traders measure how sensitive an option's price is to factors that affect its price.

The most important of the Greeks is known as "delta." Delta indicates the increase in the price of an option's price relative to the increase in the price of the underlying asset. Therefore, if an option has a delta of 1.0, it moves perfectly with the underlying stock. In other words, it gains $1 in value per every 1-point increase in the underlying asset. If it has a delta of 2.0, the option contract would move twice as much as the underlying stock, or $2 in value per every 1-point increase in the underlying asset.

An alternative way to think about delta is that it's the probability that the stock price will go beyond your strike price at expiration. When it comes to LEAPS, you typically want to look for contracts with a delta between 0.8 and 0.85, which means the probability of the option ending in the money at expiration is approximately 80%–85%.

How to Trade a LEAPS

Once you have found a LEAPS contract that meets this criteria, you want to enter your position. One key metric that investors should keep an eye on is the bid-ask spread for your LEAPS contract. The bid-ask spread is the difference between the "bid" price (i.e., where investors want to buy) and the "ask" price (i.e., where investors want to sell). When bid-ask spreads are wide, it typically means the market is illiquid, meaning that it's difficult to buy or sell your option contract at a specified price and in a timely manner.

And that's the case with LEAPS. Since not many people trade these contracts far into the future, the gap between what investors want to pay and want to sell is wide. This can be an issue for those looking to quickly exit a position, as there may not be much interest in trading for that LEAPS. That's why LEAPS investors should buy contracts only on companies they don't mind owning.

LEAPS investors should allocate no more than 3% of their investable assets to this strategy. While LEAPS are a relatively low-risk options strategy, they are still options, which means there's a good chance you may lose your entire investment. Therefore, it's best to keep your portfolio allocation small in the event your LEAPS contract expires worthless.

When I buy LEAPS, I place a 35% stop loss on the position. This is to ensure the preservation of my capital in case there's a quick downturn in the underlying stock. Assuming your trade thesis unfolds, and your LEAPS is profitable, I urge you to raise your stop loss periodically to lock in the gain. Once the contract is near expiration and in the money, I recommend closing the position to lock in the gain.

Investing Quick-Start Guide:
LONG-TERM EQUITY ANTICIPATION SECURITIES (LEAPS)

1. Buying LEAPS is akin to buying a call option. The difference is that you must find a call option with an expiration date longer than 7 months.

2. For example, you might buy (i.e., buy to open) a deep in-the-money LEAPS call that expires in 1 year.

3. Monitor the position closely.

4. If you achieve a fantastic gain, consider closing the position (i.e., sell to close) and booking the profits.

5. If the underlying stock is moving in the wrong direction, consider cutting your losses and abandoning the trade. It's a decision only you can make.

6. Once again, because these are options, I suggest that you sell the entire position before the expiration date.

CHAPTER 8

High-Yield Assets

High-yield assets are securities that issue regular payments (usually quarterly) to their holders. The most common high-yield investment vehicles are bonds, dividend-paying stocks, and other "yield-bearing" assets.

This is one of the lower-risk strategies in this book, but you should still review all the information in this chapter before investing, of course.

Back in the summer of 2016, I was sitting across a long oak table from one of Switzerland's leading independent wealth managers, Frank R. Suess of BFI Infinity. During our 2-hour meeting, we covered everything from newly elected President Trump to surging Turkish government bond yields. But we also spent a significant amount of time talking about something called "high-yield assets."

While many investors focus on high-yield assets like dividend-paying stocks and junk bonds, there are a handful of other high-risk, high-reward options at your disposal. These are often overlooked investment vehicles like double-digit dividend-paying stocks, business development companies, and real estate investment trusts (REITs).

I've learned that yield-bearing assets are just as important to my portfolio as my high-growth stocks. Why? With global interest rates near 0%, generating income from dividends is more important than ever.

But I also learned quickly that there are tons of "landmines" in this space. As I'll explain, any asset yielding 8%–10% is inherently risky.

Knowing how to spot these landmines was the difference between a steady stream of income and a potential 50% decline.

DOUBLE-DIGIT DIVIDEND-PAYING STOCKS

WHAT ARE DOUBLE-DIGIT DIVIDEND-PAYING STOCKS?

To understand double-digit dividend-paying stocks, you first need to understand dividends and how they work. A dividend is a cash payment to shareholders of some of the company's earnings. If shareholders own the company's stock before the *ex-dividend date*, they are eligible for these cash payments.

Not all companies pay dividends. Typically, dividend-paying stocks are mature companies. When these companies have "extra profit" (i.e., discretionary cash flow) each quarter after accounting for operating expenses, R&D, and interest payments, many choose to return some of that cash to shareholders in the form of dividends. This is different from high-growth stocks, which tend to keep profits as retained earnings to reinvest in the business.

One way to compare dividends across different companies and industries is to look at the *dividend yield*, or the annual dividend paid divided by the share price. The current average dividend yield for the S&P 500 is around 2%.

As a rule, the higher the stock's dividend yield, the riskier the stock. Here's an example: Let's say you're deciding between buying shares of consumer products company Kraft Heinz (KHC) and Lumen Technologies (LUMN). Kraft Heinz is one of the safest companies in the market. Dividend yield reliably increases every year, and they sell wildly popular products like Kraft Macaroni & Cheese and Heinz ketchup. The company's sales will grow along with population growth, and with such strong brands they have a lot of "pricing power." With a rock-solid balance sheet and great outlook, Kraft Heinz is a low-risk stock. As such, the company pays a modest but steady 2% dividend yield.

Lumen Technologies is another story. The company operates landline phone infrastructure in rural America. Because landline phones have been rendered largely obsolete with the adoption of cell phones, the business is in terminal decline. With a weak brand and no pricing power, Lumen Technologies is a relatively risky business. That's especially true when you realize the company has loads of debt and high interest payments. Since the stock is risky, Lumen Technologies pays a relatively high dividend of 7%.

While both companies pay a dividend, Lumen Technologies must pay a *higher* dividend yield because the opportunities for investment growth are limited and therefore the stock is riskier. The higher dividend yield is meant to compensate the investor for this elevated level of risk.

But as we've seen time and time again, a company with a low and stable dividend can be just as risky as a company with a high and unstable dividend.

Taking Kraft's Dividend to the Shredder

Kraft started paying a dividend in 2015. This came after the company merged with condiment giant Heinz (a deal arranged by Warren Buffett himself). The merger allowed them to become the fifth-largest food and beverage company in the world. With Buffett's blessing and a seemingly stable underlying business, management introduced a dividend.

From 2015 to 2018, Kraft Heinz increased their dividend at an average of 10% per year. Everything seemed to look good on the surface—by 2018 the company had a *payout ratio* of 30%. A payout ratio is the percentage of earnings paid out as dividends. It's calculated by taking the number of dividends paid per share divided by earnings per share. As a rule, any payout ratio below 80% is considered "safe." While Kraft Heinz had a high payout ratio of 112% in 2016, management had reduced the payout ratio to 30% by 2018.

It was around that time that all hell broke loose. Consumer trends had shifted in the mid-2010s toward healthier options, leaving the processed foods offered by Kraft Heinz on the shelves. Soon, this started to show up in the company's sales, which were flat between 2016 and 2018.

Despite the flat sales, Kraft Heinz kept growing earnings and raising its dividend. But these earnings were driven by cost-cutting and other financial engineering rather than by actually selling more mac 'n cheese.

Kraft Heinz continued to raise its dividend until early 2019. That's when the company could no longer meet its dividend payments. Even though Kraft Heinz had a strong brand and the backing of one of the world's greatest investors, they were forced to cut their dividend by 36%. Perhaps it was higher expenses, an adverse change in their business model, or lack of management execution, but they didn't have sufficient cash flow to service the dividend.

There's Nothing Worse Than a Dividend Cut

Investors hate being caught by surprise when it comes to dividend cuts. As a result, the stock fell 33% the day of the announcement. Despite the low and "safe" 2% dividend yield, Kraft's payments were no safer than any other company in the market.

While the story of how it got there was different, Lumen Technologies and its 7% dividend yield ended up in a similar place. The company's landline business was in serious trouble. The percentage of businesses and consumers still using a landline was plummeting.

From 2008 to 2013, Lumen Technologies started acquiring smaller telecoms that were underperforming due to the financial crisis. The plan was to increase sales—and it worked. Sales ballooned by nearly 40% per year during that 5-year stretch.

During that period, Lumen Technologies paid the hefty 7% dividend. Although the stock price stayed mostly flat, investors were happy to earn steady yield, and—as a result—it was a hot income investment. But just like Kraft Heinz, the jig was up as the company cut its dividend in 2013. This sent shares cratering over 40% in under a week.

Think about this: Kraft Heinz had a stable business and a dependable dividend. It was also backed by Warren Buffett's company, Berkshire Hathaway (BRK). Lumen Technologies, on the other hand, was in a declining business and had terrible fundamentals. And yet, both companies cut their dividend.

What is the lesson? Dividend yields can be deceiving. If a so-called safe investment like Kraft Heinz and an obvious lemon like Lumen Technologies can end up in the same place (i.e., the basement), you need more information to find a worthwhile high dividend–yielding stock. I never expected that a company that sells ketchup and mac 'n cheese and pays a steady dividend would be in jeopardy. It just goes to show that anything is possible. Business and consumer preferences can change and that was reflected in the share price, which is what happened to Kraft Heinz.

This is another reason why you want your investment portfolio to be diversified, as I have mentioned before. You can never predict what will happen when investing in the financial markets.

MAKING MONEY OFF THE CRAZIEST THING I'VE SEEN IN MY CAREER

I've been an investing professional for a long time. But the craziest thing I've seen by far in my career was when oil prices went *negative* in April 2020. That's right—oil fell as low as minus $37 a barrel on April 20, 2020. At the time, COVID-19 had brought the entire global economy to a halt. But what didn't stop was the amount of oil flooding the markets from Saudi Arabia, Russia, and other major oil-producing countries.

With tankers docked, cars parked, and airports looking like ghost towns, oil traders were stuck paying companies to store their oil. This made their "black gold" worse than worthless for a short time.

But that also briefly pushed the dividend yields of stocks like Enterprise Product Partners (EPD) well into double digits.

It's the End of the World As We Know It

Enterprise Product Partners is a North American midstream energy pipeline company. The company has 50,000 miles of natural gas, crude oil, natural gas liquid (NGL), and petrochemical pipelines stretching all over the US. Thus, when COVID-19 struck and the global economy shut down, so did much of EPD's pipeline infrastructure. The less commodities were surging through EPD's systems, the less money the company would make.

That was quickly reflected in EPD's share price. After trading around $28 at the start of the year, EPD's shares fell as low as $12.50. But the company never cut their dividend during this period. Since the company paid $1.75 per share in dividends in 2020, that means EPD's dividend was as high as 14% ($1.75 / $12.50 = 14%).

A dividend yield of 14% implies that there is something seriously wrong with the company. And in this case, the problem was that the demand for oil in the US had dried up to the point that oil traders were *paying* people to store their oil! But those savvy investors who spotted this opportunity were handsomely rewarded over the next 12 months.

Be Greedy When Others Are Fearful

Buying EPD when oil prices went negative was following the advice of Baron Rothschild, who said you should buy "when there's blood in the streets." Some of the best investments I've made were when I bought stocks that were completely out of favor at the time.

EPD was a special case. A 14% dividend yield is pretty much unheard of, as companies typically cut their payout when it grows to that level. But I had a hunch EPD was going to come out the other side as strong as ever.

And over a year later, I was vindicated. Pfizer Inc. (PFE) announced in November 2020 that they were ready to begin distribution of COVID-19 vaccines. This all but guaranteed we'd see renewed demand for oil and a bull run in oil and gas stocks like EPD.

Not only has my investment in EPD grown 64% since April 2020; I also have a 14% dividend yield locked in for life.

INVESTMENT STRATEGY:
DOUBLE-DIGIT DIVIDEND YIELD

Double-digit dividend-yielding stocks are some of my favorite high-risk, high-reward investments. Once you've learned how to assess the safety of a dividend, these can add stability and downside risk to your portfolio.

In fact, many double-digit dividend stocks are "low beta." That means many rise when the stock market falls! Plus, the longer you hold a double-digit dividend payer, the more likely it is to eventually pay for itself. Because if you hold a stock paying 10% per year for 10 years, you'll make enough in dividend to cover your original investment.

How to Identify a Good Double-Digit Dividend Stock

Double-digit dividend-yielding stocks that last (i.e., the dividends don't get cut) are typically "event driven." The dividend yield is unusually high because of some issue that has temporarily pushed the share price down.

That's in contrast to what happened in the Kraft Heinz and Lumen Technologies examples. Those businesses had to cut their dividends because they were deteriorating from a structural standpoint as fewer people bought processed foods and used landlines.

EPD was a different story. Even though COVID-19 had temporarily brought the global economy to a halt, we were always going to go back to using oil eventually. This logic made EPD a solid candidate for taking a chance on the high yield in April 2020. That's especially true since EPD had a long history of maintaining and raising its dividend yield.

But there are other factors investors need to watch when it comes to assessing the stability of a dividend yield.

1. Find the Payout Ratio

The payout ratio is the percentage of earnings a firm pays to its shareholders as dividends. The smaller the payout ratio, the safer the dividend payment. As a rule, any payout ratio above 80% is a red flag. But to reduce the impact of short-term fluctuations, I prefer to take the 3-year average payout ratio.

You can find payout ratio information on many free financial data websites, including *FinViz* and *Yahoo! Finance*.

2. Calculate the Debt-to-Equity Ratio

The more debt a company has on its balance sheet, the more vulnerable it is when economic headwinds emerge. A company with excessive debt will be more likely to have to cut their dividend when hard times hit. While acceptable levels of debt can differ between industries, typically a debt-to-equity ratio above 100% is a red flag.

Just like the payout ratio, you can find debt-to-equity data on free sites like *Finviz* and *Yahoo! Finance*.

3. Determine the Company's Free Cash Flow Growth

This is the amount of cash left over after a company pays its operating expenses and capital expenditures. Unlike earnings per share, which can be manipulated by buying back stock, free cash is a pure financial metric showing how well a company is performing.

When free cash flow is growing, that means the company has more leeway to maintain and increase dividend payments. I typically look for companies with free cash flow growth of at least 3% per year over a 5-year period. You can find this information on *Finviz*, *Yahoo! Finance*, *Google Finance*, and *Morningstar*.

How to Trade a Double-Digit Dividend Stock

As I mentioned, not all double-digit dividend-paying stocks should be bought. Many are businesses with insurmountable issues with a dividend that will likely be cut soon.

That's why you want to make sure your target is both an "event-driven" issue and meets the three criteria I mentioned earlier. Once you've found that, your goal should be to acquire shares at the best possible price.

While not as risky as some of the other topics in this book, double-digit dividend payers are still risky. I would not allocate more than 5% of your investment portfolio to any individual double-digit dividend payer. To acquire shares at the best price, I would dollar-cost average into your position over a few weeks.

Once you've acquired the necessary number of shares, you must be patient. Much like the example with EPD and the introduction of vaccines, you have to wait for the temporary setback, or "dark cloud," to lift over the double-digit dividend payer. Once the negative news fades, your dividend will be locked in at that double-digit rate. And since the "dark cloud" lifting implies the share price also rises, you'll be making money from both dividend income and share price appreciation.

As long as the underlying business is strong, you can hang on to your double digit dividend payer for many years.

Investing Quick-Start Guide:
DOUBLE-DIGIT DIVIDEND STOCKS

1. Before investing in a stock with a double-digit yield, do your due diligence and calculate the payout ratio, debt-to-equity ratio, and the free cash flow growth for the business.

2. Dollar-cost average into the position.

3. Because higher yields imply higher risk, commit no more than 5% of your portfolio to stocks paying double-digit dividends.

4. Be patient. This is a long-term buy and hold (at least 1–2 years).

5. Sell only when something fundamentally changes (i.e., payout ratio is rising or dividend is cut).

BUSINESS DEVELOPMENT COMPANIES (BDCS)

WHAT ARE BUSINESS DEVELOPMENT COMPANIES (BDCS)?

Business development companies (BDCs) are a special type of investment vehicle that gives investors exposure to private investments. BDCs invest in high-risk, high-reward asset classes like private equity, venture capital, and other investments in small to midsize private companies. That's in addition to "distressed" or high-yield companies that have difficulty securing financing.

BDCs provide a vital lifeline to these businesses. For instance, anyone who has started their own business knows how difficult that process is. And if you need to borrow money from a bank to scale your business, it can be even harder. That's partially because of major consolidation in the banking industry over the last 20 years.

The total number of US banks has shrunk by 46% since 1998. Fewer banks means that the pool of loans underwriters accept is also lower. That's one reason why the percentage of loans that are high-yield loans—known as "leveraged loans"—has tumbled from 71% in 1994 to roughly 9% today.

That has created a huge opportunity for alternative sources of financing, particularly through what's known as "private equity." Between 2009 and 2019, US private equity under management grew 170%. That's been great for the entire industry, particularly large players like Blackstone (BX).

A New Type of Private Equity

While BDCs invest in private companies, the key difference is private equity stocks only permit "accredited" investors exposure to the underlying business. This includes those who meet wealth, education, and financial knowledge requirements.

For example, Blackstone may hold positions in hundreds of private companies. But when the value of those companies rises and falls, investors do not get any direct benefit. Instead, they are exposed to Blackstone's bottom line. This gives them *indirect* access to private companies, similar to holding an exchange-traded fund (ETF) of private companies.

On the other hand, BDCs give investors *direct* access to private businesses. When the value of a BDC's "net asset value" (or total value of the private investments) rises and falls, so does the share price of the BDC. And since BDCs are required to pay out 90% of their income to investors, they often pay *huge* dividend yields.

Here's an example: Let's say both Blackstone and a BDC called Ares Capital Corporation (ARCC) invest in the same twenty private alternative energy companies. Not long after they make their investments, a new form of alternative energy starts being adopted by major economies. This may tank the value of these private investments by 50%, as demand for these "old hat" alternative energy companies falls dramatically.

In this scenario, Blackstone shares would fare relatively well. The company (and its shareholders) make money based on the *management fees* paid to the firm rather than the value of the underlying projects. Therefore, the stock falls a modest 5% to account for customers who may not return in the future.

On the other hand, Ares Capital Corp. shareholders would be hurting. Since the value of the company's publicly traded BDC is tied directly to the value of the twenty alternative energy companies, its share price also falls 50%.

So, while BDCs may carry more risk, they also carry more upside as well.

Business Development Companies and the Status Quo

Let's go back to the previous example. But this time, instead of a new form of alternative energy being introduced, let's say nothing fundamentally changes with the industry. Alternative energy demand continues to grow at a steady rate, but the value of the private companies remains relatively unchanged.

Under this scenario, Blackstone shares would grind sideways. You wouldn't see much in terms of returns, as the loans issued by the company would be priced into the stock.

That's not the case with Ares Capital Corp. Since the company is required to pay out 90% of its earnings as dividends, the company's dividend yield has surged. In fact, the company currently sports an 8.2% dividend yield! That's more than 4 times the size of the average S&P 500 dividend yield.

This structure gives BDCs a major leg up over the competition. And when you find a BDC with a strong stable of private companies, those looking to add income assets to their portfolio would be wise to check out BDCs.

That's especially true if we're in a rising interest rate environment.

BDCS, JEROME POWELL, AND THE FLOATING RATE LOANS

Investors worth their salt keep close tabs on interest rates. Since the Federal Reserve is responsible for interest rate policy in the US, these savvy investors also keep very close eyes on the Fed. This was the case when I was an analyst for an investment research firm in 2018.

That year, new Federal Reserve chairman Jerome Powell had raised interest rates three times. This was after nearly 6 years of interest rates at or near zero, also known as "zero interest rate policy" (ZIRP). Raising rates was a big deal, as the central bank had not done so since before the global financial crisis in 2008.

Central banks raise interest rates when the economy is strong. At the time, the US economy was firing on all cylinders as GDP growth hit its highest pace in 5 years, while the unemployment rate was the lowest since the 1950s.

Since I expected rates to rise and knew BDCs with floating rate loans benefited more than others, I started looking for the right stock to play so I could take advantage. I went through the 10-Ks—reports that include all the annual financial information for a company—of all the major BDCs to find which companies held my preferred asset mix.

I found that Sixth Street Specialty Lending had a whopping 95% of their portfolio in floating rate loans. Knowing all this, I expected Jerome Powell and the Federal Reserve to aggressively raise interest rates. That's why I started writing to my thousands of readers about a business development company called Sixth Street Specialty Lending (TSLX).

BDCs Love Higher Interest Rates

Rising interest rates benefit BDCs in two ways:

1. First, higher rates make it difficult for companies to get access to traditional financing options. Loan underwriters are pickier about the companies they lend to since the cost of capital is higher. This will push more businesses into BDCs.

2. Second, most BDC investments are underpinned by floating rate loans. This means that the rate of interest paid by these companies fluctuates over the life of the investment. Floating rates are almost always pegged to the yield on the 10-year US Treasury note.

As the US economy chugs along and rates rise, BDCs will benefit as their interest income rises too. This is especially true for BDCs that have a large portfolio of floating rate loans.

But the expected higher interest rates weren't the only reason to like the company.

Be Sure to Pick the Right Horse

There were many reasons to like TSLX, but the first was the quality of its assets. The company had used first-lien senior debt—investments backed by collateral—for 92% of its portfolio. That also gave TSLX control over any restructuring or asset sale in the event of default. I'm always looking for ways to reduce my risk, and that's exactly what this structure does. That made TSLX far less risky than other BDCs in its peer group.

TSLX also has an attractive mix of investments. Financial services, healthcare, and pharmaceutical investments make up over one-third of TSLX's portfolio. These are all industries where demand is inelastic. This means that people tend to be "price inelastic," meaning they will require the services of banks, hospitals, and drug companies no matter what's happening in the economy.

TSLX's portfolio is made up entirely of floating rate loans. Therefore, the interest that companies pay on their debt will rise if interest rates rise.

BDCs such as TSLX carry what I call "jockey risk." Since the portfolio of companies is picked and managed by a team, you want to have the best group of "jockeys" possible. And TSLX gets high marks on its management report card. A return on assets that is 31% higher than the industry average tells us that TSLX's team gets the most out of their portfolio of companies. A return-on-capital figure that is 20% above its peers says that for every dollar of capital invested, TSLX's team can generate more cash than its peers. That's exactly what you want to see from a BDC.

After recommending TSLX to my subscribers, the stock delivered a total return of 33% over the next 18 months. That was double the return on the S&P 500 over the same period.

BUSINESS DEVELOPMENT COMPANIES (BDCS)

I've always enjoyed researching BDCs because they're truly an under-the-radar investment. Whenever I bring up the topic with my finance friends, almost nobody has heard of the asset class.

A running theme in this book is that we want to invest in things when people don't know about them. Because if the investment is a good one, investors will eventually be enticed by the returns offered from the unique investment. When it comes to BDCs and their huge dividend yields, I expect many investors to flock to them over the coming years.

How to Identify a Good Business Development Company

BDCs give investors access to unique opportunities in the private sector. Without the BDC structure, investors would be confined to more "vanilla" investments like buying private equity companies rather than investing via a BDC. And if you're looking for a huge dividend yield, you'd be hard-pressed to find a better option than BDCs. That's especially true if the Federal Reserve is raising interest rates.

But those looking for the best BDC would be wise to keep the following three factors in mind.

1. Find a BDC with a High Percentage of Floating Rate Bonds

As I mentioned in the example, BDCs with floating rate bonds are the secret sauce when interest rates are rising. But investors looking for this information will have to do some digging.

The best place to start is making a list of the largest BDCs. Since it's a small industry, it won't take you very long. From there you'll want to look through each BDC's Form 10-K or investor presentation. This will show you the percentage of floating rate bonds. You can find information about the largest BDCs by doing a Google search. From there, you can find each BDC's 10-K in the investor relations section of their website.

Once you've ranked each BDC by its percentage of floating rate bonds, select the one with the highest figure.

2. Select BDCs with Attractive Capital Structures

In the same 10-K and investor presentation in which you find the percentage of floating rate bonds, you also want to look at the BDC's *capital structure.* This shows you how the BDC finances its business. BDCs using first-lien senior debt—investments backed by collateral—are superior to those using other forms of financing.

Note: BDCs are backed by the net asset value of the private companies they invest in. That is what makes them kind of cool when compared to how other companies are structured, such as Blackstone.

Find the BDC with the highest percentage of first-lien senior debt. In the TSLX example, the company had 92% of its portfolio in this attractive structure. This is the kind of capital structure that you want since BDCs perform better with higher interest rates. This is one of the best ways to ride that trend higher.

3. Assess the Quality of the Dividend

In the section on double-digit dividend-paying stocks, I gave you three factors to use when assessing the safety of a dividend:

- Payout ratio below 80%
- Debt-to-equity ratio below 100%
- Free cash flow growth above 3%

You will use these same factors to make sure the often high-yielding BDC has a safe payout.

How to Trade a Business Development Company

There are not many business development companies trading on the market. As of this writing, there are only twelve BDCs with a market capitalization over $500 million.

Once you've found one that meets the previously mentioned criteria and there's an accommodative environment (i.e., rising interest rates), dollar-cost average into your position over a few weeks. This will ensure that you're acquiring your shares at the best possible price.

Compared to other strategies in this book, BDCs are relatively low risk. Those looking to add an income stream to their portfolio would be wise to allocate 5% of their portfolio to the target BDC. Unless there is an exogenous shock to the market (like the COVID-19 pandemic), stable BDCs should continue producing 7%–8% per year in dividend income.

Investing Quick-Start Guide:
BUSINESS DEVELOPMENT COMPANIES (BDCs)

1. Check with your broker about how to buy a BDC.

2. Don't commit more than 5% of your portfolio to this investment.

3. After opening the position, plan to buy and hold for years. You will receive regular dividend payments.

REAL ESTATE INVESTMENT TRUSTS (REITS)

WHAT ARE REAL ESTATE INVESTMENT TRUSTS (REITS)?

Real estate is a key piece of any diversified portfolio. The asset gives investors exposure to two key forms of return:

1. Capital appreciation if the value of the property increases in value
2. Income from monthly rental payments

But as anyone who manages real estate properties can tell you, it's *a lot* of work. Managing property taxes, maintenance fees, and other costs associated with owning real estate can often turn into a full-time job.

That's why I prefer to use something called a "real estate investment trust" (REIT) in lieu of owning property. A REIT is a unique business structure that requires the company to pay out 90% of its income as dividends. This makes them great yield-bearing assets for income investors. In fact, REITs can pay dividends as high as 10%. And as we've discussed in both the double-digit dividend-paying stock and business development company sections, those who can figure out which dividend yields are solid can achieve massive gains.

In addition, REITs trade just like stocks. Unlike owning a piece of real estate, REIT investors get both the income (via high-dividend yields) and capital appreciation (from rising unit prices) just like if you owned a piece of actual real estate. That's all without the high capital costs and hands-on management that goes into owning a real estate property.

The Advantages of Owning a REIT

Let's use an example. Let's say you wanted to add real estate exposure to your portfolio. You've never heard of a REIT, so you decide to go the traditional route and buy an investment property in Cleveland, Ohio.

Since it's a smaller city and interest rates are favorable, you get a good deal on a $100,000 30-year fixed mortgage. You plan to rent this house to college kids near the local university and stay in the house yourself in the summers. You grew up fixing things around the house with your family, so you don't have to worry too much about upkeep on the property. And since you live in Cleveland, you can easily stop by and work on the house if necessary. You expect to earn about 7% in annual income in addition to any capital appreciation on the property, which has risen in value 5% per year since 2010.

Then something unforeseen happens: a global pandemic. Since students no longer feel safe on campus due to the virus, demand for your investment property dries up. And although you could sell the property, real estate prices are tanking so you would be taking a loss on the property.

This is an example of how illiquid real estate properties are. Unlike a share of stock, it's very difficult to convert your real estate investment into cash. Buying physical real estate is a long-term investment. And if you aren't careful—or simply have bad luck—it can go south relatively quickly. If that happens, you can get stuck holding a piece of property that's underwater—or worth less than the mortgage you're paying—for many years.

Real Estate Investment Trusts Fix This

Let's try another example. Let's say you want to add an investment that's tied to student housing to your portfolio. But instead of actually buying an illiquid physical property that you have to manage, you buy a REIT called American Campus Communities (ACC).

The REIT manages and develops student housing properties throughout the US. This gives you exposure to the same trend you bought your property for in the previous example. In this case, you still benefit from the capital appreciation in student housing and earn a slightly lower 5% yield on your money with 5% annual gains on the REIT units. Plus, instead of being tied to one property in the city you live in, you get exposure to hundreds of student housing properties spread around the country.

And while the yield is slightly lower than what you'd earn by owning the physical property, you're happy to pay that small 2% fee. Because with ACC, you don't need to manage the property and can sell your property at any time.

This came in handy when you invested in your student housing REIT. Because when you realized that the contagious virus would negatively impact universities—and thus student housing—you were able to sell your position without issue. If you had bought the physical property, you would have been stuck holding an illiquid asset.

SUN COMMUNITIES AND THE GRAYING BABY BOOMERS

Back in 2017, I was in Napa Valley, California, on a research trip. Unfortunately for me, I wasn't researching the region's namesake wines. Instead I was looking at trailer parks, or, as the business owner called them, "manufactured homes." But this wasn't a normal trailer park; this community was more akin to a luxury resort. And since these homes cost nearly $300,000 less than "site-built" homes, there was strong demand for the product.

I was looking at trailer parks in Napa Valley because a REIT I was researching called Sun Communities Inc. (SUI) owned it. The company specialized in trailer park communities for retirees. And—at least on the surface—the company seemed strong in my analysis. At the time, the baby boomer generation was starting to retire. In fact, it was estimated that 12,000 boomers were retiring every day in the US. But there was a wrinkle in this story: Baby boomers had little saved for retirement. According to a study from the Transamerica Center for Retirement Studies, the median retirement savings for the boomers was a measly $150,000.

As you can imagine, this wasn't enough to buy that dream house on the beach...but it was sufficient to buy a manufactured home in a nice community. Studies showed one in three boomers had no money saved for retirement. And of the ones who did, nearly half had less than $10,000.

But what many of these non-savers did have was a wholly owned home. And according to a Duke University professor I spoke with, many owners were expected to sell their site-built homes and move into trailer parks—I mean "manufactured homes."

I smelled an investment opportunity, so I decided to dig deeper.

Moving Into the Trailer Park

Not surprisingly, the park was attracting lots of baby boomers. Many tenants were retiring boomers who sold their site-built homes at the highs to live in manufactured homes.

I wasn't the first to connect the dots on this. One early mover into this market was the Oracle of Omaha himself, Warren Buffett: His holding company Berkshire Hathaway bought Clayton Homes for $1.3 billion in 2003. At the time, Clayton Homes was the largest builder of manufactured homes in the US.

Buffett was right to like manufactured homes. Sales for Clayton Homes had risen 10 years in a row and were accelerating as more boomers retired. But the way I saw it, I wanted to own the *real estate* these homes were built on, not the company making the homes.

For one, manufactured homes were one of the most profitable segments in the real estate sector. Property owners measure a property's profitability with net operating income (NOI). NOI is equal to all sales from the property minus any operating expenses. And I was happy to find out that manufactured home REITs had one of the highest average NOI of all REIT segments.

There were two more things to like about manufactured homes:

1. First, the supply of these homes is finite.
2. Second, despite being the most affordable housing option in America, manufactured homes carry a stigma. That made it hard to get permits to build new communities. This challenge is known as "not in my back yard," or NIMBY for short. While not ideal for people buying manufactured homes, it's great for those who own the land.

Making Moves in the Manufactured Home Market

There are two components to the manufactured home industry:

1. The first is the *manufactured home* itself. This is typically wholly owned by the individual who lives in the home after buying the property from a company like Clayton Homes. And since the average tenant stayed in a manufactured home for 12 years or more, you didn't have to worry about a person picking up and leaving the property. That time frame is only slightly less than that for single-family homes, where—according to the National Association of Home Builders—the average person spends 13 years in the same home.
2. The second is the actual *land* the home sits on. This is typically owned by a management company. Tenants prefer this, as management takes care of water and sewer hookups, a foundation, trash removal, and other amenities.

After speaking with management and understanding the underlying factors driving the business, I decided to recommend the business to my readers. And in the subsequent 3 years, the 5% dividend paying trailer park returned a total of 128% (includes both dividends paid and capital appreciation for the stock).

INVESTMENT STRATEGY:
REAL ESTATE INVESTMENT TRUSTS (REITS)

For most investors, owning REITs instead of physical property makes sense. Not only can you own different types of properties like student housing and trailer parks, but you can also buy and sell easily because they trade like stocks. And since you get both the dividend income and the capital appreciation offered by physical real estate, you get all the best features of real estate investing. But you want to keep a few things in mind when selecting a REIT, which we'll discuss in this section.

How to Identify a Good REIT

As with the other high-yield assets discussed in this chapter, you need to make sure that the REIT you choose benefits from long-term demographic trends. My former boss John Mauldin often said that economic growth is equal to population growth and productivity growth. While the latter increases roughly 1% every year, population growth can be a bit less predictable (depending on which country you're in).

Find real estate trends that aren't stopping any time soon. From there, you need to make sure that the REIT you choose has a sustainable dividend yield. As we discussed in the Kraft Heinz example in the section on double-digit dividend-paying stocks, a dividend cut is a death sentence for any dividend-paying stock.

But if you use the following three factors, you'll have much better luck investing in REITs.

1. Evaluate Demographic Trends

As in both the American Campus Communities and Sun Communities examples, investors need to keep a close eye on the underlying demographic trends fueling the real estate market. That includes long-term secular trends like the baby boomers retiring in addition to an influx of millennials attending college. That's in opposition to other secular trends, like fewer people shopping at brick-and-mortar real estate (which is a negative for mall REITs).

To find this information, you want to look at US Census data to determine the general trend for each demographic. Understanding the "tectonic plates" of the real estate market can help you avoid pitfalls that you might otherwise encounter.

2. Look for Higher Funds from Operations (FFO) Margins

One of the most-watched metrics for traditional stocks is earnings per share (EPS). This is the amount of earnings an investor is entitled to per share of the company they own. But for REITs, you instead use something called "funds from operations" (FFO). Unlike EPS, FFO includes depreciation and more accurately shows a REIT's bottom line. Just like a higher net income margin is attractive for most stocks, the same logic applies to higher FFO margins.

Hence, when looking for REITs, I'd gravitate to businesses with consistently higher FFO margins. You can find this information in a REIT's 10-K.

3. Determine the REIT's Funds from Operations (FFO) Payout Ratio

Much like a traditional payout ratio that uses earnings per share, funds from operations (FFO) payout ratio tells you how much of a REIT's FFO is spent on a dividend.

When it comes to dividends, I always look for the safest option. That means I only buy REITs with an FFO payout ratio below 80%. You can find FFO payout ratio information in the REIT's 10-K.

How to Trade a REIT

Once you've found a REIT that meets the previously mentioned criteria, dollar-cost average into your position. This is to make sure you get into the position at the best possible price.

Compared to other strategies in this book, REITs are a relatively low-risk endeavor. Depending on how your portfolio is constructed, allocating 5% to REITs makes sense.

Once you open your position, you'll want to keep track of how your REIT does each quarter. After all, if the FFO margin or payout ratio begins to decline, you may want to reconsider holding the REIT. That's especially true if the secular trend you're investing in also starts to falter.

Investing Quick-Start Guide:
REAL ESTATE INVESTMENT TRUSTS (REITs)

1. After buying the REIT from your broker, dollar-cost average into the position.

2. After buying, if the position is in an uptrend, buy and hold. Periodically monitor the REIT to make sure it is moving in the right direction (i.e., higher).

3. Sell only if something fundamentally changes with the REIT.

CHAPTER 9

Alternative Assets

An alternative asset is any investment that doesn't include stocks, bonds, or other "traditional" assets like cash. While the term casts a wide umbrella, some of the most popular alternative assets include things like memorabilia and fine art. To avoid losing money in this high-risk, high-reward asset class, I'd recommend reviewing this chapter closely.

As a youngster growing up in Northeast Ohio, I was obsessed with baseball. At the time, my hometown Cleveland Indians (now the Guardians) were one of the hottest teams in baseball, making it to the World Series twice (before losing in classic Cleveland sports fashion). Sports were everything to me and my friends, and naturally we started collecting sports trading cards and other collectibles.

But it wasn't only because we loved these sports stars; we were convinced that the cards would be "worth" something one day. In my mind, owning these collectibles was a surefire way of making money in the future. Whether it was my Ken Griffey Jr. rookie card, first edition Charizard Pokémon card, or vintage Star Wars action figures (in the box, of course), the idea that a collectible could be worth more in the future was innate.

As I grew older, I put away these childish things. Many of these items were sold at garage sales or collected dust in my parents' attic. Little did I know that many of these collectible items actually would be worth money one day. In fact, the increase in value of some of these items would even outpace the S&P 500.

Collectibles, wine, and fine art fall into a broad investment bucket known as "alternative assets." If you learn how to invest in this asset class responsibly, you can earn great returns.

MEMORABILIA

WHAT IS MEMORABILIA?

One of the hottest alternative asset classes right now is memorabilia. Memorabilia is any object that people save for historical preservation. Like my Ken Griffey Jr. rookie card, collectors save and treasure these objects as a reminder of the people they admire. Whether it's a home run ball caught at a World Series game or a Michael Jordan rookie card, this $5.4 billion market has been making investors rich for years.

There are typically two types of memorabilia investors. First, there are the amateurs who collect for sentimental reasons. They have a nostalgic connection with a physical piece of history, and to fully express that nostalgia, they buy a piece of memorabilia. While they usually don't have access to the high-end memorabilia market, amateurs are able to afford minor pieces.

Then you have the second type of investor: wealthy individuals. These high-end collectors bid on pieces of memorabilia at auction houses like Christie's. The goal is to diversify their investment portfolios with the expectation that the pieces will increase in value.

Whether you're an amateur or high-end collector, it's never been easier to invest in alternative assets like memorabilia. That's especially true since this trend kicked into high gear during the COVID-19 pandemic. With so many people cooped up inside for long stretches of time, many began sifting through old boxes in search of memorabilia. Now that online auction houses on eBay, Collectable, and others are more accessible than ever, it's never been easier to match buyers with sellers.

What's astonishing are the returns on memorabilia. For instance, PWCC—a leading marketplace for trading cards—publishes a Top 100 Index for the most valuable trading cards. Between 2008 and 2020, the Top 100 Index cards returned a whopping 264%—compare that to the S&P 500 return of 110% over the same period. Other memorabilia indexes like the GCI 250 display similar returns. Since its advent in March 2018, the index is up 71%, which is roughly equal to the S&P 500 return of 68%.

In short, the broader memorabilia market has delivered solid risk-adjusted returns over the last decade.

Money Talks in the Memorabilia Market

Many of these pieces in the memorabilia market are selling for millions. For instance, here are the top five most expensive pieces of sports memorabilia:

- Original Olympic Games manifesto: $8.8 million
- Babe Ruth 1928–1930 jersey: $5.6 million
- Babe Ruth 1920 jersey: $4.4 million
- James Naismith 1891 Rules of Basketball: $4.3 million
- Daniel Lucius Adams's Rules of Baseball: $3.2 million

Multimillion-dollar prices would typically price most investors out of the market. After all, not many individual investors have $3.2 million to spend on a century-old piece of paper. However, with the advent of something called "fractionalization," anyone can own a piece of these timeless heirlooms.

For example, let's say that we have two investors: Reginald and Joe.

Reginald is a portfolio manager for a multimillion-dollar sports, media, and entertainment hedge fund. His job is to go around and acquire rare pieces of memorabilia for his fund to hold. This gives his fund's investors access to rare items, thereby diversifying their portfolios. Because Reginald has deep-pocketed investors, he's able to buy the rarest collectibles and wholly own them via his fund. When the value of these collectibles rises, so does the net asset value (NAV) of his fund, which pleases his investors.

Now, Reginald's portfolio is worth $20 million. Since the value of these assets keeps rising, he expects them to deliver returns that beat the S&P 500 for the next decade.

On the other end of the spectrum you have Joe. The middle-aged New York native has always been a fan of collecting baseball cards. During his 20 years of collecting cards, he's accumulated a number of rare cards, including a LeBron James rookie card he found in a pawn shop years ago. While he's spent much of his expendable income on collecting cards since he was a kid, Joe's portfolio of cards is worth a mere $5,000.

Here we have two people doing the exact same thing: collecting memorabilia. The only difference is that one is better capitalized than the other, allowing him to take advantage of more lucrative opportunities in the memorabilia market.

While this is the way the memorabilia market (and many other alternative asset markets) worked for years, technology platforms have leveled the playing field.

Technology and Memorabilia Are Merging

Let's introduce a new player into the memorabilia market: twenty-three-year-old Asher. Asher has long been a fan of investing in the memorabilia market. Unlike both the hedge funder Reginald and the individual investor Joe, Asher invests in the memorabilia market using a service called Traceable.

Traceable offers *fractionalization* of the memorabilia market. For instance, when an investor wants to invest in a share of a small-capitalization stock like Etsy Inc. (ETSY), that investor never considers buying the entire company. Instead, Etsy sells "shares" in its company. This allows anyone to have access to this market. Unlike many pieces of memorabilia, Etsy has fractionalized its capital structure to attract more investors.

The same concept is used in Traceable. Let's say Asher is a huge fan of Michael Jordan. He heard of a card that has a piece of Jordan's jersey in it, which is now selling for $37,000. Asher is just out of college and clearly cannot afford a $37,000 purchase. However, just like investors who can buy shares or "fractions" of Etsy's business, Asher can buy a fraction of this Michael Jordan card. In fact, Asher can invest as little as $25 and own a piece of his favorite playing card.

While Traceable is a fictional fractionalization company, there are tons of new companies offering this service today (we'll discuss the specifics later in this chapter). First, I want to tell you a story of how some lucky investors hit it big during the latest memorabilia boom.

CASE STUDY:

THE BALLAD OF BRADY HILL

Every asset class has a leader. Whether it's Jeffrey Gundlach in the bond market, Warren Buffett in value stocks, or Cathie Wood in high-growth stocks, each investment has their standard-bearer that fellow investors look to for guidance and wisdom. In the memorabilia market, that person is Brady Hill.

Like many investors in the collectibles market, Hill got his start collecting baseball cards as a youth. He was a huge fan of New York Mets slugger Darryl Strawberry. Thinking he was going to be the next big thing, Hill started collecting all of the Darryl Strawberry memorabilia he could find. That was until his dad gave him sage advice: Sell the Darryl Strawberry cards and buy Mickey Mantle.

Hill was initially put off by his dad's advice. At the time, it looked like Strawberry was set to be the next big thing in baseball. In that event, didn't it make sense to stock up on his memorabilia now while it's cheap? Begrudgingly, Hill took his father's advice and sold his Darryl Strawberry memorabilia and bought a Mickey Mantle card.

This turned out to be great investment advice. While interest in Strawberry's memorabilia took a dive after a drug possession suspension in the middle of his career, the allure of Mickey Mantle continued to grow.

The Birth of "The Kid"

During a visit to the National Sports Collectors Convention as a youth, Hill was one of the few youngsters to have his own table. This quickly earned him the nickname "The Kid," because not many other kids had the quality cards he displayed on his table.

Hill got so good at collecting that he ended up selling his entire collection to buy his first car. Then he put himself through Louisiana State University. The only card Hill decided to keep was a 1954 Topps Hank Aaron rookie card; at the time, Aaron was Major League Baseball's all-time home run leader.

Like many kids making the transition into adulthood, Hill set aside his collecting hobby. He focused on starting his own T-shirt printing business called Greensource. Nearly a decade later, Greensource became one of the largest T-shirt printing companies in the US.

As it turned out, Hill was destined to be a collector. In the mid-2010s, fate would bring him back in touch with his childhood passion.

"The Kid" Returns

During a move to New York, Hill went through an old safe deposit box. In that box was the Hank Aaron rookie card he decided to keep when he went off to college.

He sent the card to get "graded" by a professional. This is a process whereby a third-party assesses the condition of an item. All rare collectibles are ranked on a numerical grading system. Once the grade is established, the collectible is sealed so it can never be corrupted by human oils again. After Hill sent in his Hank Aaron card, the company graded it a 7.

Hill quickly listed the card online. Instead of selling it directly, he ended up trading another collector for a 1969 Topps Mickey Mantle rookie card. At the time, the Mantle card was worth more than the Aaron.

From there, Hill went on a buying spree. He took his father's advice and didn't chase shiny new collectibles. Instead, he stuck with tried-and-true cards such as the vintage prewar sets, the 1914 Cracker Jack collection, and the high-grade Babe Ruth rookie cards.

Hill continued to acquire more and more rare cards. When the trading card boom took off in 2020, Hill's longtime hobby turned into a big investing win. Now his card collection is valued in the multimillions.

INVESTMENT STRATEGY:
MEMORABILIA

Investing in the collectibles market definitely falls under the high-risk, high-reward investing umbrella. At the highest level, investors are making huge bets on the trajectory of assets that are little known outside their tight-knit communities. These multimillion-dollar transactions reflect how strongly investors believe in the long-term trajectory of the market.

How to Identify a Good Memorabilia Investment

The advent of fractionalization in the collectibles market has opened up an entirely new market for investors. Those retail investors with smaller bank accounts can now participate in the upward momentum in the collectibles market. Now that the COVID-19 lockdowns have kicked this alternative asset class into high gear, the near-term picture looks bright for investors.

However, fractionalization has not changed how you assess which collectibles to buy. In fact, the lessons that Brady Hill learned from his father early on in his career still ring true today. Here are some tips to follow.

1. Stick to the Classics

When "The Kid" was starting his investing journey, he nearly made a fatal error in the collectibles market: He went for the "new" thing. He figured that Darryl Strawberry would be the next big thing in baseball and wanted to go all in. If he had done this, his collectibles would've lost nearly all their value, as Strawberry would eventually tarnish his career and thus the value of his collectibles.

Instead, Hill's father pushed him to buy "classic" collectibles like the Hank Aaron and Mickey Mantle rookie cards.

When choosing a collectible to buy—whether fully or via a fractionalization platform—always stick to tried-and-true collectibles. A home run ball or jersey from Babe Ruth will always retain its value and likely grow even *more* valuable over time. By sticking to these classics, you eliminate a major risk associated with investing in collectibles.

2. Invest Only in "Mint" Items

When searching for collectibles to buy, keep your focus on "mint" or pristine items. These museum-quality items hold their value much better than their worn counterparts.

Investors should pay close attention to the "grade" issued for each item. Once an item is graded and sealed, there is less ambiguity in its value. I'd recommend investing only in collectibles with a grade of 8.0 or higher.

GRADE YOUR ITEMS

In the event you've bought or discovered a collectible that has value, you may want to get it graded immediately. Each type of collectible has its own grading agency. For instance, the prime grader for sports cards is PSA, while the premier comic book graders are CGC and CBCS.

As I said earlier, I'd avoid buying ungraded items. It's best to stick with collectibles that have years of provenance and have been thoroughly vetted before purchasing.

3. Invest Only in Scarce Items

Whether it's baseball cards or non-fungible tokens (which we'll cover in Chapter 11), the key to any collectible's value is its scarcity. If there are fewer items in existence, it is more likely that it will retain its value.

That is a concept you see across the economic spectrum. For instance, one of the central bullish cases for bitcoin is that the cryptocurrency has a 21 million supply limit. The same can be said for gold, as 244,000 tonnes have been discovered, which would fit stacked back-to-back in two city buses.

When choosing your collectible, make sure to find scarce items with only a few in existence. This could be something like the golf ball Tiger Woods hit to clinch his first Masters championship, or the ball that Hank Aaron hit to take the top spot on the all-time home run list. These are the kinds of items you want in your collection.

How to Trade Memorabilia

Those who want to trade collectibles fall into two camps: wholesalers and fractional buyers.

Wholesalers

For wholesalers—or those buying the entire collectible—do your homework and check all the earlier boxes before making your purchase. Once you've verified the item is classic, in mint condition, and scarce, you want to make sure your collectible is stored in ideal conditions.

Some items—like baseball cards—need to be stored in low-humidity environments to avoid cracking the card. If you don't follow this advice, the value of the piece may erode over time. You will probably need to sit on your collectible for many years before it appreciates in value, so proper storage is key. For those who want to dig deeper into the collectibles market, I'd recommend reading *Kovels' Guide to Selling, Buying, and Fixing Your Antiques and Collectibles.*

Fractional Buyers

Fractional buyers have a much easier road. For one, those buying fractional pieces of collectibles operate in a much more liquid market. As we've discussed a few times in this book, lack of liquidity can be a major hurdle for investors looking to sell their investments. Collectibles—unlike stocks and bonds—are illiquid since there are only a few buyers and sellers. In fact, once you hit collectibles over $10,000, the market for buyers and sellers shrinks significantly.

For those buying and selling fractional amounts of collectibles, however, the market has much more liquidity. To become a fractional buyer, you need to sign up for a sports memorabilia exchange like Collectable, Otis Wealth, Rally, or Dibbs.

Once you've found a collectible that's classic, mint, and scarce, allocate roughly 1% of your portfolio to the asset. While collectibles do offer upside, it's best to keep these investments small since there's a chance the asset could stagnate and never generate the gains you expect. By keeping your investments small and manageable, you get the potential upside of a high-risk, high-reward investment without tying up capital in an asset that doesn't generate any investment income. In addition, ideally, you'll diversify into multiple collectibles to give exposure to potential upside in different assets like trading cards, classic cars, and comic books.

Investing Quick-Start Guide:
MEMORABILIA

1. Take the time to study the memorabilia you are interested in. You don't want to make the rookie mistake of overpaying for an item. Do your due diligence.

2. Speak to investors and collectors to learn which items are most popular, and what is considered a good price. Put another way, do your research.

3. It's important that you do not get emotional about any item. Most importantly, don't fall in love with a particular piece, or you may overpay.

4. The key is to learn how an item is graded. Aim to buy pieces with higher ratings (8.0 or higher is the best) and lower prices. This means patiently waiting for the right piece to appear. Stick to the "classics," and it is hard to go wrong.

5. It's better to have a few pristine items than many mediocre ones. Focus on buying items in mint condition. Even better, find items that are scarce. You should be able to sell them for top dollar.

6. Be sure to store the item in a safe place. It's essential that it retains its value, which also means taking good care of it. Some collectibles, like baseball cards, need low-humidity environments.

FINE ART

WHAT IS FINE ART?

Investing is all about parking your money somewhere today so that you can take more money out in the future. While many investors choose to focus on traditional assets like stocks, bonds, and commodities, alternative assets like fine art can give investors diversification not found in traditional assets.

This isn't a new concept. For example, think about the Medici family in Florence, Italy. The family amassed a huge fortune in the 15th century thanks to its double-entry bookkeeping system. By the end of his life, Cosimo de' Medici—the patriarch of the family—was one of the wealthiest people in Italy.

While his lineage included four popes, his most well-known investment was in the arts. To this day, the art collection accumulated by the Medici family—including works by Michelangelo, Raphael, and da Vinci—is housed in the Uffizi Gallery in Florence. Many of these works are considered priceless and have maintained their value over the last 500 years.

The Medicis of today also use art as an investment.

Some Investments Never Go Out of Style

In the 2010s, there was a resurgence in art as an investment. Within a couple of years, some of the biggest art collectors in the world were hedge fund managers. The irony was not lost on me; these were the world's best investors, and they saw an opportunity to enhance the returns of their own portfolios in an area not traditionally associated with Wall Street.

Near the top of that list is billionaire fund manager Steve Cohen. As the head of family office Point72, Cohen has added works by Picasso, Andy Warhol, and Jeff Koons to his billion-dollar art portfolio.

And he's not alone. Billionaire fund manager Dan Loeb is also a patron of the arts. Not only does Loeb have rare works from Basquiat, Mike Kelley, and Richard Prince in his collection; he also acquired a 9.3% stake in one of the most exclusive auction houses in the world—Sotheby's.

I make a habit out of tracking the moves of the world's best investors. When you look at the data, it makes sense that these fund managers are piling into the art market. Since 1995, the contemporary art market has returned 14% per year. That's nearly double the return on the S&P 500 and triple the return on US government bonds.

Not only are returns higher, but the $70 billion fine art market also offers investors of all stripes a novel way to diversify their investments. Compared to bonds, the returns on art are often superior depending on interest rates.

Plus, it's never been easier for individual investors to participate in the art market.

Average Joes in the Fine Art Market

At the highest end of the art market, you have recent painting sales like Leonardo da Vinci's *Salvator Mundi* and Picasso's *Young Girl with a Flower Basket*, which sold for $450 million and $115 million, respectively.

Most people don't have hundreds of millions lying around to invest in the art market. In fact, the best approach to investing in fine art is to make it 5% of your total portfolio. With the advent of fractionalization (discussed earlier in this chapter), the dream of owning a piece of fine art has become a reality even for the non-superwealthy. Platforms like Masterworks, Yieldstreet, and others give investors the option to buy a sliver of a million-dollar work of art.

For instance, let's say that the Masterworks management team acquires a piece of art from the artist Banksy. The work shows a silhouette of the *Mona Lisa* holding an AK-47 machine gun and a target in the center of her forehead. Masterworks pays $250,000 for the piece and holds the physical painting in their vaults.

Banksy is one of the most famous artists of the 21st century. His work appears in galleries all over the world and—while he's anonymous—his work is beloved. While a collector like Loeb or Cohen can spend $250,000 on a piece of art, the average Joe does not have that type of expendable income.

That's where fractionalization enters the equation. Many of these websites have minimum investments (usually $1,000), so investors can buy "pieces" of their favorite artwork. Instead of owning an entire Banksy for $250,000, you can own 1% of the work for $2,500. That's the power of fractionalization.

The best part is that you can trade your position like a stock. That means if the value of the Banksy work underlying your position rises 100% to $500,000, your position—which is now worth $5,000—can be easily sold.

Unlike the traditional art market, fractionalization platforms provide liquidity to a formerly illiquid market. As I'm about to show you, those with a keen eye for the art market can make loads of money using these platforms.

A PENSION FUND DIVES INTO THE ART MARKET

One of the oldest retirement structures is known as a "pension plan," or "defined benefit plan." These plans are employer-sponsored retirement plans that pay employees after they complete their employment. The employer is responsible for managing and maintaining the plan. After the employee retires, the employee (or their surviving spouse if they die) receives monthly payments for life.

While pensions are often associated with blue-collar workers like teachers and police officers, they represent a massive amount of assets. For instance, the California Public Employees' Retirement System (CalPERS) managed nearly $500 billion in assets in 2020. That was nearly 3 times larger than the assets managed for Ray Dalio's Bridgewater Associates, the largest hedge fund in the world.

Those managing pension funds are typically risk-averse investors. The goal is to generate market returns of 7%–8%, growing their asset base in order to fund the retirements of hundreds of thousands of workers. While safe investments are the norm, some pension systems—like the British Rail Pension Fund—break the mold and invest in alternative assets like fine art.

Sotheby's to the Rescue

In 1974, many developed economies were experiencing rapid inflation. That included the United Kingdom, whose inflation rate was as high as 17%. Inflation rates of this magnitude presented issues for pension funds, which had to invest loads of cash every month. If inflation was eating away at their purchasing power, they needed to experiment with other methods of generating returns.

That pushed British Rail Pension Fund managers to delve into an alternative asset class: fine art. The fund decided to invest £40 million ($70 million)—or 3% of the fund holdings—into a basket of different pieces of fine art. The fund partnered with famed auction house Sotheby's, which agreed to help the fund identify artworks that would increase in value. In exchange, the pension fund would run any acquisitions and sales of fine art through Sotheby's.

The fund went on a buying spree. With the help of Sotheby's, they purchased 2,400 pieces of Chinese porcelain, African tribal art, Impressionist paintings, and a host of objects made from precious metals.

The Grand Experiment Comes to an End

While inflation cooled in the early 1980s, the art market continued to boom. Impressionist paintings from artists like Vincent van Gogh saw a resurgence in demand. This was partially fueled by Japanese art buyers, who flocked to art because of a favorable currency environment following an international agreement known as the Plaza Accord.

This was all great news for the British Rail Pension Fund. After acquiring a wide-ranging collection between 1974 and 1980, the value of their pieces surged. While the fund began selling off its assets in the early 1990s, the art collection returned 13.1% per year between 1974 and 1999. That bested even the S&P 500 over the same period.

The gains were fueled by its highest-quality holdings, including the Impressionist paintings and works from Pablo Picasso. On the other hand, rare coins and European paintings—a more niche market—performed poorly and dragged down the overall returns. According to Sotheby's, the fund's Impressionist collection's return between 1974 and 1990 was a whopping 400%!

While the British Rail Pension Fund's managers claimed they would never invest their pension assets in art again, one thing was clear: The first large-scale investment in the art market by a public fund was a success.

INVESTMENT STRATEGY:

FINE ART

The British Rail Pension Fund experiment would be difficult for an individual investor to re-create. The fund had nearly unlimited capital to invest in a wide variety of different collections. This means they could afford the best items across the entire market. The pension fund also had the assistance of Sotheby's, one of the most respected art houses in the world. Still, other opportunities are available for an average investor—we'll cover those in this section.

How to Identify a Good Fine Art Investment

Some would contend that—while art is clearly a great high-risk, high-reward investment—the capital requirements needed to make it worth your while are simply too high. While I understand this conclusion, fractionalization of art on platforms like Masterworks and Yieldstreet has leveled the playing field. If you apply the lessons of the British Rail Pension Fund to these novel platforms, you, too, can generate great returns in the art market.

1. Prioritize Quality over Quantity

When the British Rail Pension Fund decided to break into the art market, they bought a diversified basket of different artists and collections. This is a classic investing approach, as you don't want to put all your eggs in one basket.

Although I'm a fan of diversification in most asset classes, I would not necessarily want you to sacrifice investing in quality art for the opportunity to spread your bets among less-rare pieces. For instance, the best-performing artworks for the fund were classics by well-known artists like Van Gogh, Picasso, and Renoir. When these pieces were first acquired, they were already household names that only became more famous as time went on. According to Sotheby's, 86% of Andy Warhol's pieces sold at auction have increased in value by 14% between 2003 and 2017.

Name recognition matters in the art world. While it can be tempting to "buy low" on a lesser-known artist, history shows it's better to pay more for an established artist.

2. Hold for the Long Term

Many of the chapters in this book show you how to invest in assets that deliver quick returns. In the art world, however, patience is a virtue.

For instance, there is a famous saying related to art investing that goes, "You get your money back in five years, it doubles in ten years, and multiplies thereafter." You may not see great returns in the first few years of your investment. It's possible it will stagnate and even underperform. But—as we saw in the British Rail Pension Fund example—the long-term returns are hard to argue with.

This is especially true for those collectors looking to delve into the illiquid physical art world, as it can take years for a work to sell at auction.

3. Remember: The Rarer the Better

One issue the British Rail Pension Fund ran into was the low returns on its rare coins. While rare coins certainly have their own niche market, the problem is that these items are not scarce. There are hundreds if not thousands of rare coins in existence, which can drive down their overall value.

On the other hand, there is only one *Jim Crow*, the 1986 painting by renowned artist Jean-Michel Basquiat. This "scarcity" increases the artwork's value, in contrast to how the "excess" number of rare coins limits their value.

How to Trade Fine Art

Investors looking to enter the lucrative high-risk, high-reward world of art investing should first research the art market you want to invest in. For instance, the demand for Chinese antiques is wildly different than the market for digital art like non-fungible tokens (which we will cover in Chapter 11). You should familiarize yourself with the major players in each art market, historical price trends, and other factors that drive sales in the market.

Once you have found an art market you're comfortable with, I would recommend allocating no more than 5% of your investable assets to art. This is much easier if you're using fractional services like Masterworks, Yieldstreet, or Otis, as you can buy stakes in multiple works and diversify your bets.

After you have built up your position, simply hold it for many years. If you're investing in high-quality art (e.g., Picassos, Basquiats, Warhols, etc.), there is little downside risk. However, there's a good chance the value of this art will not appreciate for many years. While it can be frustrating to see your investment not move around much, trust that the long-term growth outlook in demand for high-quality art is bright.

Investing Quick-Start Guide:
FINE ART

1. Do your research by visiting galleries or art shows such as Art Basel in a city near you. Search online for artists or art that appeals to you. Art is very personal; be sure to find art that "speaks" to you. Make a list of the artists that you like.

2. Be on the lookout for sales or limited-edition projects from the artists that you follow. Decide if you want works created by "emerging" or "established" artists.

3. Focus on higher-quality pieces and be selective about potential purchases.

4. Sign up for fractionalization platforms like Masterworks, Yieldstreet, or Otis to diversify your holdings.

5. Plan to hold any purchases for the very long term (i.e., years or decades).

CHAPTER 10

Day Trading Strategies

"Day trading" refers to any strategies that involve holding an asset for less than a day. It is a notoriously difficult way to trade, as investors often succumb to their emotions, causing them to make rash decisions (and lose money in the process). However, if you use the tools in this chapter, you will drastically increase your odds of having success using this high-risk, high-reward strategy.

When people first start investing, many want to be day traders; there's a certain mystique associated with the term. Day traders rarely hold long-term positions and primarily depend on technical analysis to gain an edge in the market.

Many new investors see day traders in movies and social media and assume that's how investing works. That couldn't be further from the truth. In fact, the most proven way to create wealth in the stock market is to hold strong companies over many years and let their gains compound. As Warren Buffett said, "Our favorite holding period is forever." This time-tested buy-and-hold strategy is the approach that most investors are wise to adopt.

Nonetheless, I know that many of you want to learn how to day trade. That is why a book on high-risk, high-reward investing is the perfect place to discuss this strategy.

Before we discuss it, however, you need to know the truth: Studies show that only a small percentage of day traders generate meaningful income. The data can vary, but most imply that one in five day traders fail within their first year. That's roughly double the failure rate for college and 3 times higher than the first-year failure rate for restaurants.

There have certainly been day traders over the years who have had lots of success. I'm going to show you how they did it and—maybe—you can do it too.

The following are three popular short-term intraday trading strategies that you should consider. I begin by showing you how to take advantage of earnings surprises.

EARNINGS SURPRISES

WHAT ARE EARNINGS SURPRISES?

Every 3 months, US publicly traded companies report their quarterly financial results. These results greatly affect stock prices. A report of an "earnings surprise" to the upside can be a boon for the shares. Conversely, an earnings disappointment to the downside can tank a company's stock overnight. Trying to predict whether a stock will "beat" or "miss" is a common day trading strategy.

As we've covered multiple times in this book, stocks are priced based on their earnings. Whether it's the expectation of how much a stock will grow in the future or previous earnings performance, earnings and the "earnings multiple" are the keys to understanding what drives stock market returns.

For instance, let's say Microsoft (MSFT) shares are trading at $300 per share. The company generated $8 in earnings per share over the last year. That means that Microsoft shares trade at a *trailing earnings multiple* of 37.5 ($300 / $8).

When it comes to investing, you shouldn't care as much about what a company did in the past. Instead, you want to focus on where the company is headed. That's why analysts use something called "forward earnings multiples." This is the multiple that investors believe that a company such as Microsoft will trade at in the future. Generally, the forward earnings multiple will be lower than the trailing multiple. That's because forward multiples are calculated based on a company's earnings projections and are thus not as reliable as trailing earnings.

For instance, let's stay with the earlier example, in which Microsoft earned $8 in earnings per share last year. By next year, the "consensus analyst" opinion is that the company will increase earnings 12% to $9 per share. If the stock is still trading at $300, that means Microsoft trades at a *trailing earnings per share* of 37.5 ($300 / 8) and a *forward earnings per share* of 33.3 ($300 / $9).

Here's Where Things Get Interesting

We now understand how stocks are priced based on earnings, trailing multiples, and forward multiples. Let's return to the previous example. Microsoft trades at $300 with the consensus analyst estimates claiming the company will earn $9 in earnings per share next year. It's now "earnings day," and traders are patiently waiting after the market closes to see how Microsoft performed this quarter.

There are three things that can happen:

1. First, Microsoft releases their earnings report and it shows that the company met its consensus analyst estimate of $9. Since this was expected by the market, the stock is flat after hours. There was no earnings *surprise* so the stock is priced as it should be.
2. Second, there's another scenario known as an "earnings miss." Let's say that when Microsoft releases its financial statements, the company reveals that a major decline in cloud computing revenue weighed on its earnings performance. As a result, Microsoft's earnings per share came in at $6. This would set off a firestorm for Microsoft stock. Since analysts were expecting earnings per share of $9 and the actual figure came in 33% lower, that means that Microsoft "missed estimates." This is also known as an "earnings miss." Since investors hate to be surprised with bad news, in this example the market punishes Microsoft's shares by sending them down 15% the following day.
3. A third scenario that can unfold is an "earnings surprise." Analysts are expecting Microsoft to deliver $9 in earnings per share. But let's say that a surge in demand for Microsoft Office software last quarter caused earnings per share to surge to $12 per share. This means that Microsoft surprised analysts with better-than-expected news.

Instead of an *earnings miss* that caused Microsoft shares to sink, an *earnings surprise* causes Microsoft shares to surge. Since the company topped estimates by 33%, Microsoft's "forward earnings" estimate also rises, which causes the share price to surge by 15%.

What Has Your Company Done for Me Lately?

Keep in mind that the Microsoft example is simplified. There are a multitude of factors that can impact a company's share price after earnings are released other than earnings per share.

For instance, to spur an upside move in a stock, a company can do something known as "raise guidance." This is when a company announces that their internal calculations show that the company will make more money than expected in future quarters. Analysts like to see a company's business accelerate at a faster pace than investors or the company had expected, as it's a good sign the business is performing well.

However, the flip side is also true. Even if a company "beats" estimates on both revenue and earnings per share, it will all be for naught if the company lowers guidance.

In the end, the investing community cares about what happens in the *future*, not in the *past*. That said, being able to predict if a business is performing better than what the investment community or the "consensus" is currently forecasting can be a profitable (yet difficult) investment strategy.

That's why there are a ton of companies offering services to help investors forecast such "earnings beats."

CASE STUDY:

PROFITING FROM "THE EYE IN THE SKY"

Hedge funds and analysts are always looking for ways to gain an edge over their competitors. Early in my career, I heard stories of hedge funds that sent junior analysts to count cars every evening at companies they were researching. The idea was that each car represented a fixed dollar amount the company was earning.

If each car is worth $50 and 50,000 cars visit a store per quarter, that means the store generates $2.5 million. If the company has fifty stores, that implies a revenue estimate of $125 million in revenue for the quarter. If that figure was above analyst estimates, the hedge fund would open a large position in the company in anticipation of an earnings surprise. But if it was below estimates, the same hedge fund would initiate a short position.

The problem with this approach is that it takes a lot of manpower. Sending a highly paid analyst out to count cars in a parking lot isn't necessarily the best use of that analyst's time. As with many things these days, technology has made this process much easier.

Capitalizing on the "Alternative Data" Boom

James Crawford got his start in tech working at Google. His role was to develop an artificial intelligence (AI) model that allowed Google to scan millions of books and make them searchable. He quickly learned the value of the technology, which could be used to scan satellite imagery as well.

Armed with his idea, Crawford left Google in the early 2010s to start a new company, Orbital Insight. The company was at the forefront of something known as "alternative data." During the 2010s, stock market indexing had become very popular, as hedge funds kept underperforming the S&P 500. In fact, between 2009 and 2014, hedge funds underperformed the S&P 500 every year.

Crawford's customers included several multibillion-dollar hedge funds. These major players were searching for any possible edge.

That's exactly what Crawford provided. His company sold a detailed analysis of cornfields to predict how much a crop would yield (i.e., crop yield). This directly impacted the commodities market, where many hedge funds traded futures. Orbital Insight satellites also analyzed imagery of dozens of Chinese cities to give traders independent data on the strength of the Chinese property market. In the same way that hedge funds sent analysts to count cars at stores, Crawford's satellites measured the number of cars at Walmart and Home Depot to estimate demand.

Orbital Sets Its Sights on a Clothing Store

The first major test of Crawford's technology came in November 2014 with an analysis on discount clothing company Ross Stores. The company was slated to report earnings in November, and Orbital had been monitoring activity at multiple Ross Stores parking lots.

According to the company's analysis, Orbital Insight expected the firm to generate revenue above the consensus analyst estimate of $2.55 billion. According to Orbital Insight's research, Ross Stores' revenue would be closer to $2.56 billion. While that may seem small, this translates to a "top line beat" and can cause a jump in the share price.

That's exactly what happened: Ross Stores' revenue estimates came in even higher than Orbital Insight's forecast with a figure of $2.6 billion. This proof-of-concept was a major turning point for the alternative data industry. By 2018, funds were spending as much as $650 million on alternative data with the industry growing at 75% per year.

The results were hard to deny. According to a study from Greenwich Associates, 72% of investment firms claimed that alternative data not only improved their analysis; it also helped generate 20% of their returns.

INVESTMENT STRATEGY:
EARNINGS SURPRISES

You probably don't have millions to shell out to an alternative data company such as Orbital Insight. The company's customers are mainly well-capitalized hedge funds with plenty of money to throw at finding an earnings surprise. But this section can help you make the most of opportunities that are out there for an investor like you.

How to Identify a Good Earnings Surprise

Individual investors are certainly not completely helpless when it comes to finding earnings surprises. As is common in the legend of David versus Goliath, individual investors often have an advantage over their larger peers when investing. They can be nimbler and have more real-world experience than institutional money managers.

If you use the following parameters, you should drastically increase the odds of making money on an earnings surprise.

1. Look for Stocks with a History of Earnings and Sales Surprises

One of the best research firms for locating company earnings history is Zacks .com. Leonard Zacks, the founder, surmised that companies that have delivered earnings surprises in the past are likely to repeat the feat in the future.

The perfect way for an investor to find companies that have consistently delivered earnings surprises to the upside is to see which companies have done so in the past. You want to find stocks that have surprised multiple years in a row, with the earnings often coming in double the estimates.

2. Avoid Stocks with Inconsistent Earnings History

It's in a company's best interest to deliver earnings surprises. Most companies keep their earnings estimates conservative to trigger an earnings surprise.

After all, most executives have stock and options tied to their stock performance and obviously stand to benefit from an earnings surprise.

When a company continually delivers variable earnings—whether above or below expectations—it means management is inconsistent. Investors like to see smooth and steady growth in business activity, as massive fluctuations can lead institutional buyers to hit the "sell" button.

Just as you want to focus on companies with lots of earnings surprises, you want to avoid companies with a muddy earnings history.

3. Focus on Smaller Stocks

Companies of all sizes can deliver an earnings surprise. Whether it's trillion-dollar or $1 billion market capitalization companies, most will likely see a nice bounce if they deliver an earnings surprise.

However, the subsequent gain on an earnings surprise will be much higher for a small-capitalization company. Those firms are typically under the radar relative to the trillion-dollar firms. Therefore, much of the institutional money has yet to realize the value in a small company.

You want to get in before the big institutional money flows in. That's why you'll want to keep your earnings surprise search confined to stocks between $100 million and $1 billion in market capitalization.

How to Trade an Earnings Surprise

The risks associated with using this strategy depend on whether you have a long-term or short-term time horizon for holding the position. If you're investing in a $10 billion market capitalization stock in hopes of capitalizing on an earnings surprise, the strategy is relatively low risk. Even if the surprise does not come to fruition, you are still holding a relatively large company, and shares should recover (assuming there isn't a major earnings miss).

In this scenario, allocating 3%–4% of your portfolio is fine. The more comfortable you are holding this stock for the long term, the more capital you can allocate.

On the other hand, if you are going to gamble on an earnings surprise for a stock with a $100 million capitalization, you must be more cautious. Smaller stocks are much more volatile, and an earnings miss can send shares plummeting.

If you plan to invest in a small stock with hopes of achieving an earnings surprise, limit your allocation to 1%–2% of your investment portfolio. This way you still have exposure to the upside associated with the surprise without blowing up your account if your analysis is incorrect.

If an earnings surprise occurs, you should see a strong upward move in the stock's volume. This will likely be 2–3 times more than the average daily volume. If the results are superior, you may want to hang on to this stock position for the long term. Upward earnings surprises are often a catalyst for other investors to accumulate the stock. Therefore, after the stock surges because of the surprise, the stock may continue trending higher (this is called a "post-earnings drift"). Many investors choose to "average up" their positions after a positive earnings surprise.

On the other hand, if this is simply a short-term trade, you may want to close out your position the day the earnings surprise is announced. Shares often retreat the day after a strong upward move, so it's a good idea to cut your position if you don't plan to hold for the long haul.

Investing Quick-Start Guide:
EARNINGS SURPRISES

1. Allocate no more than 4% of your portfolio to the earnings surprise strategy.

2. Find a company that you think may potentially deliver an earnings surprise, perhaps using Zacks.com.

3. After you have identified a stock candidate, use DCA to scale into the stock 3–4 weeks before the earnings announcement. It may take a couple of weeks to build up a full position.

4. Once you have the position, wait patiently for the earnings announcement.

5. If the earnings announcement is to the upside, take advantage of the surge in demand for the shares and sell. This is if you are in a short-term position and don't plan to hold the shares long-term.

6. If you are in a long-term position, hold as the trend moves higher. Use stop losses as gains are made.

SHORT SELLING

WHAT IS SHORT SELLING?

Short selling—or "shorting"—is a strategy that allows you to make money on an investment when the price falls. This is contrary to how most people invest. For instance, let's say I want to buy shares in Visa Inc. (V) because the economy is doing well. I'm convinced that more people are going to use credit cards to buy things. If I'm right, that should translate to more transaction fees for Visa (and thus higher sales and earnings), which should cause the company's share price to rise over the long term (or so I expect). To complete this trade, I buy 100 shares of Visa at $200 per share in my brokerage account and hold for years until Visa hits my target price. If my idea works and shares rise to $400 3 years later, I made a 100% return on my investment.

Shorting is the opposite of a long-only strategy. For instance, let's say that you think that people will buy fewer clothes in stores over the next 5 years. Because more people shop on e-commerce platforms, there will likely be less demand for in-person shopping. That means brick-and-mortar retailers like Children's Place (PLCE) may struggle, which should translate to a lower stock price. To test this idea, you decide to "sell short" 100 shares of Children's Place at $30 per share. If the thesis comes to fruition and shares fall to $15 years later, you close your trade with a 50% gain. The concept behind short selling is rudimentary: Instead of buying low and selling high, you are selling high with the intention of buying back lower and pocketing the difference.

While this is a general explanation of shorting, the underlying process for how this works is slightly more complex.

Stamps Are So 1900s

To "sell short" an asset, you are not simply buying a position in a stock and making money when the value falls. Instead, you are "borrowing" those shares and returning them at a lower price.

Let's use an example: Imagine that a friend of yours collects rare stamps. You believe that stamp collecting is a dying hobby and that the value of his stamps will fall. That's when you decide to sell short your friend's stamps.

To do this, you walk to your friend's house and ask if you can borrow a few of his stamps. Your friend doesn't mind, and lets you borrow several of his prized stamps for a small fee. He tells you that the market value of these stamps is currently $100, and you need to take extra good care of them since they're the nicest in his collection. You agree and take the stamps into your possession.

Unbeknownst to your friend, you take those stamps to a pawn shop and immediately sell them for the current market value of $100. Then you wait for the value of the stamps to decline. This happens sooner than you expect, as the US Postal Service announces that they will begin reissuing many of the stamps in your friend's collection. Since the stamps are now far less rare, their value plummets to $50.

You go back to the pawn shop where you sold the stamps and "buy back" the same stamps for $50. Since you sold the stamps for $100 and they're now worth $50, you pocket the $50 in profit and return the formerly rare stamps to your friend.

Investors can apply the same idea with stocks. Let's circle back to the example of Children's Place (PLCE). If you wanted to bet that the stock would fall, you would "short" the shares by borrowing shares from your broker for a small fee. If your thesis comes to fruition and shares fall, you can then "buy back" or "cover" your short position and return the shares to your broker.

While this sounds like an ideal scenario, things can also go haywire when shorting stocks.

The Great Stamp Collecting Revival

Let's go back to the stamps example. You believe the value of stamps will fall. To profit from this idea, you borrow your friend's stamps for a small fee, sell them to a pawn shop for $100, and wait for their value to decline.

But your thesis was incorrect. In fact, not long after you sell the stamps to the pawn shop, prominent *YouTube*r David Dobrik reveals that he's starting a stamp-collecting company. While he never revealed it to his fans, he's been a collector of stamps for years and wants to share his passion with the world.

Suddenly people all over the world are buying rare stamps. The value of some rare stamps doubles, perhaps even triples overnight on auction houses like eBay. Unfortunately, the stamps that you sold to the pawn shop are now worth $400. Since you believe the value will keep rising now that they have Dobrik's endorsement, you buy the stamps back, taking a 300% loss on your investment.

Shorting is one of the few strategies in investing where you can lose more than 100% of your investment. If you buy a stock at $100 and it goes to $0, you simply lose 100% of your investment. That's bad enough. But with shorting, your potential losses are infinite!

However, many of the world's most savvy investors have used shorting to generate massive gains. One such notable investing legend is Jim Chanos.

JIM CHANOS AND THE LARGEST BANKRUPTCY IN US HISTORY

One of the hottest stocks in the 1990s was an energy company called Enron. From humble beginnings in Omaha, Nebraska, Enron had grown to one of the largest companies in the world. The company was headed by Kenneth Lay, a well-connected businessman with close ties to former US presidents George H.W. Bush and his son George W. Bush.

The company made its fortune by laying pipe and electricity lines in addition to infrastructure development all over the continental US. Unlike traditional energy companies, which simply transported natural gas and oil around the country, Enron dabbled in ancillary businesses like broadband Internet and even ran a quasi–hedge fund known as Gas Bank.

In January 2000, Lay and his team announced they were going to start trading on a "high-speed fiber-optic network." Since this was near the height of the dot-com bubble, many investors cheered. At that time, nearly all Internet-related stocks surged. While Enron's stock price was $40 before this announcement, it would hit price levels as high as $90 per share in the summer of 2000.

But one hedge fund manager—Jim Chanos—noticed something was amiss with the Wall Street darling Enron.

Chanos Smells Something Fishy

Back in the 1990s, Jim Chanos was running his hedge fund, Kynikos Associates. The bespectacled Yale-educated investor started his fund in 1985 with an aim to short struggling companies into the ground.

He was having a lot of success. Chanos spotted irregularities at companies like Tyco, Drexel Burnham Lambert, and others well before Wall Street caught on. He had a knack for spotting companies whose underlying businesses seemed sketchy. When Chanos made an announcement that he intended to take a short position on a stock, the share prices of those stocks invariably fell.

Chanos first started looking into Enron in 2000 and noticed that it was strange how Enron seemed to be creating these new revenue streams out of thin air. Enron had a multitude of different businesses, from pulp futures to something called "weather risk management." To Chanos, it didn't seem feasible that any company could deal in so many disparate industries.

Chanos was suspicious when he realized Enron was using something called "mark-to-market accounting." This form of bookkeeping allows businesses to price their assets based on the future value of their accounts. Therefore, if Enron held a $50,000 futures contract in soybeans and a financial model says the contract will be worth $100,000 in the future, Enron accountants could mark the contract as a $100,000 asset on the company's balance sheet. This contrasts with "mark-to-model" accounts, which take the present value of the asset.

But this wasn't the only irregularity that made Chanos skeptical about Enron.

One of the Greatest Trades of All Time

Chanos and his team of forensic accountants uncovered troves of irregularities in Enron's financial statements. In Chanos's view, Enron was simply a giant leveraged hedge fund earning low returns on their capital.

Chanos acted on his concerns by opening a massive short position in Enron in November 2000. At the time, Enron was the darling of Wall Street and wasn't yet on any short seller's radar. As a result, it was easy for Chanos to borrow shares from brokers. Chanos believed this would be a profitable trade, and he was proved right.

A month after Chanos set up his short position, all hell broke loose. From December 2000 to December 2001, Enron's stock price went from the mid-$80s to $0. A year after Chanos initiated his short position, Enron filed for Chapter 11 bankruptcy.

As for Chanos, he pocketed over $500 million in profits, netting his firm one of the greatest trades in investing history.

INVESTMENT STRATEGY:
SHORT SELLING

Not everyone has the forensic accounting skills of Jim Chanos—but you can still find success with this investing method using the suggestions in this section.

How to Identify a Good Stock to Short

Day traders can use shorting strategies akin to those used by Chanos. Once you are given clearance from your broker, you may "sell short" a position you believe will decline in value. While the mechanics of shorting are easy, making money with this strategy is challenging.

If you're looking to make Chanos-style gains, however, you want to use the following suggestions.

1. Find a Stock with Collapsing Earnings

Not every short opportunity will be a "sexy" Enron-level fraud. Instead, most short selling opportunities are in companies whose earnings have stopped growing.

Share prices are based on a variety of factors, including how much the company earns, share supply and demand, and a company's future earnings. If you plot a stock's price and its earnings growth, they typically align over time. Companies with growing earnings tend to see their share price rise, while companies with falling earnings tend to see their share price fall.

The first thing you want to do when looking for a short is to identify a company where earnings have declined multiple years in a row. This could be due to secular trends (e.g., Amazon rendering brick-and-mortar retail obsolete) or poor management (e.g., JCPenney).

2. Look for Stocks That Benefit from One-Time Events

One of the best ways to find short ideas is to look at companies that had a recent one-time windfall. For instance, a company called Lumber Liquidators (LL) had a surge in demand after Hurricane Sandy in 2012. Investors bid up the company's stock in anticipation of the flurry in demand for lumber.

A short seller may see this as a one-time opportunity that cannot be repeated. Unless there's another hurricane, a stock such as Lumber Liquidators should "mean revert" (i.e., fall back down) once earnings normalize. By finding companies that benefited from these one-time events, you increase your odds of putting on a profitable short position.

3. Choose a Liquid Stock

If you want to initiate a short position on a company, you first need to make sure you can borrow the shares from your broker. Like the earlier example where you borrowed stamps from your friend, you need to borrow shares from a broker and pay a fee to do so.

If your short idea is popular, you may have to pay a higher fee to borrow these shares. For example, you may have to pay a "stock loan fee," which is approximately 0.5% of the amount borrowed (subject to change). The more people that short a particular stock, the more that percentage rises.

By finding a short that's under the investing community's radar, you may find it cheaper and easier to borrow the shares.

How to Trade a Short

There are multiple ways to work shorting into your investing process. First, you can go the Jim Chanos route and bet against companies you believe will fail. This process involves borrowing the shares from your broker and immediately selling them in the market.

Before you are allowed to short, you must set up a margin account with your broker. That's in addition to any other necessary permissions the broker requests. I recommend allocating not more than 3% of your investment portfolio to short positions. Your losses can balloon rather quickly if your short thesis is incorrect. By keeping your position small, you avoid wiping out your brokerage account. Keep in mind that to avoid disaster, experienced short sellers monitor their portfolios closely. They also use stop losses or option hedges to prevent a small loss from turning into a large loss.

Day traders can also short but in a different manner. For instance, if you believe the market is due for a pullback, you can "hedge" your portfolio by selling short an index ETF such as the SPDR S&P 500 ETF (SPY) or the Invesco QQQ Trust (QQQ). If you want to fully hedge your portfolio, you can short an equal amount of the S&P 500 or Nasdaq index relative to your portfolio. While you will have to pay a small fee to do so, it will be worth it if markets are in freefall and you want to keep your account hedged.

Once the dust settles and you're comfortable going "long" with stocks again, you simply close your short position with your broker.

Investing Quick-Start Guide:
SHORT SELLING

1. Because of the potential for unlimited losses, understand that shorting is a very high-risk strategy.

2. Once you have identified a potential short, ask your broker if there are enough shares available to short. If yes, allocate not more than 3% of your portfolio to this strategy.

3. To open the position, select "Sell to Open." Some brokers have a "Sell Short" tab.

4. After selling a stock short, place a 30% stop loss on the position. This is an important step, as it limits the amount you could potentially lose on the position. Managing risk is the key to success in using this strategy.

5. Even with the stop loss in place, watch the position closely.

6. If the short position is successful, move your stop loss down to lock in at least a 25% profit. As the stock falls, keep moving the stop loss lower to lock in additional gains.

7. Eventually, the stop loss will be triggered, and hopefully you have locked in a hefty gain.

8. To close the short position, select "Buy to Close."

FUTURES TRADING

WHAT IS FUTURES TRADING?

Many day traders use a strategy called "futures trading." If you thought selling short was high risk, wait until you read about trading futures. This strategy is for experienced traders only!

Here's how it works: When you own a futures contract, you agree to buy or sell a set amount of a commodity or financial asset at a specific price on a specific date in the future. The best way to illustrate what futures are and how they work is to use an example.

For instance, let's say we have two people: Gerald and Ronald. Gerald lives in Cleveland, Ohio. Every Sunday, he goes to his local Giant Eagle grocery store and buys five cans of corn. Each time Gerald arrives in the canned vegetable aisle, he sees the corn and grabs it. While the price may change by a few cents each week, the corn typically costs approximately $2 per can.

The picture is less clear for Ronald, as he's the farmer who's producing the corn Gerald is buying. Ronald owns acres of farmland in rural Ohio and sells his crops every few weeks to a processing company. That company takes Ronald's corn, processes it, cans it, and sends it off to the Giant Eagle grocery store. Soon, it's on Gerald's dinner table.

Unlike the consistent prices Gerald sees when he buys corn at Giant Eagle, the "spot price" or "cash price" for corn is volatile. Ronald, however, is harvesting most of his corn at once, along with the other farmers in his agricultural community. When everyone harvests their corn at once, the supply of corn rises quickly while demand stays constant. Every time we see this dynamic (i.e., rising supply and constant demand), the prices of those goods fall.

Even though Ronald and the rest of the farmers are harvesting at once, the processing company doesn't want to buy all the corn at once. This would entail storing the corn at their facility, which would add to the company's cost. Instead, farmers like Ronald store the corn and buy and sell their supply throughout the year.

Here's Where Futures Come Into Play

Now let's talk about how futures come into play. Instead of the farmer and food processor buying and selling corn directly, the two buy and sell corn contracts.

The food processor agrees to buy 100 bushels of corn from Ronald the farmer 6 months from now at a fixed price.

This is a mutually beneficial transaction for both parties. Ronald is able to sell a significant amount of his corn at a future date and lock in that price. And the food processor is happy to lock in that price and hedge against future swings in the price of corn. This means that neither party is stuck with whatever the market price is in the future. It also helps keep prices steady for people like Gerald, who simply want to buy corn at a stable price when needed.

What's interesting is that Ronald may enter into a futures agreement with the food processor before the corn is grown! Ronald sells a fixed amount of his anticipated harvest in the future to the food processor. That means the food processor can acquire corn at a better price, and they're happy to do so. Since Ronald can lock in that price, a collapse in the price between the contract signing and harvest won't ruin his business.

Here's where game theory comes into play. Let's say between the time the contract is signed and the sale date, a massive drought hits the Midwest. While Ronald's crop is spared, many farmers were not so lucky and therefore had lower harvests. Since the supply of corn fell and demand stayed constant, it means that the price of corn rises.

The food processor is happy he signed that futures contract, as he locked in a relatively low price months before the drought. But Ronald isn't so thrilled; corn prices have doubled since he and the food processor signed the deal, thus pushing up the potential selling price. That said, Ronald did not sell *all* his corn on that futures contract, and he still sells some of his supply at the new, higher price. This offsets some of his losses in the futures market, although he is still in the red overall.

Let's look at another scenario. Say a new technological advancement in farming doubled corn yields this year. Since the supply of corn surged and demand remained constant, the price of corn fell from the time Ronald and the food processor entered into their agreement. In this case, Ronald is happy, as he already locked the food processor into that future price. While the food processor wishes he had waited to buy his corn, he still has other farmers to buy from at the current price.

Futures As a Risk Management Tool

As the example shows, both buyers and sellers in the commodities market can use futures to *hedge* their crop. Hedging is an investment strategy that helps to offset losses or gains for a complementary investment. For Ronald and the food processor, each was trying to hedge the future buying and selling in the corn market by using futures contracts.

Traders can also use futures contracts to speculate on the movements of stock indexes, currencies, and commodities. For instance, let's say that an investor thinks that the price of silver—currently trading at $20 per ounce—is going to rise to $25 in the next 6 months. To initiate this trade, the trader buys a $25 6-month silver futures contract at a price of $5,000.

If the trader speculates correctly and the price of silver rises, that contract will also increase in value. In fact, if the price rises above $25 after 6 months, the trader can sell that contract for a tidy profit.

Let's say the trader is incorrect. Instead of rising to $25, the price of silver falls below $20 by the expiration date. In this case, the futures trader loses his entire $5,000 investment.

Futures trading is an extremely high-risk, high-reward strategy. But if used effectively—like the subject of our case study—you can learn to make money on both the upside and downside of a price swing.

CASE STUDY:

TIM LUONG AND THE "TRUMP TANTRUM"

On election night in November 2016, the US was learning that underdog presidential candidate Donald Trump would be the next president. Polling before the election showed that Trump had a minimal chance of winning. In fact, most polls gave him only a 5% chance of defeating establishment candidate Hillary Clinton.

Trump's win came as a surprise to most investors. While it looked as if Trump would win in traditionally conservative states, people were shocked to see him win the "blue wall" swing states of Wisconsin, Michigan, and Ohio.

If there's one thing that financial markets hate, it's negative surprises. It was no wonder that S&P 500 futures markets were crashing in the overnight session. While a longtime businessman, Trump was an outside figure with few connections in Washington. Nobody knew what type of policies he would implement, and without such clarity investors began to panic.

But one smart futures trader saw this unfolding and decided to act.

Striking While the Futures Irons Are Hot

Tim Luong is a twentysomething futures trader. His company, Stock Navigators—which he runs with his dad, Tom Luong—teaches individual investors about trading in the futures market.

Tim saw that the markets were incredibly volatile the night of the election. He closely tracks the S&P 500 and saw that the stock index had broken key technical levels. When that happens, it usually means that downside pressure will likely take over and push the index lower.

That's exactly what happened. Fortunately for Tim, he was short an S&P 500 futures contract. While the stock index was falling, his position was rapidly increasing in value. Once the price began to hit new levels of support and stabilize, Tim closed his short position for a massive gain.

While he'd nailed the downward move, it was his *next* action that turned this from a good trade to one of his best.

Playing Both Sides of the Field

The S&P 500 had crashed more than 5% in the overnight futures market session. Investors feared what a Trump presidency could bring and were therefore selling in a fit of panic. By the morning, however, cooler heads had prevailed. Many people realized that Trump and other Republicans were typically "pro-business" and "pro–Wall Street." Therefore, having Trump in office could be a good thing for markets.

Tim saw this dynamic unfolding as well. On the morning after Election Day, Tim went long with an S&P 500 futures contract. This was great timing as well, as the S&P 500 finished up 1.1% on the day.

All in all, Tim had played both sides of the market wagering with futures contracts. By the time he had closed the position, he had netted more than $30,000 in 2 days. This shows that if your ideas are right, and you position correctly, you can make serious money trading futures.

INVESTMENT STRATEGIES: FUTURES TRADING

There's an old saying: "Luck is when preparation meets opportunity." That is a good descriptor of how Tim Luong played both the *short* side and the *long* side during the surprise US presidential victory of Donald Trump. This section will help you invest in futures in a similarly smart way.

How to Identify a Good Futures Contract

Tim and his father had run a futures trading education company for years. He had lots of experience in this subject and was able to put that know-how to work during a very unusual bout of volatility in US stocks.

While Tim had plenty of experience and knowledge about futures before putting this trade on, it doesn't mean a less-seasoned investor couldn't do the same. If you follow the following three criteria, you can increase your odds of making money in the futures market.

1. Make Use of Technical Analysis

Before delving into this high-risk, high-reward market, make sure to have a trading plan in place. To successfully day trade in the futures market, you need to have a solid grasp of technical analysis.

Technical analysis is a trading strategy that focuses on charting and price trends to forecast where a security's price is headed. While some claim technical analysis is "voodoo," there are countless examples of successful traders who use this strategy to generate substantial returns.

When it comes to day trading in the futures market, you need to understand the patterns and other technical indicators (e.g., relative strength index [RSI], moving average convergence divergence [MACD], etc.) to be successful. Technical analysis provides day traders with a clear plan and risk management technique.

Before day trading futures, make sure to read about technical analysis and related strategies. That includes reading books like *Technical Analysis of the Financial Markets* by John J. Murphy and *All about Market Indicators* by Michael Sincere.

2. Pick One Trading Instrument

There are four standardized markets for trading futures: commodities, currencies, stock market indexes, and interest rates. Before beginning your journey day trading futures, you want to pick one of these markets and stick with it.

The best futures market for beginners is the E-mini Russell 2000 Index Futures Contract (RTY). This is a small-capitalization US stock index made up of the 2,000 smallest public companies. Because this index isn't as mainstream as the S&P 500 E-mini, most likely you will be trading against amateur investors.

The goal is to trade one security repeatedly to learn its intricacies. As you gain experience, you will see the same patterns, which you can profitably trade.

3. Understand Both Sides

Most investors tend to go for "long" stocks. This means that they buy and hold companies and expect their shares to rise over the long term. Day traders are not shackled by this long-term outlook. They trade in and out of positions in a single day, trying to exploit short-term movements in the security's price.

To be successful, day traders need to know how to play both the "long" side and the "short" side of a trade. Futures traders need to use the technical indicators to make short-term bets on a security's price action. Whether your indicators and oscillators imply the security's price is going up or down, a futures trader needs to know how to take advantage of these tools.

This is easier said than done, as traders tend to develop a bias toward either going long or going short on a security. If you want to be a top futures trader, you need to suppress or altogether eradicate that bias—whether it's for going long or short—and trade what the charts tell you.

How to Trade the Futures Market

One thing that you need to know before delving into the futures market is that futures use *leverage*. That means the gains and losses in the contracts you trade are amplified. While that does make the market riskier, it also means that you can potentially make a lot of money with only a little money.

For example, before trading one futures contract, let's say you funded your account with $15,000. With $15,000 in your account, you could buy one futures contract and potentially make a $300–$500 profit per day. If the futures contract is trading at $4,500 and moves to $4,501, you don't make $1. Instead, you make $50 because of the leverage involved with the contract.

It can also move in the other direction. If the futures contract falls from $4,500 to $4,499, you may lose $50. Leverage is one of the reasons why futures are very high risk and very high reward. Any investor's portfolio should be made up of primarily long-term positions; thus, those who want to learn futures trading should allocate no more than 5% of their investable assets to futures trading. This is important: People with smaller trading accounts—less than $25,000—should avoid futures because losing money via a leveraged trade could decimate your trading account.

Investing Quick-Start Guide:
FUTURES TRADING

Note: I can't stress enough that this is an extremely advanced strategy that takes a lot of trial and error and experience to be successful. Do not trade futures contracts unless you first learn how to day trade stocks and options. This is only an introduction to this strategy to give you an idea of what to expect if you decide to try it.

1. To trade futures, you must first find a broker that allows it (only a handful do at this time). In the United States, Interactive Brokers, TD Ameritrade, TradeStation, E-Trade, and Charles Schwab allow customers to trade futures. Ask your broker if they have a futures trading platform.

2. Allocate only a limited amount of capital to futures trading because it is extremely high risk.

3. Practice trade for as long as it takes until you are comfortable trading futures.

4. Use your brokerage scanning program to find securities and opportunistic setups (i.e., patterns). Use technical analysis to enter and exit positions and to identify overbought or oversold securities.

5. The simplest strategy is to buy oversold securities and sell when near overbought levels. Investors can measure this by looking at the 14-day relative strength index (RSI). A reading above 70 on RSI tells investors the stock is overbought and it may be time to sell. A reading below 30 means the stock is oversold, which is typically a good time to buy. Warning: Practice this strategy before using real money.

6. If there is an intraday gain, sell your position quickly. Don't forget that when day trading futures, all positions must be closed before the end of the day with no exceptions. Risk management is essential when trading futures, or when using any strategy in this book.

CHAPTER 11

Advanced Strategies

In our final chapter, we're going to cover some of the highest-risk investments currently available to individual investors. These include the buying and trading of non-fungible tokens (NFTs) and the rapidly evolving space of yield farming.

Keep in mind that this chapter was written within 12 months of these assets coming into the mainstream consciousness. By the time you read this book, it's possible that the rules of these markets (and how to successfully trade them) have changed. Still, this chapter should at least give you the basics necessary to have success in these high-risk, high-reward markets.

While writing this book, I kept coming across strategies that were—as people say in video game parlance—the "final boss" in terms of risk. These are often strategies and assets that didn't exist as recently as a year ago. In fact, these high-risk, high-reward investments are so new that there's no guarantee they'll be around even a few years from now! That's why I wanted to silo these strategies at the end of the book.

You don't want to take these sections lightly. While I'm giving you step-by-step instructions on how to use these strategies in the safest manner possible, you must know that *all* of the strategies in this chapter could result in you losing *all* of your investment in them. For that reason, you need to size your position correctly to prepare for that possibility. And as a rule, I wouldn't allocate more than 1% of your investable assets to any of these strategies.

Because, as you'll learn in both sections of this chapter, *risk comes at you fast*. And even some of the world's most successful entrepreneurs have been burned using these high-risk, high-reward investments.

NON-FUNGIBLE TOKENS (NFTS)

WHAT ARE NON-FUNGIBLE TOKENS (NFTS)?

It's always interesting to see an industry turned on its head. And that's exactly what happened with the art world after the introduction of non-fungible tokens (NFTs).

NFTs are a form of "smart contract" (see Chapter 2) that proves or certifies ownership of a digital asset. They can be exchanged and traded just like cryptocurrencies, and held through other applications like "staking." Most NFTs are also stored on the Ethereum blockchain; however, other chains like Solana, Ronin, and Wax also have active NFT blockchains.

Most importantly, NFTs represent ownership of photos, videos, audio, or any other type of digital file. It's notoriously difficult to keep track of who owns digital files. These assets can be copied and shared easily, so proving ownership of the asset can be tricky. NFTs solve this issue, as these assets are "non-fungible" (i.e., they cannot be changed), and thus ownership is guaranteed for whoever shows they are the rightful owner of the NFT.

Let's focus on the key operative word in NFT: *fungible.* If I take a $20 bill out of my pocket and want to trade it for another $20 bill or two $10 bills, neither of us has a problem with that. That's because US dollars are fungible assets. US dollars, commodities, and even bitcoin can be exchanged for each other without issue.

Now let's look at something that's *non-fungible.* Let's say I ordered a limited-edition copy of a book about building skateboards from a friend of mine. There were only fifty copies of the book created, but I was able to buy the fourth copy. Since this work is unique and is marked as "4/50 copies," it is non-fungible. Nobody can claim they have the fourth copy of this book, because I have proof of ownership from its creator.

Even though other people have access to the book (and even have their own copies), because I can prove I have the fourth copy, it is unique and cannot be changed or replaced by another copy. Even if you took a picture of every page of the book with your phone, printed out the pages, and created your own book, you still would not have the "original" copy. That's because this book is *non*-fungible.

When you apply this concept to the art world, you can see how NFTs are fundamentally transforming the way art dealers and investors do business.

"Minting" a Non-Fungible Token

One way to think of NFTs is that they are digital tokens or collectibles. They can represent trading cards, clips from NBA basketball games, or even JPEGs of CryptoPunks (more on that later).

When you buy an NFT from a marketplace like OpenSea, you can show proof that you are the rightful owner of the digital asset. This isn't so different from how the traditional art world works. For instance, while in Paris a few years ago I took a tour of the Louvre to see Leonardo da Vinci's *Mona Lisa.*

The *Mona Lisa* is arguably the world's most recognizable painting. It was created by one of the most influential artists in history, has been authenticated by the world's top art historians, and is prominently placed in a world-renowned art museum.

Yet, anyone can look up a picture of the *Mona Lisa* on their phone and take a screenshot. They can even print out and frame a rendition of the *Mona Lisa* and hang it on their wall. They could even commission an artist to paint a replica of the *Mona Lisa*!

But without *proof* that it's the original *Mona Lisa*, a replica does not have much value. Even if it's a direct copy of da Vinci's masterpiece, nobody would pay $850 million—the work's valuation in 2020—for the copy of the painting.

From *Mona Lisa* to Instagram

We can apply this same concept to digital art. An artist in Los Angeles named Alexa Meade was one of the first artists to sell NFTs. Her work involves painting people and capturing these "living paintings" as images, transforming three-dimensional reality into two-dimensional abstraction. She posts her images on her widely followed Instagram account and displays them in galleries all over the world.

Anyone can take a screenshot of Meade's artwork for free. But only those who buy the corresponding NFT for that artwork can claim ownership over the work. For example, let's say Meade creates or "mints" an NFT of an artwork called *Color of Reality*. Once the NFT is minted, it generates the following:

- A fingerprint or "hash"
- A token name
- A token symbol

This *Color of Reality* token is then stored on the Ethereum blockchain, with this "transaction" being the first for the NFT. Since blockchain data cannot be changed (i.e., it's non-fungible), that information is secure. It proves she created and owns the NFT. When Meade goes to sell the *Color of Reality* NFT, a new transaction is recorded on the blockchain proving that the person who paid her is now the rightful NFT owner.

While Meade or any of her fans can share the image of *Color of Reality*, the person who paid for the NFT is the actual owner of the image. And if you buy the right NFT at the right time, you could make a 10,000% return in short order.

CASE STUDY:

HOW CRYPTOPUNKS TURNED A JPEG INTO $12 MILLION

I've always been fascinated by Western art history. The Renaissance was spurred by the rediscovery of ancient Greek and Roman teachings in the wake of the bubonic plague. This was followed years later by Impressionism, which was made possible by portable premixed paint and other technologies that allowed painting outdoors. This movement bled into the contemporary art movements led by Andy Warhol and his Pop Art aesthetic.

2020 brought the advent of a new movement: cryptoart. And just like technological advancements enabled previous art movements, the same can be said for cryptoart.

The seed for the cryptoart movement was planted in June 2017 by two Canadian software developers at their firm Larva Labs. They had written a piece of software that automatically generated 10,000 unique 24×24 pixel images that they called "CryptoPunks." These small, 8-bit-style pixelated images of aliens, zombies, and apes took inspiration from such disparate sources as Ridley Scott's *Blade Runner* and electronic music artists Daft Punk.

But it wasn't so much what these images looked like that made them valuable. Rather, these CryptoPunks would be the first works in a new movement called "cryptoart." At the center of this movement was the new technology of non-fungible tokens.

The Dawn of the Cryptoart Movement

All CryptoPunks are distinct. Some are male, while others are female. Some wear glasses; others have pigtails. While they share similarities in form and style, each has unique features that can't be duplicated.

But unlike a picture you'd buy and hang in your house, these works exist only in the digital space. While you could print out an image of a punk, you only "own" the image if you purchase the corresponding non-fungible token. The ownership is enshrined in code on the Ethereum blockchain, where nobody can hack or falsely claim that they are the rightful owner.

The Larva Labs project inspired something called the ERC-721 standard. This was developed by those working on the Ethereum network to ensure rightful ownership of digital assets. The ERC-721 standard created a "smart contract" on the Ethereum blockchain for anyone who bought and owned a digital asset. And since the Ethereum blockchain is a distributed ledger, anyone has access to the owner of the NFT at any time.

This was a first in the art world. And like with anything that's rare and increasing in demand, the prices of these CryptoPunks have skyrocketed in value.

CryptoPunks Go Mainstream

As mentioned earlier, the CryptoPunk movement went mainstream when two developers at Larva Labs created 10,000 CryptoPunks. They gave away 9,000 of them for free because—at the time—there was little to no interest in the project.

But then something odd happened; fans started collecting these "punks." Much like traditional art, owning a punk became a status symbol in the cryptocurrency world. If you owned a punk and displayed it in your *Twitter* profile, people knew you were "in the know" when it came to cryptoart. Some even displayed their NFTs in Decentraland, an Ethereum-based virtual world.

Not long after, a bull market in NFTs began. While a mere $2 million worth of NFT sales happened the first week of January 2021, that figure hit $175 million by March 2021. These sales included everything from NBA highlights to—you guessed it—CryptoPunks. In fact, CryptoPunks were so popular that by June 2021 they were selling for $12 million each! (That is not a typo!)

The prices were exorbitant. But just as people would pay top dollar for an original Andy Warhol—which kicked off the Pop Art movement—art collectors were willing to pay millions for the works that started the modern cryptoart movement.

NON-FUNGIBLE TOKENS

NFTs are a very new high-risk, high-reward investment. Not everyone is convinced NFTs are an investing trend that will stand the test of time, with some comparing them to a speculative bubble. As a result, the parameters for determining which projects are good investments are largely undefined. It also means you need to be extra careful how you approach investing in this market. Based on recent history, you might call this market the "Wild West." This section will help you try to make the most of it.

How to Identify a Good NFT Investment

In the CryptoPunk example, the NFTs were clearly bid up since they were the first NFTs to gain widespread adoption. Think of CryptoPunks like a "rookie card" for the cryptoart movement. But one thing is clear: Digital assets are here to stay. Today, most young people don't care about buying an antique vase from the early 19th century. They'd much rather own a piece of popular culture, such as one of the first CryptoPunks. And with fractionalization—which we discussed in Chapter 9—coming to the NFT space, many people will soon be able to buy a piece of these iconic cryptoart projects.

While it can be difficult to value and determine which NFTs are the best investments, you can use the following three factors to tip the scales in your favor.

1. Stay on Top of Google Trends

As we covered in Chapter 9, recognizing which part of the market cycle we're in can help you enter your NFT position. And one of the best ways to gauge sentiment is by using Google Trends.

This free database allows you to see how many people are searching for a specific keyword on Google. The more people that are interested in NFT projects, the higher the search cache will be for "NFT."

Your goal should be to wait until your NFT search hits a trough. Since I believe that NFTs are likely here to stay, *you may want to wait until fewer people are talking about NFTs*. That will correspond with a lower Google Trends score and likely lower prices.

On the flip side, you don't want to buy NFTs when they are abuzz in social media. If you buy because FOMO took over, it's very likely you will be buying at high prices.

2. Look for Scarcity and Good Artist Reputation

Once you've determined via Google Trends that it's a good time on a "macro" level to buy an NFT, you want to find an NFT project that's scarce.

For the most part, NFTs have no tangible or physical value; 99.9999% of NFTs are going to be worthless. But 99.9999% of all art is worthless, which has no bearing on the market itself.

Just like in the traditional art world, an NFT's value is defined by what other people are willing to pay for it. And that value stems from the scarcity of these NFTs. For instance, the CryptoPunks minted only 10,000 NFTs. That means there are only 10,000 CryptoPunks that will ever exist. There is a finiteness to that, which is one reason their prices have risen so rapidly.

While these items are scarce, they also come from a reputable NFT project. This was the case with the artist Beeple, who sold an NFT for $69.4 million in March 2021. Beeple had built a massive social media following for nearly 15 years prior to his sale. Since he's a respected visual artist, the value of his art and reputation is long-lasting, and so is the value of his NFT.

In addition, a prospective NFT investor will want to see how active this artist is on his social media platforms, particularly *Twitter* and *Discord*. The larger the following and the more active the social media community, the higher the likelihood of success with your NFT investment.

3. Aim for Popular, Highly Liquid, and "Gameified" Projects

Liquidity represents how easy it is to buy or sell an asset. For instance, a blue-chip stock like Alphabet (GOOGL) is a *liquid* asset since you can easily buy or sell it on an open market. On the other hand, an apartment building is an *illiquid* asset because there are only a few people in the area who would be willing to buy or sell a multimillion-dollar property.

The same concept applies to NFTs. If you spend $2,000 on a piece of digital art, you want to make sure there is a buyer on the other side of the transaction so you can unload that high-risk investment for a profit. That means you want to stick with popular NFT projects with a large following on social media and in the cryptoart realm, particularly on *Twitter* and *Discord*.

Lastly, NFT projects that have been "gamified" will also be longer lasting. These projects allow users to purchase, earn, and then own in-game assets (including NFTs). This feature supports the underlying ecosystem of the NFT-gaming project and gives users playing the games a reason to come back. This dynamic supports the underlying price of these in-game NFT items, reinforcing the tokenomics of the NFT-games' ecosystem.

How to Trade an NFT

Those investing in non-fungible tokens need to start by making a list of NFT artists. These can be as well-known as the CryptoPunks all the way down to more niche artists like Alexa Meade. From there, you want to track price performance for these projects during NFT bull markets and keep an eye out for future NFT "drops."

The bull runs should be tightly correlated with Google Trends activity. If activity is high, it's best to put your list of top NFT projects on the back burner. However, when Google Trends activity and NFT prices inevitably collapse, take advantage of the pullback and buy your favorite projects.

Once your NFT is secured, sit and wait. Keep in mind that we are operating under the assumption that NFTs are not a passing fad. Hence, when a bull market in digital assets appears, you will already have exposure. One particular strategy you can use is to sell when sentiment hits a new high along with extreme prices.

Those who want to buy NFTs can use marketplaces like OpenSea, Rarible, and SuperRare. Because of the high-risk, high-reward nature of NFT investing, you want to make sure to keep your position small. There's a chance that even the most reputable projects may fade into obscurity. That's why you want to make certain you avert blowing up your account if the trade doesn't go your way. For that reason, I'd keep any NFT position at less than 1% of your total portfolio.

Investing Quick-Start Guide:
NON-FUNGIBLE TOKENS (NFTs)

1. Go to an NFT platform or marketplace. You will notice that prices are not listed in US dollars but are listed as a percentage of cryptocurrency (usually ether or Solana, depending on the exchange). For a review of ether and Ethereum, read Chapter 2 on cryptocurrencies.

2. Decide what kind of NFT you want to buy (there are many to choose from, including digital art, land in virtual worlds like Decentraland, and sports highlights on NBA Top Shot).

3. Set up your digital wallet so you can store your digital assets.

4. After you have bought your NFT, store it in your digital wallet.

5. When you want to sell, return to any NFT marketplace and list your NFT. Keep in mind that the NFT market is very illiquid, so make sure you're comfortable with potentially never selling your NFT.

YIELD FARMING

WHAT IS YIELD FARMING?

The cryptocurrency market is rapidly evolving. New hot trends in this market will undoubtedly pop up in the future. My first foray into cryptocurrency investing came in 2017. Back then, most investors were focused on investing in smart contract platforms like Ethereum and Cardano. In 2021, however, most investors turned their attention to non-fungible tokens (NFTs), which—at the time—were surging in value.

In 2020, a new crypto trend emerged called "decentralized finance," or "DeFi" for short. DeFi projects use blockchain and smart contracts to cut out financial intermediaries. This is intended to create brokerages, exchanges, banks, and other traditional financial services without the use of a centralized authority.

DeFi was born out of the Ethereum blockchain. In 2018, Ethereum was one of the first blockchains where people could build protocols and other applications using smart contracts. As we covered in Chapter 2, it's best to think of Ethereum as the "operating system" on which blockchain protocols are built. In this case, users are building DeFi projects on top of the Ethereum blockchain. This opened a whole new wave of products and services that were enabled by blockchain technology.

Although the Ethereum blockchain ushered in a wave of new DeFi applications (including "yield farming," which we will talk about in a few paragraphs), it's important to remember that bitcoin was the first DeFi project. As discussed in Chapter 2, bitcoin, the world's first cryptocurrency, was intended to allow people to exchange money digitally outside of the traditional banking system. Bitcoin cut out the middleman in the money transferring process. And DeFi intends to have the same effect on a host of other financial services.

And one of the most interesting applications of decentralized finance is something called *staking*.

A New Way to Earn Interest

Staking is a high-risk strategy that allows cryptocurrency owners to earn interest on their digital assets. When you "stake" your cryptocurrency, your assets are locked in what's known as a "liquidity pool" for a set period.

In exchange for locking up their digital assets, those staking their cryptocurrencies earn interest via transactions fees, interest from lenders, and other methods. The more cryptocurrency you "lock up" in a liquidity pool, the more interest you'll earn.

Staking is important for a few reasons. In Chapter 2 we discussed "proof of stake" tokens that use "consensus mechanisms" to verify transactions on the network. This is to make sure that people aren't spending their cryptocurrency more than once, which would be a security violation.

Many of these consensus mechanisms that verify transactions are actually "pools" of staked cryptocurrency. These pools validate a block of transactions from which you are paid a transaction fee.

In traditional finance, a centralized authority like a bank verifies every transaction on a payment network. Since the goal of cryptocurrency is to create a decentralized financial ecosystem, these pools take the place of the centralized authority.

Yield Farming Is Staking on Steroids

Let's say that you are the creator of a cryptocurrency called ElonMoon. For ElonMoon to have any chance of success, you need to provide liquidity for the ElonMoon market.

Liquidity is a measure of how easy it is to buy or sell an asset. For instance, a share of Apple Inc. (AAPL) is a *liquid* asset since you can buy or sell your shares at the click of a button. On the other hand, the vintage Bob Seger poster in your living room may only have a few interested buyers on the planet and is therefore an *illiquid* asset.

Many new cryptocurrencies are illiquid. There are simply not many buyers and sellers for the digital asset, especially if it recently embarked on an *initial coin offering (ICO)*. This is the process whereby a cryptocurrency starts trading on exchanges and is akin to an initial public offering (IPO).

Traditionally, when you launch a cryptocurrency, you will have "whales" (large holders of the cryptocurrency tokens) using automated trading software ("bots") to buy and sell your cryptocurrency. This is to ensure that new entities making transactions with your cryptocurrency can do so easily.

DeFi applications changed this process. Anyone planning to hold a cryptocurrency for the long term could now "lend" their cryptocurrency to a liquidity pool. The platform on which you're lending can redistribute those crypto assets to customers interested in using their products. "Yield farmers" benefit because the platform pays them a portion of the fees gained from user transactions. Like bitcoin, there is no middleman since this process is automated via smart contracts.

Staking and yield farming accomplish their goals of removing middlemen from a traditional financial transaction. When done properly, these processes can earn interest—sometimes as high as 100%! Considering that traditional bank accounts yield a measly 0.01% a year, it's no wonder that many speculators are drawn into the world of crypto staking.

But there's a reason the returns are so lucrative for this new technology. And as I'm about to show you, even the savviest of techies can get scammed in the staking market.

CASE STUDY:

MARK CUBAN HEADS TO THE YIELD FARM

Mark Cuban is one of the world's best-known entrepreneurs. Cuban made his billions by identifying technology trends before anyone else and capitalizing on them. That includes Broadcast.com, which he sold to Yahoo for $5.7 billion near the height of the tech bubble.

Although known as the owner of the NBA franchise Dallas Mavericks and the host of *Shark Tank*, Cuban is also an early adopter of DeFi. He was especially interested in *yield farming.* Cuban contends that yield farming isn't that much different from investing in high-dividend stocks or junk bonds that offer high yields. While yield farming offers returns 10–20 times those of dividend-paying stocks, Cuban rationalizes that those yields are to compensate for the risk.

Cuban has long documented his foray into yield farming on his website *Blog Maverick*. In fact, on June 13, 2021, he wrote an essay titled "The Brilliance of Yield Farming, Liquidity Providing, and Valuing Crypto Projects." In this blog post, Cuban wrote glowingly about a cryptocurrency project called Iron Finance that—at the time—was delivering triple-digit yields.

Unfortunately for Cuban, this DeFi project would soon lose 99% of its value overnight.

Clash of the TITANs

Iron Finance is a *stablecoin* protocol backed by a cryptocurrency called TITAN. A stablecoin is designed to be pegged to either a specific cryptocurrency, a fiat currency (like the US dollar), or a precious metal.

Tether is the world's largest stablecoin owned by Bitfinix. It is permanently pegged to $1, meaning every tether is backed by $1. While stablecoins are meant to stick to $1, their structure often causes them to fluctuate between $0.98 and $1.02.

For Iron Finance, their stablecoin was backed by TITAN. And to supply liquidity for this platform, Iron Finance was offering astronomical yields. In fact, at its peak, users who staked their ether—the token for Ethereum—were rewarded with an average percentage yield (APY) of 347%!

On the Iron Finance platform, users could either mint or convert tokens. These tokens were then locked into a liquidity pool for TITAN-UCSD (a stablecoin that's common in the currency world). For staking their tokens, users were paid interest in the form of IRON tokens. Enticed by these yields, even billionaire Mark Cuban couldn't help but dip his proverbial toe into the market. But as Cuban posted in his blog, the reason the yields are so high is because these platforms are so risky.

The First Large-Scale Crypto Bank Run

At its peak, those yield farming a TITAN-MATIC pairing on Iron Finance were earning $400 per day for every $10,000 invested. While the money was flowing, the key risk was that the TITAN token would lose its value and thus cause IRON to crash.

And that's exactly what happened. Within 1 week of Cuban's blog post extolling the benefits of yield farming, TITAN started to implode. By June 17—4 days after Cuban first posted about the project—TITAN's value had fallen to $0. Yes, you read that right—ZERO!

The reason for the crash? A classic *bank run*. Similar to what happens in the traditional finance world, banks cannot allow customers to redeem all their money at once. After all, these institutions use fractional reserve banking, whereby banks loan out many more dollars than they hold in their coffers. If everyone tries to get their money at once, the bank can't meet demand since the money has already been loaned out.

This is precisely what happened with Iron Finance. Large investors removed their tokens from the Iron Finance liquidity pool, causing the value of TITAN to plummet. This caused other holders of TITAN to pull their funds as well. With no liquidity, the IRON stablecoin temporarily lost its US dollar peg.

While it briefly recovered, Iron Finance had to mint tons of TITAN to meet the demand from all the people trying to redeem their funds. This increasing supply and demand phenomenon erupted in a negative feedback loop, ultimately sending the token to $0.

Unfortunately for Cuban, he lost a few hundred thousand dollars in the process. For those who don't have the financial resources of a billionaire, a trade like this could lead to unspeakable financial hardship. That is why it's so important to devote only a small portion of your funds to this revolutionary but risky product.

INVESTMENT STRATEGY:
YIELD FARMING

When an investment seems too good to be true, it usually is. When I first read about yield farming and how people were making up to 300% for staking their cryptocurrency, I couldn't help but be suspicious. Any investor considering diving into yield farming should remember that it's one of the highest-risk, highest-reward strategies in this book. That's one reason why investors should be very cautious before delving into this strategy.

How to Identify a Good Yield Farming Investment

If you choose to proceed with yield farming, just know there's a chance—like what happened to Mark Cuban—that you could lose your entire investment. High-risk, high-reward investing is all about managing risk. When it comes to yield farming, you want to make sure you're sizing your position correctly.

Although yield farming can return serious gains in a short period, you can also generate serious losses. Even billionaire tech entrepreneurs like Mark Cuban aren't immune to the wrath of the yield farming market.

If you follow these guidelines, you'll have a much better shot at finding a legitimate yield farming project.

1. Assess Project Reputation

The cryptocurrency community is rife with scams. For instance, tokens are regularly "pumped and dumped" by Internet communities looking to use coordinated buying to push up a cryptocurrency's price. This is meant to draw unsuspecting people into the market who "FOMO buy" into the asset. And once enough unsuspecting people have bought, there will be a coordinated dump or "rug pull" of the cryptocurrency.

These rug pulls are most common with small cryptocurrencies. For that reason, you need to do your research before deciding on a cryptocurrency to yield farm. You also only want to use cryptocurrency on platforms that are reputable.

After speaking with multiple experts, I learned that a couple of the most trusted DeFi platforms are Harvest Finance and SushiSwap. Harvest Finance is especially good for yield farming since the platform is designed to automate the complex yield farming process. It's also been around for many years, so its platform has an established reputation.

While I prefer Harvest Finance over SushiSwap, both platforms aggregate different projects looking for loans. In fact, both platforms conduct a great deal of the due diligence involved with staking cryptocurrencies, making it less likely you'll be the victim of a rug pull.

2. Look for High Transparency

There are thousands of cryptocurrency projects offering prospective yield farmers large yields that help add liquidity to their tokens. As you may discover if you do your due diligence, well-known projects typically offer the lowest yields, while lesser-known projects offer higher yields. This is by design, as lesser-known projects must compensate users with higher yields to attract investment to their liquidity pools.

One clue when deciding in which pool to stake your cryptocurrency is to see how transparent these lesser-known projects are with their customers. You can also measure transparency by going to the cryptocurrency's website to see who is involved with the project. If the team is anonymous, it's very possible the project is a scam and should be avoided.

However, if the project is run by former Google engineers with visible faces and active *Twitter* accounts, it is unlikely that you will be "rug pulled" by that project. As always, it's essential that you do your research before investing in any of these products.

3. Determine Annual Percentage Yield

Most "high-yield" dividend-paying stocks pay at most 10% per year (see Chapter 8 if you want to learn how to find these stocks). When it comes to yield farming, however, you can often find an annual percentage yield (APY) that is higher than 100%.

APY is the amount of return you'll get in a single year if the yield is maintained. If you staked $1,000 worth of Ethereum on a yield farming platform and it had an APY of 100%, you would receive $1,000 in yield over the period.

The catch with yield farming is that these triple-digit returns usually aren't sustainable. In fact, prospective yield farmers should avoid yields of this magnitude because the risks associated with them are too high.

Protocols willing to pay triple-digit yields are hyper-risky projects. The reason they pay such high yields is because it's the only way they can attract cryptocurrency to their liquidity pools. Those looking to stake and yield farm their cryptocurrency should instead target yields in the 25% range. While it's tempting to assume more risk, I'd be wary of any yield over 50%.

How to Invest In Yield Farms

I want to stress to you that investing in yield farms is truly a high-risk, high-reward strategy. This is also a new technology that is rife with issues and other scams. If you choose the wrong platform to stake or the wrong cryptocurrency liquidity pool, **you can lose your entire investment**. Yield farms are also not FDIC insured, so if the exchange fails, you will not be reimbursed.

That means you want to conduct a lot of due diligence on both the yield farming platform and underlying cryptocurrency protocols before you dive headfirst. While targeting an APY of 25%–50% is recommended, you still want to be mindful of your position size. As mentioned before with these high-risk investments, I would allocate not more than 1% of my investable assets to yield farms. While there is the potential for high returns, there is simply too much risk to invest heavily in this new, largely untested market.

After finding which cryptocurrency pool meets the criteria here, you may want to build out your position. Most yield farms do not offer the ability to dollar-cost average, so you will have to put down your investment all at once. On many exchanges, you will be required to "lock" your cryptocurrency for a set period of weeks or months. Typically, the longer you lock your cryptocurrency, the higher the yield.

From here, you want to keep an eye on your investment. If liquidity surges into the protocol, the APY will fall and you'll need to rebalance into another liquidity pool.

Investing Quick-Start Guide:
YIELD FARMING

While the potential to earn steady income is attainable, it is also possible to get trapped into a yield farm scam (e.g., read about what happened to Mark Cuban in this chapter). Be cautious.

1. You must own a cryptocurrency to "stake" your currency.

2. The most common coins to stake are low-volatility stablecoins.

3. Take the stablecoin and add to the liquidity pool that you want to lock up your funds with. There are companies (e.g., Harvest Finance, Sushi-Swap, Uniswap, PancakeSwap, etc.) that make this process very easy.

4. Once you are yield farming, you should receive income nearly every day.

5. You will be paid in the currency that you provided liquidity for.

6. Many yield farmers move funds to different DeFi platforms to chase after the highest yields.

Conclusion: If You're Going to Do Something Risky, Do It Smart

My goal from the outset with this book was to help the next generation of investors navigate the challenging world of high-risk, high-reward investing. Most of the classic investment books were written long before the flood of retail investors poured into the market. As far as I can tell, this is the only book of its kind ever written, and I'm happy this new cohort of investors can use this book as a guide as they meet the unique investing challenges presented by the latest market trends.

I feel an immense amount of duty pulling this project together. While most of my career was spent working in senior analyst positions for various investment research companies, the last 2 years was spent sharing all the knowledge I've accumulated over my career by creating content for an enthusiastic young audience.

But the more my audience grew, the more horror stories I read of people gambling on high-risk investments they didn't understand. Whether it's options, cryptocurrencies, or some newfangled asset class that will likely have been invented in the future, you need to know the safest ways to use these high-risk strategies. It's vital that you first understand the risks and—most importantly—how to manage those risks.

As I outlined in the beginning of the book, if you're going to do something risky, you need to do it smart. Simply YOLOing into a position because you saw a post on *Reddit* is no reason to risk your hard-earned money.

And while some online forums—like WallStreetBets—often glorify such losses, these actions have real-world consequences for people. Exulting "loss porn" comes from a place of immense privilege for the people posting about their thousands of dollars in losses. The reality is that most people cannot afford to gamble thousands on risky strategies.

In addition, many people see others losing money in the markets and it scares them away from investing. Or worse, they follow bad advice for their first investment, lose money, and avoid investing ever again. Investing is not like going to the casino; it's one of the greatest ways to build wealth. And the fact that only 50% of Americans own stock is reflective of how many view the investment community.

My hope is that even if these stories helped a handful of people avoid losses and grow confident enough to start their investing journey, then this was all worthwhile.

Acknowledgments

First off, I want to thank Michael Sincere for editing and providing mentorship while developing this book and helping me see it all the way through.

I also want to thank the people who took time out of their busy schedules to tell me their investing war stories. This includes Tim Luong, Genevieve Roch-Decter, and E.B. Tucker. Also thanks to Maxine Ryan for answering my questions on the constantly changing world of decentralized finance. Also, thank you to Brad Vitou and Justin Spittler for shedding light on the initial public offering process.

I want to thank Patrick Reagin and Jared Dillian for helping me navigate the business side of the publishing industry.

Importantly, I want to thank those people who gave me opportunities throughout my career. This includes Walter Block, Fergus Hodgson, Ed D'Agostino, Helena Woodruff, Dan Steinhart, and Dawn Pennington. Without all of you taking a chance on a kid from Northeast Ohio, I wouldn't be publishing this book today.

I want to thank my family—Pat, Terry, and Katie—for supporting me through this entire project. And a special thanks to my partner, Alexis Reck, for all the much-needed pep talks throughout this process.

I'd also like to thank Rebecca Tarr Thomas and Peter Archer for putting this project together.

Last but certainly not least, I'd like to thank all my fans. Without you none of this would be possible, and I'm forever grateful for the opportunity to teach you all about investing.

Index

About the Author

Robert Ross's unique style of clear and direct stock research helped him build a massive following in the investment research industry. He started his career at investment research company Mauldin Economics and quickly rose through the ranks to become the youngest chief analyst in the industry. Today, more than a million investors turn to Ross every month for his take on investing, economics, and personal finance. Between his social media followers on TikTok, Instagram, and Patreon and profiles in *Time*, *Business Insider*, and the *Daily Mail* (London), Ross uses his platform to promote fundamentally sound investing habits for people of all ages. Ross has a degree in economics from Loyola University New Orleans, and lives in Los Angeles.